China Stands Up

In 1949, Mao Zedong made the historic proclamation that 'the Chinese people have stood up'. This statement was significant, undoubtedly reflecting the changing nature not only of China's self-perception, but also of its relationship with the rest of the world. In terms of reducing the imperialist presence of the West and Japan within China, and reasserting China's territorial integrity and legal sovereignty to the outside world, Mao and China can indeed be seen to have successfully 'stood up'. However, the development of China's position in the hitherto Western-dominated international system has been more ambiguous.

In *China Stands Up* David Scott examines the PRC's presence in the international system, from 1949 to the present, and also looks forward to the future, asking:

- How do we define the rise of China?
- How does China see its role in the world?
- What shapes China's role?
- How do international actors view China's role in the international community?
- Has China risen in any real sense?

Engaging with a rich tapestry of sources and imagery, ranging from governmental, media, academic and popular settings, and bridging the divide between history and international relations, this book will appeal to students and scholars of both these fields, as well as those interested in Chinese politics and foreign policy.

David Scott is Lecturer of International Politics at Brunel University, UK.

China Stands Up

The PRC and the international system

David Scott

 Routledge
Taylor & Francis Group
LONDON AND NEW YORK

First published 2007 by Routledge
2 Park Square, Milton Park, Abingdon, Oxon OX14 4RN

Simultaneously published in the USA and Canada
by Routledge
270 Madison Avenue, New York, NY 10016

Routledge is an imprint of the Taylor & Francis Group, an informa business

© 2007 David Scott

Typeset in 10/12pt Times NR MT by Graphicraft Limited, Hong Kong
Printed and bound in Great Britain by Antony Rowe Ltd, Chippenham, Wiltshire

British Library Cataloguing in Publication Data
A catalogue record for this book is available from the British Library

Library of Congress Cataloging in Publication Data
Scott, David, 1952–
    China stands up : the PRC and the international system / David Scott.
        p. cm.
    1. China—Foreign relations—1949– I. Title. II. Title: PRC and the international system.
    DS777.8.S3 2007
    327.51—dc22
    2006038771

ISBN10: 0-415-40269-7 (hbk)
ISBN10: 0-415-40270-0 (pbk)
ISBN10: 0-203-94746-0 (ebk)

ISBN13: 978-0-415-40269-9 (hbk)
ISBN13: 978-0-415-40270-5 (pbk)
ISBN13: 978-0-203-94746-3 (ebk)

Contents

Epilogue **167**

Back to the future: 1949 revisited 167

Acknowledgements

The first and most important acknowledgement goes to my wife Clare. A trained archivist, history postgraduate, and above all partner in life; her love, support and encouragement over the years made this possible. My thanks also to the anonymous reviewer of the original manuscript whose warmth and helpful suggestions moved this forward at an important time. From a distance, various figures have attracted me with their sweep of events allied to their sensitivity to nuances and feelings. Previously, as a student, I was taken with the breadth of academic and humanistic vision of Martin Wight and Jaroslav Krejci. Currently, as a researcher and reader, I am engaged from afar with the style of writing and ideas of Arnold Toynbee, Paul Kennedy, Akira Iriye and Jonathan Spence.

Transliteration and word order

In the text and bibliography, Romanization of Chinese (Mandarin) terms generally follow the current *Pinyin* system, rather than the older Wades-Giles system. Thus, Mao Zedong appears rather than Mao Tse-tung, etc. Two exceptions are the more familiar older rendering of Chiang Kai-shek and Sun Yat-sen rather than their less familiar Pinyin rendering of Jiang Jieshí and Sun Yixian. Traditional Chinese and PRC usage of family name followed by the personal name is generally applied, exemplified with politicians like Deng Xiaoping and scholars like Deng Yong. However when Western personal names are present, Western name order is used. Consequently, Richard Hu appears as Richard Hu, whereas Hu Jintao appears as Hu Jintao, etc. Book titles remain as published, as do quotations.

Prologue
Time, space and memories re-written

On 21 September 1949, Mao Zedong made one of the iconic speeches of the twentieth century. That day, he stood before the First Plenary Session of the Chinese People's Political Consultative Conference and made his famous declaration *zhongguo renmin zhancilai le* 'the Chinese People have stood up', prefixed by the equally revealing assertion 'our nation will never again be an insulted nation'.

The 'standing up' metaphor entered into the lexicon of China's International Relations and political jargon. In 1965, China's Chief of Staff, Luo Ruiqing, used the metaphor to judge that 'in founding the great People's Republic of China, the long suffering Chinese people stood up like a giant ... the triumph of the Chinese revolution drastically changed the world balance of forces' (1965: 31). Deng Xiaoping used this metaphor to conclude his formal resignation letter in September 1989 that 'since the Chinese people were able to stand up, they will surely be able to stand firm forever among the nations of the world' (1984–94: 3.313). Elsewhere that month, it was a transformation of the Chinese people that 'they felt inferior for more than a century, but now, under the leadership of the Communist party, they have stood up' (3.317). Indeed, such was its resonance that subsequently Mao's 'standing up' speech became associated not with the September Conference meeting but with the formal proclamation of the People's Republic of China, the PRC, made by Mao at Tiananmen Square on 1 October 1949.

Mao's speech was iconic in the way in which China's past, present and future experiences were welded into a collective national panorama. In retrospect, it indicates key drives that have shaped PRC foreign policy since 1949. Mao's standing up was in part an 'internal' issue, that is, having stood up to imperialist presence of the West and of Japan in China, Mao was now reasserting China's territorial integrity and legal sovereignty to the outside world. In this sense, Mao and China had indeed successfully stood up. Mao's standing up was also in part an 'external' issue, one that was not finished in 1949. It was of course relatively simple enough, from its position of domestic power, for a PRC-led China to stand up and end the Western presence 'within' China during the PRC's immediate consolidation of power 1948–50 (Hooper 1986). What was far more complicated was to end that dominatory Western presence 'outside' China, in the international system at large. Here, 1949 was the start of a process that is still going on vis-à-vis China and the world. For Zhang Yongjin, the establishment of the PRC in 1949 was 'one of the most significant events in twentieth century world politics' which 'helped reshape the political and strategic balance in the post-war international system, and has since exercized profound and lasting influence in the evolution of international relations in the second half of the twentieth century' (1998: 17). One can say that China has indeed been 'standing up' for over the past half century, attracting more and more attention within the International System. China's sense of herself standing up has interacted with others' sense of China's standing up, a complex, at times volatile, and certainly significant issue.

Within Mao's speech, varied strands were woven together, 'encoding the personal experience of individual shame and [national] racial humiliation in the language of Marxism–Leninism' (Fitzgerald 1999: 16, 18). In Mao's speech, the immediate 'standing up' had been inside China, to the 'defeated . . . Kuomintang reactionary government backed by American imperialism' (Mao Zedong 1977: 15). Mao's vision, whilst wrapped in Marxist rhetoric was intensely Sino-centric, 'the Chinese people, forming one quarter of humanity, have now stood up . . . we have very favourable conditions: a population of 475 million people and a territory of 9,600,000 square kilometres' (16, 18).

Looking to the past, Mao asserted 'the Chinese have always been a great, courageous and industrious nation, it is only in modern times that they have fallen behind' due to 'oppression and exploitation by foreign imperialism and domestic reactionary governments' (17). As to the future, 'ours will no longer be a nation subject to insult and humiliation' (17), but instead would 'foster its own civilization' (17). Socio-economic forces were combined with cultural-civilisation undertones where 'an upsurge in economic construction is bound to be followed by an upsurge of construction in the cultural sphere' (18); that is 'the era in which the Chinese were regarded as uncivilized is now ended. We shall emerge in the world as a nation with an advanced culture' (18). The practical side of this was that 'our national defence will be consolidated . . . and no imperialist will ever again be allowed to invade our territory again . . . we will not only have a powerful army but also a powerful air force and a powerful navy' (18). Consequently, 'let the domestic and foreign reactionaries tremble before us' (18). Various cycles of time, to evoke Fernand Braudel's *Annales* framework, can be seen, be it the immediate past Century of Humiliation, the longer-term past Middle Kingdom glories and the future post-1949 hopes for China on the world scene, i.e. in the international system.

What can be emphasised is that China has long been a challenge to the international system in terms of what it did, and could, represent and do. China has not fitted into easy categories and expectations, 'the anomalous position of the PRC in international society in that period constitutes one of the greatest anomalies in the history of international relations of this century' (Zhang Yongjin 1998: 18). China has often been a 'problem' for the world and the world has often been a 'problem' for China. Indeed, 'the experience of China's interaction with international system clearly shows there exists a fundamental uneasiness in how China relates to the world . . . a highly problematic relationship between China *and* the world' (Deng Yong 2000: 42). This was true enough when China was on its knees during its Century of Humiliation; it has been all the more true as the PRC started standing up *in* and standing up *to* the international system, a 'modern international system [which] has actively discouraged non-Western countries from gaining leadership roles' (Nayar and Paul 2003: 95).

The relationship between the international system and China has been a long running issue for China, 'a long lived tension in dealing with the outside world' (Hunt 1996: 10). This cuts both ways as 'how China relates to the international system has been a perennial issue besetting both the Chinese nation and the world since China was forcibly drawn into the European-centred international system in the mid-nineteenth century' (Deng and Wang 1999: 11). There has been 'the perpetual theme of China *vis-à-vis* the world . . . in this century' (Zhang Yongjin 1998: 3) and into the twenty-first century, in which 'the uniqueness of China's case is also seen in its constant challenge to the legitimacy of the existing international system' (4); and in which 'few countries have experienced changes in its foreign relations as tumultuous as China has, and few nations have embarked upon a more turbulent quest than that of China in search of its rightful place in the universal international society' (4). This relationship was to be an ongoing issue from 1949 through to the present, and indeed for the future.

As China stood up to survey the international system in 1949, what was the PRC trying to be, what international environment did it perceive, and how have such perceptions developed since 1949? The same question can be asked with regard to the international system vis-à-vis China – how did it perceive the PRC and how have such perceptions developed since 1949? History and international relations converge in terms of disciplinarity (Gaddiss 1996, Kennedy and Krasner 1997, Elman and Elman 1997, 2001), and mutually inform each other here. Underneath, both challenge and response are perceptions of the challenger (China) and of the challenged (the international system); perceptions of and from the past, around the present and to the future. How tall did China actually stand in terms of objective quantitative power, how tall did she 'seem' to stand in terms of subjective attributed power, in her own right and in comparison to others? Actual power intertwines with potential power, 'for at least the last half-century, China has been good at trading on the supposed strength of its future prospects' (Buzan 2004: 148–9), its 'bluff impact of size' (Ramo 2004: 37), or 'the Beijing bluff . . . in keeping this impression alive without having to prove it' (Moller 2006: 145). In a word, and in the world, images count.

1 Images in international affairs and their legacy for China

This book deals with relations operating between the PRC and the international system. In doing so, questions of imagery are prominent, as are related questions of national identity and indeed international identity – both for the PRC and the international system vis-à-vis the other. Power and perceptions are entwined, as IR (International Relations) realism and its geopolitical bent is complemented by IR constructivism and its focus on images and perceptions.

Cultural-ideational (image-related) factors in international affairs

In recent years there has been interest and focus by some historians on how seemingly intangible cultural-ideational factors affect tangible foreign policy, 'diplomatic history in the expanded field' (Stephanson 1998). Akira Iriye welcomes how 'a cultural approach to diplomatic history can start with the recognition that nations like individuals . . . develop visions, dreams and prejudices about themselves and the world that shape their intentions'; so that, alongside IR realism issues of security and trade, 'one will also have to consider the mind-sets of leaders and peoples' (1990: 100, 101; also Iriye 1979, Sampson 1987, Wang Jisi 1998: 501; Gerald Chan 1999: 139–61). An evocative twist was given in Iriye's talk of images and diplomacy with regard to the US and China, and their mutual 'storehouse of images' that could be given 'privileged status' in times of 'war, peace, or situations inbetween' (Iriye 1988: 39).

IR theory has seen analogous developments, where 'events in the post-Cold war world . . . are forcing scholars to take socio-culturally based identity factors more clearly' (Ollapally 1998: 253; also *Millennium* 1993). Classic IR security dilemma paradigms are based on the mutual effect of actions as mediated through perceptions and images of the other's intents and actions. Harold Isaac's *Scratches on the Mind* (1958) had already looked at perceptions and how 'images . . . get somehow cranked into the process of policymaking' (1972: xxviii). Alongside the traditional paradigms of IR realism, social Darwinian state competition, and of IR liberalism-functionalism, state co-operation within international frameworks, comes the 'promise' (Hopf 1998) and 'new prominence' (Guzzini 2000: 148) of IR constructivism, with its focus on constructed images of oneself and others in the international arena. Robert Jervis's work on *Perceptions and Misperceptions in International Politics* (1976), his 'logic of images in international relations' (1970) can be used here. Such concerns were central to David Shambaugh's classic study *Beautiful Imperialists. China Perceives America, 1972–1990* and the 'image structures' (1991: 283) and 'perception gaps' (302–3) in play. Others have used such image angles for looking at China's relations with the USSR (Rozman 1987) and Japan (Whiting 1989). Geopolitics and geoeconomics can be complemented, though not necessarily replaced, by geoculture and indeed geopsychology! Government statements can be complemented by sources from academia, the media, literature and cyber-space (Pillsbury 2001a), to reconstruct what Raymond Williams has generally dubbed these 'structures of feelings'.

Thus, in looking at the period from 1949 to the present, and into the future, this study argues that various ideational strands deeply affect tangible actions and events at play between China and the world – then, now and probably in the future. Perceptions and misperceptions, national identity and national memory, images of oneself and the Other, International Relations as Iriye-style intercultural relations, strategic culture, civilisational claims and clashes, 'yellow' and 'white' racial categorisation, identification and alienation, affirmation and rejection, nationalism and internationalism – such intangible yet pervasive ideational factors are all at play. In short, 'often images and symbols rather than cold logic and analysis are the currency of international relations' (Buszynski 2004: 7). Yu Bin, for one, considers that such a 'cognitive/image orientation' represents 'new ground that could open the way to an understanding of the deeper structure of Chinese thinking and its impact on China's foreign behavior' (1996: 246, 247). Of course, whilst perceptions and misperceptions face one with the perceived, they also face one with the perceiver. Images shed light in two directions, the observed and the observer. As Peter Gries puts it, 'who do we see? A cuddly panda or a menacing dragon? Westerners interpreting Chinese foreign policy, like subjects staring at inkblots during a Rorschach test, frequently reveal much more about themselves than they do about China' (2005a: 235; also Rotter 2000: 1216). Here one can note images of a menacing worrying 'Red China' in the 1950s–60s giving way to more cooperative reassuring 'Pacific Rim' tropes of the 1970s (Cumings 1997); indeed reflecting China's own shifts but also reflecting the contextual rise and fall of what China would come to call 'Cold War mentalities' at play in the West and in academic circles.

Images and perceptions give a state more or less general credibility and appeal. Indeed in this sense there has been very deliberate international political marketing going on by the PRC, in effect 'selling China' to the world, nation branding as it has striven to shape how the world sees it and responds to it. There has always been 'China's concern for its international image' (Foot 2001: 15), whether it be 1960s rhetoric on the PRC as an inspirational beacon for world revolution, or the 1990s emphasis on China as a responsible Great Power. Image is shaped in part through actual power. Yet if China was standing up after 1949, then standing up in what sorts of power terms? Whilst there are the traditional 'hard' (quantifiable military and economic) power elements to consider, there is also what Joseph Nye calls *Soft Power* (2005: 5–18) to take into account for states around the world, and for China (88); i.e. that more diffuse credibility, prestige, image-related and model-emulating aspect of a state that may indeed give it influence and thus a degree of power within the international system. The linkage is of course not a tight explicit quantifiable one. Nevertheless, John Gaddis wondered if 'international relations, in its preoccupation with measuring and quantifying [hard] military and economic [hard] power, did not leave out certain other forms of power' at play in the modern world 'namely the power of ideas' (1996: 40–2), be they formal ideologies or informal images.

Images, of oneself or of others, are entwined with questions of *identity*, a theme of general interest in International Relations (Bloom 1990, Krause and Renwick 1996, Hall 1999). At a general level, Peter Katzenstein argues that 'issues dealing with norms, identities and culture are becoming more salient' (1996: 2) in consideration of national security issues. Friedrich Kratochwil and Yosef Lapid's *The Return of Culture and Identity in IR Theory* (1996), is complemented by Masaru Tamamoto's sense that 'culture and identity have been salient and obvious factors in shaping the history of international relations' (2003: 193). National identity becomes a focus not so much on the raw power of the national state but rather on 'the way in which a people, and especially a policy-making elite, perceive the essence of their nation in relation to others' (Scalapino 1993: 215). Consequently, national identity 'influences attitudes and policies alike, being the psychological foundation for the role and behaviour patterns of a country in the international arena. National identity helps to define threat and opportunities' (215).

Here, China has been compared to having a 'quest over its national identity, in terms of establishing it for China and in terms of establishing it for the international system' (Dittmer and Kim 1993: 1–31). Zhang Yongjin reckoned that, post-1949, 'few nations have embarked upon a more turbulent quest than that of China in its search of its rightful place in the universal international society' (1998: 4). This crucially reflected China's sense, its image, of what it thought its rightful place was, and what the international system was ready to give China, which in turn reflected how that international order was constructed. Deng Yong has been explicitly 'drawing on constructivist theory in international relations' in order to analyse China's setting in the International System where 'the state's identity in international relations is acquired, constructed and reconstructed' (2000: 44). Leszek Buszynski's look at *Asia Pacific Security – Values and Identity* argues that 'identity matters in international relations – no more so than in the Asia Pacific region which is home to deeply distinctive and proud cultures. To ignore the imprint of Chinese civilization upon Beijing's foreign or security policy would be unforgivable' (2004: 1). Questions of identity are then central to this study. As China stood up in 1949, and afterwards, what image did China have of its proper identity and thereby role in the world, what image did the world have of China's identity and thereby role in the world?

Images affect and reflect *collective memory* (Halbwachs 1992, Confino 1997) of the past. IR and History concerns converge as 'memory, history, and strategic alignments are inextricably and perception-wise linked' (Gong 2001: 49). Past and present are both involved, 'remembering and forgetting . . . give countries national identity . . . remembering and forgetting are creating history' for the future, in which 'remembering and forgetting [history] issues will provide the vocabulary for and the battlefield on which strategic alignments in the contemporary world will turn. . . . the way in which peoples and countries remember and forget [history] will structure the international system' (Gong 2001: 45, 48, 57). Like images, 'collective memory cannot be adequately defined at any given time' though 'it is known by its effects . . . in this sense memory is the source of the image building power that cultures demonstrate when complicated issues of international relations are made comprehensible to mass audiences' (Buszynski 2004: 7). As Consuelo Cruz puts it 'how nations remember their pasts affects how they 'make [or attempt to make] their futures' (2000: 276). One's place in the world is an objective and subjective thing, what one's position is and what one hopes its position should be and will be. One's place in the world looks back to what it has been, as well as forward to what it might or could be.

The relevance of this is that 'only by tracking down past images can we begin to understand present day actions' (Wilkinson 1990: 29), a comment made about Japan, but equally applicable to China. Here History intersects again with international relations, Michael Hunt arguing that 'history is essential and central, not optional and incidental, to an understanding of Chinese foreign policy' (1996: 2). Paradoxically, there is 'the future of the past' (25) at play for China and its foreign policy. This study brings in three particular collective memories in operation. For China, its collective memory has revolved around 'the history of remembered grievances and of cultivated glories, that is, the Century of Humiliation and the Middle Kingdom, which 'serve as a rich repository of inspiration' (Fitzgerald 1999: 51) for the PRC. For the international system its collective memory has revolved around China as a great opportunity but also a great threat, its population being seen as a hugely promising market for western economies but also providing the manpower for the biggest industrial workforce and military pool on the globe, in short a Yellow Peril to be found in any Chinese awakening. Each of these images interacts with each other.

'The Middle Kingdom'

Even in the twenty-first century, 'one can better understand China's external relations, even today, by turning back the pages of history to ancient times' (Kornberg and Faust 2005: 7). After all, if questions of 'strategic culture'

(Johnston 1995, Lantis 2005, Scobell 2005) have any validity, then China's past is very much at play in the present, concerning Chinese attitudes and world view on war and peace. Jonathan Spence looks at 'the once and future China' in order to draw out 'what of China's past could be a harbinger for its future' (2005). From a Chinese perspective, Wang Gungwu argues that 'to most Chinese leaders, it is a measure of a world at disequilibrium if China does not have a place of respect commensurate with its size and history' (1999: 46). The 'history' in mind is China's Middle Kingdom paradigm, where she stood up tall and towering over her region.

Before the intrusion of Western imperialism, East Asia had been a virtually self-contained regional system. China, *Zhongguo* (The Middle Kingdom/ Central Country), culturally and politically dominated the region, shaping a world order as far as she knew (Fairbank 1968). This was a 'normative' (Cranmer-Byng 1973: 68) world view of enduring consequences. Indeed, as Paul Kennedy noted in his macro-survey of Great Powers, 'of all civilizations of premodern times, none appeared more advanced, none felt more superior, than that of China' (1988: 4). External and internal perceptions were mutually matched, reflecting China's real strength in quantifiable power and qualitative civilisation terms. It was not a militaristic centralised system, Chinese pre-eminence was not a heavy presence for its neighbours, she was more an arbiter than occupier. However, 'the "international relations" of China with surrounding areas, and with non-Chinese peoples generally, were colored by the concept of Sinocentrism and an assumption of Chinese superiority . . . such Sinocentrism and the Chinese world order were unusual and maintained for centuries' (Zhao Suisheng 1998b: 16, 19).

This Chinese pre-eminence as the Middle Kingdom involved other junior states giving deference and tribute, whilst receiving legitimising investiture and gifts in return, but also being left pretty much under their own rule. David Kang sees this as a distinctive interstate system, a restrained hierarchic system, with China's senior prestige and civilisational *soft power* being its characteristic rather than military *hard power* enforcement (2001; also Zhang Yongjin 2001). Iriye reckoned that this was 'a system of interstate relations based on morality and personal interaction, not on force and impersonal laws' (1979: 119).

Francesco Carletti was typical of early European contact with China, in 1598 noticing a confident Sinocentric population, 'they believe themselves to be full of all knowledge, to have an abundance of everything good, and to have no need of anything' (1965: 152) and a powerful realm, the 'fifteen provinces of China, each of which, in its hugeness and fertility, might be better to be called an entire kingdom' (155). China's concept of itself as the Middle Kingdom was alluded to, 'the Chinese . . . call it *Ciuco* or *Chiuquo* which means the kingdom set at the center of the entire earth' but where cultural pre-eminence and respect meant 'for that reason they have no desire to acquire other regions, but are content with their own' (162). That restraint was also coupled with the sinews of military power, 'fortresses and garrisons many millions of soldiers on foot and mounted . . . 1,043,141 soldiers and 487,471 horse . . . further they have armed vessels all along the coasts of the sea, which form an infinite number of ships' (162). China, under the Ming and then Qing dynasties, was well able to keep the West at bay and control its relationship with the outside world on its terms.

China could expect, and received, equal and courteous diplomatic treatment from European powers. Indeed, European missions complied with Chinese court rituals on showing formal respect in its *kow-tow* ceremonies, and accepting Chinese conditions concerning trade and contact. In 1655, the first Russian mission to reach Beijing was told, 'no one from your country, located far away in the northwest, has ever reached the Middle Kingdom. Now you show your sincere longing for Our civilization by sending an envoy to present to us your native products as tribute' (Fu Lo-shu 1966: 15–16). The Dutch 'tribute' mission of 1686 was told 'every ball of mud and foot of earth for foreign countries is but a particle of dust flown from the Middle Kingdom' and that 'every spoon of water, every hoof print filled with water in strange lands has its origins in the falling dew of the Celestial Household' (Wills 1984: 168–9) of China.

At the time, China was more than a match for European powers, where the power of the 'Manchu' Qing dynasty was at its height during the reigns of Kangxi, 1669–1722 and Qianlong, 1736–96. The Qing Empire was able to evict upstart Russians from the Amur Basin in the seventeenth century, a military advantage reflected in 1689 with the Treaty of Nerchinsk, the first Treaty signed by China with a Western power, and one signed from a position of some military strength. China was strong enough to expel European missionaries in 1725. Qianlong projected Qing power into Central Asia, as well as launching successful campaigns against Burma 1766–70, Vietnam 1788–9, and Nepal 1790–2. British attempts to open trade and diplomatic links were blocked. In 1763, 'to control the foreign barbarians' Qianlong restricted trade, 'Our Empire rules the four seas and our interior produces practically everything we need . . . trade benefits the foreigners only. The Celestial Empire does not depend on the trifling articles they import' (Fu Lo-shu 1966: 229–30). The emperor could rightly claim in 1777 that 'at the present time Our Empire is at her peak. The various barbarians fear and live in awe of Our power so that they dare not show disobedience' (278–9). From such a position of strength, Qianlong famously dismissed British attempts to establish an embassy at Peking in 1793, and with it more economic access to China. China's central and dominant position as the Middle Kingdom was still apparent at the start of the nineteenth century.

Pride in China's achievements and standing were not lost in China. Such possibilities were a source of hope for young Mao Zedong in 1919, where 'the world is ours, the nation is ours . . . the Chinese people of several hundred million . . . our Chinese people possesses great intrinsic energy . . . the great union of the Chinese people must be achieved' (1969: 162, 164). Consequently, 'we must all exert ourselves, we must all advance with the utmost strength.

Our golden age, our age of brilliance and splendour, lies ahead!' (164). Sun Yat-sen's horizons partly lay in the past, with his talk in 1924 about China's 'single, pure race . . . the greatest population and the oldest civilization' (1929: 12). Yet Sun used the past as a map for the future, where China 'will be equal to ten great powers . . . and will then be able to recover her predominant national position' (146) held in her Middle Kingdom days of glory. In 1942, Sun Fo the President of the *Yuan*, considered 'after our victory over Japan, China will command even greater respect in the world . . . our greatness will again be restored'; that is, 'we shall not only regain our status of fifty years ago – that of the senior State in Asia – but we shall regain the leading and stabilising role in the Orient that was ours for more than two thousand years' (1944: 152–3). 'Fifty years ago' would take China to its pre-1894 defeat by Japan, 'two thousand years' ago back to the heights of the Middle Kingdom pre-eminence.

Commentators have picked upon this Middle Kingdom paradigm. Chen Jian argues that during the Cold War, 'Mao and his comrades . . . wanted to change China's weak power status, proving to the world the strength and influence of Chinese culture. In the process, they would redefine the values and rules underlying the international system', that is, 'in short, they wanted to restore China's *central* position in the international community . . . as the Central Kingdom' (2001: 47). Analysis of current PRC policy has continued this linkage, that 'the ambition of Chinese leaders is to restore their nation to its traditional place as the Middle Kingdom, the suzerain of Asia to which other nations must pay homage', not so much through 'conquering their neighbours with military force', but 'rather to acquire such political and economic power that no major decision would be made in any Asian capital without Beijing's approval' (Halloran 1998: 56). Perhaps most telling was David Lampton's 'insider access' observations of China during the 1990s over 'the almost universally expressed desire of Chinese to economically, culturally and politically resume their "rightful place". . . in the region, and ultimately the world . . . a vision shared across generations, walks of life, and system levels' (2001: xi) in China. For Michael Hunt, 'recollections of the imperial past' served 'as a standard (or perhaps a national myth) of cultural achievement and international power and influence to live up to' (1984: 38–9).

Consequently, the phrase has been coined, of China's 'Middle Kingdom mentality'. This is no abstract concept for 'the Middle Kingdom mentality implies the re-emergence of China's traditional geo-political importance' (Song Xianlin and Sigley 2000: 56). It is also of geocultural importance, with Singaporean commentators agreeing that 'this ancient imperial mentality seems to have some bearing on certain recent geo-political trends emanating from China . . . this Middle Kingdom mentality cannot be totally neglected today' (Cheow 2004b: 7; also 2004a). It is the combination for Ralph Cossa, of China's 'sheer size, and middle kingdom mentality . . . that poses the greatest challenges' (2004: 1–2) to the international system. Indeed, for Martin

Jacques, a 'Middle Kingdom mentality' (2005a) may have been beneath the virulent racially-nuanced criticisms of 'black' Secretary of State Condoleezza Rice in 2005. Elsewhere the PRC's 'deep-seated "middle kingdom" mentality makes them condescending towards their darker-skinned Southeast Asian neighbors, former tributaries who dwell in China's maritime "South Sea" backyard' (Ching Chi'ien-peng 2004: 171).

Mentalities or not, in structural terms, China's previous Middle Kingdom periods of glory mean that China's standing up presents a return to older patterns. China is not rising, rather she is re-emerging. For the American media 'it is easy to forget that China is a place of grand ambition . . . Yet for centuries, China was the world's most advanced civilization . . . Today, China aims to reclaim the grandeur of its past . . . China has become a juggernaut'; in other words 'in its people and its policies, China today is infused with a profound sense of destiny, a steely determination to regain primacy in world affairs. The rest of the world is just beginning to digest what that might mean' (Newman 2005). For politicians like House International Relations Committee Chairman, Henry Hyde, 'now, as this new century dawns, China has reemerged into its traditional position of influence in Asia and the world' (House Select Committee 2006). This was China's glorious past, yet there is also Hyde's sense of the 'the Chinese people . . . still suffering a sense of victimization from the periods of unequal treaties, the Opium War, the Nanjing massacre' (House Select Committee 2006), which indicates the other reference point for China, its Century of Humiliation.

'The Century of Humiliation'

Despite its centuries of pre-eminence as the Middle Kingdom, China had also been subject to cyclical patterns, of the dynastic falls as the 'Mandate of Heaven' was periodically withdrawn before China's next recovery to pre-eminence. Consequently, China went into economic, military and dynastic decline during the nineteenth century, resulting for Zhang Yongjin in 'the subjection of China in world politics' as 'the hallmark of China's international relations' (1998: 10; also Scott forthcoming). The upshot was an extended period where China was politically, militarily and legally pushed around by outside powers, for just over a century from 1842 to World War Two. This was its *bainain guochi* (Century of Humiliation) at the hands of the West, with Japan joining in after 1895, and encapsulated in Alexis Krausse's *China in Decay* (1898). The result was stark, 'the humiliation, impotence, and rage felt by China's elites in the face of colonial representations of their country and their people. This humiliation knew no political boundaries' (Fitzgerald 1997: 61). Distrust of the West, of the unequal treaties, and of international law was equally high (Wang Dong 2003). This is why William Callahan argues that 'Chinese identity and security are shaped by the historical insecurity of national humiliation' (2006: 187). Chinese political leaders reacted against this humiliation, 'in the twentieth century, all Chinese leaders', from Sun Yat-sen through to Jiang Zemin 'have shared a deep bitterness resulting from China's humiliation' and have been 'determined to blot out that humiliation and restore China to its rightful place as a great power . . . pursuing the similar goal of national greatness' (Zhao Suisheng 2004: 70).

Sun Yat-sen, in his 1912 *Republican Manifesto* lamented about 'the anguish-causing lessons taught them by Foreign Powers' which had brought '[the Chinese] people beneath the contempt of the world' (Bland 1912: 53–5). A decade later and Sun was still lamenting in 1925 about 'the standing of our nation in the world . . . the poorest and weakest state in the world . . . we are despised' (1929: 12). In 1943, Chiang Kai-shek's *China's Destiny* considered the unequal treaties as 'a national humiliation' so that 'not until all lost territories have been recovered can we relax our efforts to wipe out this humiliation . . . we must work still harder . . . in order to catch up with other nations . . . fulfilling the new destiny of the Chinese nation' (1947: 34, 104–7).

Chinese communist leaders evoked the Century of Humiliation on many occasions. The Chinese Revolution of 1949, whilst undeniably Marxist–Leninist in its ideological wrapping, was also very much focused on 'China and the quest for dignity' (Fitzgerald 1999), that is, in reversing not just the conditions but also images imposed on China during its Century of Humiliation. For Jusuf Wanandi, Chinese communist leaders 'were still over burdened by history, which placed so many chips on their shoulders regarding relations with the region and with the world, especially the West', in which 'the psychological complexities stemming from this historical burden have made the Chinese very defensive and reactive to even the smallest things that impact their national interest' (2004: 38). This is not too surprising in retrospect, since Mao Zedong, born in 1893, and Deng Xiaoping, born 1903, spent over half their long lives witnessing China's humiliation at first hand during the first half of the twentieth century before being able to lift China up on her feet in 1949.

Mao Zedong recalled to Edgar Snow his early memory of those times, how as a 14/15 year old c.1907/8, 'I began to have a certain amount of political consciousness, especially after I read a pamphlet telling of the dis-memberment of China', which 'told of Japan's occupation of Korea and Formosa, of the loss of suzerainty in Indo-China, Burma and elsewhere', from which 'after I read this I felt depressed about the future of my country and began to realize that it was the duty of all the people to help save it' (Snow 1937: 133). As head of the Propaganda Bureau for the United Front 1925–6, Mao put forward the slogan *Quxiao bupingdeng tiaoyue* 'Cancellation of the Unequal Treaties' as a way of awakening the masses. Even in 1940, in the middle of war with Japan and with Chiang Kai-shek's Guomindang regime, Mao could still lament how 'after having inflicted military defeats on China, the imperialist countries forcibly took from her a large number of tributary states, as well as a part of her own territory' (1969: 375). The swathe of territory and number of countries identified by

Mao was impressive enough, what was also significant was the abject humiliation of China where 'even a miserable little country like Portugal took Macao from us' (375). A much larger country had been Russia, the biggest imperialist robber, with Mao Zedong famously complaining in 1964 that 'about a hundred years ago, the area east of [Lake] Baikal became Russian territory and since then Vladivostok, Khabarovsk, Kamchatka and other areas ... we have not yet presented our account for this list' (Lawrance, 1975: 145; also Deng Xiaoping 1984–94).

Political considerations maintained the impact of the Century of Humiliation in Mao's China. According to Chen Jian, 'the role of revolutionary foreign policy in Mao's continuous revolution [1950s] must be understood in the context of the Chinese people's "victim mentality"', where 'during modern times, the Chinese people's perception of their nation's position in the world was continuously informed by a conviction that political incursion, economic exploitation and military aggression by foreign imperialist countries had ... humiliated the Chinese nation' (2001: 12). This 'profound victim mentality' (203) generated from China's century of humiliation at the hands of the West in the nineteenth century, was a national 'feeling' able to be used by Mao to generate domestic support of Chinese external affirmation, as well as for regime consolidation.

Deng Xiaoping also often referred to the Century of Humiliation as an experience shaping China and against which the PRC had striven since 1949. In 1984 it was a question that 'for more than a century after the Opium War, the Chinese people were looked down upon and humiliated by foreigners. But China's image has changed since the founding of the People's Republic ... it is the People's Republic that has changed China's image' (Deng Xiaoping 1984–94: 3.70). Words and images mattered, for 'in 1949 China put an end to its history of humiliation, and the Chinese nation stood up' (3.264), the Chinese people, 'felt inferior for more than a century, but now under the leadership of the Communist Party, they have stood up' (3.316), a deliberate invocation of Mao's 'standing up' phrase.

Though slightly more removed from the Century of Humiliation than Mao and Deng, newly appointed General Secretary Hu Yaobang (Deng's protégé), was direct enough, telling the CCP National Congress in 1982 that 'being patriots, we do not tolerate any encroachment on China's national dignity ... having suffered aggression and oppression for over a century, the Chinese people will never again allow themselves to be humiliated as they were before' (1982: 29, 30). The CCP leadership also used memories of the Century of Humiliation to full effect during the 1990s in its national humiliation discourse and Patriotic Education campaign discussed by William Callahan and others. The recovery of Hong Kong in July 1997 was important, not just economically but psychologically. Premier Li Peng evoked 'our memory of the humiliation and the struggle of the Chinese nation in modern history ... the return of Hong Kong has wiped out the century-long national humiliation' (1997: 24). President Jiang Zemin asserted 'the occupation of Hong Kong is an epitome of the humiliation China suffered in modern history . . . the return of Hong Kong marks an end to the 100-year national humiliation of China' (1997b: 27), its recovery representing *xuechi* 'redemption' (Wang Dong 2003: 422) of that national humiliation. Hu Jintao's foreign policy advisor, China's emerging Kissinger, Zheng Bijian, personally recalled how 'as a Sichuan native, I remember my father once told me that when they hear, far away from the capital in Southwest Sichuan, about the Eight Allied Forces' occupation of Beijing, they all burst into tears. Deep in their hearts, the people felt so humiliated' (2005: 83).

The legacy of that period was 'China's firm belief that its political security must never be subjected to interference by foreign powers again . . . as China today seeks to wipe out a "century of humiliation"' (Ong 2002: 21, 22). Its memory runs deep, 'without doubt, "the century of humiliation" has been impaled in the minds of China's security policy-makers and it has also left an indelible mark on the Chinese masses' (143). The authors of *Interpreting China's Grand Strategy: Past, Present and Future* (Swaine and Tellis 2000) felt that 'China's modern history of defeat, subjugation, and humiliation at the hands of the West and Japan has produced an acute Chinese desire for international respect as a great power' (4). History created geo-emotional undercurrents, as 'China's humiliation at the hands of the West and Japan . . . gripped the imagination of three generations of Chinese and stung them into an ever more critical analysis of the international order' (Hunt 1984: 3, 38–9) after 1949. This is no matter of history, it affects current international relations. Japanese commentators warn 'there is no greater threat to the world today than the emergence of a major power in possession of a victim mentality . . . can China readily dispel the humiliation and victim mentality it has harbored since the mid-19th century?' (Funabashi 2003).

China's images of past humiliations and glories are closely linked to each other, 'the century of humiliation, which constitutes the negative pole of Chinese experience is inextricably joined to a positive pole defined by recollections of the imperial past, especially in the guise of its great dynasties' (Hunt 1996: 27; also Ness 2002: 140, Funabashi 2003). Chen Jian reckons that because it forms 'such a sharp contrast with the long-lived Central Kingdom concept, the Chinese thus felt that their nation's modern experience was more humiliating and less tolerable' (2001: 12), what Maria Hsia Chang (2001: 205) sees as an exacerbating 'particularly acute' contrast. Similarly, Callahan notes 'Chinese people feel that they are unique in national humiliation. Only China can go from so high a civilisation to be the lowest of the low, the Sick Man of Asia, and back again' (2004a: 206). It is China's coming back after 1949 that is the heart of this study, but a China coming back with what images and what hopes? Meanwhile China's Middle Kingdom heights had also generated perceptions in the outside world of China's latent and potential strength, a recognition that slid all too easily into fears of China as the Yellow Peril, a long featuring archetype in Western images of China.

'The Yellow Peril'

One of the ironies in China's Century of Humiliation was that China's potential strength, its size, resources and population continued to attract outside attention. Even when China was prostrate and occupied in the wake of the Boxer Revolt, Westerners like Robert Hart were nevertheless warning from Beijing in 1900, 'that the future will have a "Yellow" question – perhaps a "yellow peril" – to deal with, is as certain as that the sun will shine tomorrow' (1900). China had, for many decades before 1949, been seen by the outside world as an enigma, one that was important, difficult to read, but one that inherently posed a threat to global stability through its potential strength, if awakening and standing up. In many ways it can be summed up by Napoleon's famous and often supposed judgement that 'China is a sleeping giant. Let her lie and sleep, for when she awakens she will shake/threaten the world'.

By the later decades of the nineteenth century, as China struggled to modernise and signs of 'China's Awakening' were perceived in the West, there had arisen discernible fears of China amongst public and politicians, 'that strange recurrent nightmare known as the Yellow Peril' (*Atlantic Monthly* 1899). This was what Edward Said's *Orientalism* would come to term the 'Other', something that was simultaneously inferior yet also a threat, something to be defined and thereby controlled by the West. It was 'a foundational, essentialist discourse on an entire geocultural area and its inhabitants' (Lyman 2000: 687), leaving its legacy in which 'events of the last century live on, refracted and distorted through nightmarish dreamscapes about Oriental menaces and . . . phobias in the West' (Hevia 2003: 249–50).

The Yellow Peril was based around *China's Menace to the World* (MacGee 1878), in Vladimir Solovev's words of 1888, China was 'an alien, hostile world that threatens us more and more . . . a dark cloud approaching from the Far East' (Lukin 2003: 83). Images abounded, the image of the Chinese masses 'silent and persistent . . . ants that destroy the strongest timbers while the householder sleeps' (Whitney 1880: 137), and ready to sweep out from China across Asia and beyond. Around the Pacific there was widespread discussion, assumptions and fears at that time surrounding China's potential – forcefully expressed in the political debates in the American and Australian legislatures. The New Zealand Parliament, in debating and sanctioning the *Chinese Immigrants Bill*, was treated to lengthy arguments by former Prime Minister George Waterhouse that 'when an empire like China, with its 400,000,000 of people, begins to move, it is time for other nations to begin to look out' (New Zealand 1881: 213). The long-term future was one of China's rise, where 'those who come after will have to settle with China itself, which will be one of the greatest powers on earth' (214).

Rudyard Kipling was struck by 'the Chinese question' as he travelled around the Pacific in 1889, a question that was 'too large to handle alone' (1900: 1.333) and where 'they [the Chinese] will overwhelm the world' (1.274).

The very alien 'Otherness' of Chinese culture and its demographic potential combined to give not only a geo-economic but a menacing geo-political threat. The Boxer uprising was James Miller's *China. The Yellow Peril: At War With the World* (1900). The Yellow Peril, whilst couched in geo-cultural and geo-economic terms, was also seen in military terms. China's demographic weight was central: Kipling writing at Guangzhou/Canton, 'the March of the Mongol is a pretty thing to write about in magazines' but 'hear the tramp of the feet on the granite blocks of the road . . . Watch the yellow faces that glare at you . . . and you will be afraid, as I was afraid' (1900: 1.305–6). The March of the Mongol was an image invoked by Kipling at Penang, Hong Kong and Canton, and was taken from Dunlop's widely read profile *The March of the Mongol*. From his own military background Dunlop warned 'there is no room to doubt as to what is to be the dominating power of the future in the Far East of Asia. The Chinese . . . crushing and supplanting the rival populations of East Asia . . . the doom . . . is sure and inexorable' (1889: 44). For Dunlop, it was a 'vision' of China 'awe-inspiring and sublime' of 'hundreds of millions' of Chinese rising 'from weakness into power' to 'the grand and ever increasingly startling strains of the mighty March of the Mongol' (45). Such talk of the 'Mongol' was of course evoking that still older spectre, Genghiz Khan and his Mongol onslaught across Eurasia in the thirteenth century, with whom China could be merged in the blurred Western psyche, Chinese masses and Mongol hordes equated with each other (Young 1891: 430).

The challenge might not be just for European colonialists. America was also under threat, 'the coming question will be Asiatic. It belongs to the next generation . . . the oldest and the youngest of civilizations, face to face, America and China . . . come it will' (Young 1891: 431). Similar clashes were foreseen in Australia, with Charles Pearson's widely read *National Life and Character. A Forecast* reckoning that 'fifty years hence [i.e. 1940s] . . . China has taken its inevitable position as one of the great powers of the world' (Pearson 1893: 49). Demographic weight would be conclusive for China, 'the most populous country must ultimately be the most powerful, and the preponderance of China over any rival – even over the United States – is likely to be overwhelming' (130). The Yellow Peril looked to the future. Arthur Brown's *New Forces in Old China*, felt that 'the problem of the future is plainly the problem of China' with 'something appalling in the spectacle of a nation numbering nearly one-third of the human race . . . majestically rousing itself . . . No other movement of our age is so colossal, no other is more pregnant with meaning' (1904: 6, 1). In that setting, and with specific regard to discussing the question 'is there a Yellow Peril', he felt 'we observe the changing march of world powers' and 'tomorrow . . . some new Jenghiz Khan . . . with the weapons of modern warfare in his hands, and these uncounted millions at his command' (317). Currently 'there is not a statesman in Europe to-day who is not troubled with dire forebodings regarding these teeming hordes, that appear to be just awakening from the torpor of ages' (318). Thus, 'all see that the next few decades are big with possibilities of peril . . . the overshadowing problem . . . the relation of China to the world's future' (318–19).

Literary images reinforced and reflected this geopolitical geocultural unease about China's potential, as in Matthew Shiel's *The Yellow Danger* (1898). In Russian circles, such perceptions of 'tidal wave' posed by the 'yellow race' were prominent in Solovev's apocalyptic *Short Tale of the Anti-Christ* centred on how, 'the immense population of China' had been mobilised 'to establish the true Middle Kingdom over the whole world . . . all the European States submitted as vassals to the domination of the Chinese Emperor' (1900). Jack London's *The Unparalleled Invasion*, though composed in 1907, was set in 1976 with its 'menace of the twentieth century – China, old China, rejuvenescent, fruitful, and militant' (1993: 2.1240). After flooding across Eurasia, this impending Chinese global hegemony was only defeated by advanced germ warfare carried out by the United States! Sax Rohmer's Fu Manchu figure, the 'advance guard of a cogent yellow peril . . . the yellow peril incarnate' (1913: 250, 23), merely consolidated this existing image of China.

Rohmer's continuing inter-war novels about Fu Manchu matched the continuing undercurrents of unease about China, despite China's own slide into warlordism, internal fragmentation and rivalry between Communist and Nationalist/Guomindang forces. Griffith Taylor reckoned 'we shall see in the next fifty years a new China', in which 'when we realize that the Chinese have the natural resources at their disposal which are unrivaled (except in North America), it is obvious that only unremitting diligence, thrift, and sobriety will enable the white man to resist the "yellow peril"' (1921: 97). In 1931, Nathaniel Peffer's *China. The Collapse of a Civilization* emphasised 'the first and fundamental fact concerning China is that it contains nearly a quarter of the human race, in population it is the largest race in the world' (1931: 1). Underneath its current weaknesses, 'China seethes and heaves, rushes forward turbulently . . . there will be a new configuration . . . this is certain' (9), one which 'may well be more rugged and forbidding than the soft China that yielded so easily to the vigorous and aggressive intruder in times past' (9). The new landscape came in 1949. Even as China was enveloped in Japan's advances into China in 1937, Rohmer, the creator of Fu Manchu, pondered about 'future saviours in China . . . one wonders if a Kubla Khan is about to arise: one who by force of personality will weave together the million threads and from his loom produce a close-knit China. Should this occur, what then?' to which his answer was 'the Pacific slopes of America would be deeply interested. And Australia would follow the policy of such a Yellow Emperor with keen attention' (1938) and dread. Mao in 1949 perhaps came to represent such a Yellow Emperor?

Chinese sources, though mostly weighed down by the immediate humiliations faced by the Qing Empire, had been able to express threatening sentiments and feed such Yellow Peril nightmares. China's suave diplomat,

Zeng Jize, aka the 'Marquis Tseng', was widely known in the West through his profile *China, the Sleep, and the Awakening*. In it, he pointed to 'the awakening of 300 millions to a consciousness of their strength . . . the toiling millions that stay at home to provide the sinews of war. The soldiers are but the outer crust, the mailed armour of a nation' (Zeng Jize 1887: 4, 8). Chen Jitong, China's military attaché in Paris, worried Solovev by his warning in 1888 that 'we will get from you everything we need, all the technology . . . you are yourselves providing the means whereby we will vanquish you' (Lukin 2003: 83). Chinese nationalists were ready to beat the racial drum. Zou Rong's call in 1903 was to 'you 400 millions of the great Han race . . . you are a fifth of the peoples of the globe . . . you possess the omen of the Yellow Peril [*huanghuo*], you possess the might of the sacred race' (1903: 46). Domestic struggle would have its external benefits, 'to take its place as a powerful nation on the globe . . . in the new world of the 20th century . . . China is to be a great country in the world and play the leading role. Stand up for Revolution' (46–7). Within Chinese Communist circles, racial analysis was discernable. Thus, in 1924, Li Dazhao reckoned 'the races on a world scale have come to confront each other . . . the struggle between the white and coloured races will occur' (Meisner 1967: 190). A renewed pan-Asiatic Yellow Peril theme could be seen as something to rejoice in. Typical was Huang Zhenxia's 160-page poem *Huangren zhi xue* (Blood of the Yellow Race), penned in 1931, 'Hide, frightened European dogs!/ Topple, Muscovites imposing high buildings!/ Roll, Caucasian yellow-haired heads/ . . . The Yellow Peril is here!/ The Yellow peril!/ Asian warriors' bloody maws are devouring men' (Dikotter 1992: 161–2).

The war years brought the West and China together against Japan, but underlying images of China as a potential, and bigger, challenge still remained. Amidst the trials and tribulations of conflict, April 1945 had Payne's assertion in *China Awakes* that 'China is on the verge of self-discovery. It is true that she is awake at last, but at what cost have these blood-rimmed eyes been opened! Better almost would have been to sleep this western nightmare away' (1947: 87). The end of World War Two saw the next and final confrontation between the Communist and the Guomindang parties, and their respective visions for China. Theodore White and Annalee Jacoby's perception in *Thunder Out of China* was that 'for half a century the world has fretted about the "China problem"; statesmen of great powers have spent decades of their lives pondering China's role in their imperial plans' (1946: 316). For the next half century, the world continued to fret. On the other hand 'from a Chinese point of view the problem is different: What can China do about the world? What can she do about the aggression of her neighbors?' for 'China cannot plan and cannot hope until she lives in a world that treats her as an equal, not as a subject' (316). China and the world had their images of themselves and each other to be played out when the dust settled in the Chinese Civil War, in effect concluded as Chiang Kai-shek fled to Taiwan.

For the first time since 1911, there was one effective government in power across the Chinese landmass, the People's Republic of China. A new China was facing the world, a world long wary of an Awakening China, a new China profoundly aware and affected by its preceding Century of Humiliation and distant days of glory as the Middle Kingdom, a West in which images of the Yellow Peril lurked in the collective subconscious.

2 China 'leans to one side' in the Cold War

The Chinese Revolution of 1949 reverberated around Asia and indeed the world. For the first time in over a hundred years, events in China seemed to have dramatically and decisively moved in ways that the outside world (i.e. the West, Japan, and even the Soviet Union), found difficult to shape, or indeed at times understand. This was in an international setting in which alignment was expected and pushed for. US President Harry Truman set this out in his defining Cold War speech to a joint session of Congress, that 'at this moment in world history nearly every nation must choose between alternative ways of life' (Truman 1947: 179). His outlook was matched by Secretary of State Dean Acheson's comments on 27 February 1947 that 'only two great powers remained in the world . . . the United States and the Soviet Union. Not since Rome and Carthage had there been such a polarization of power on the earth' (Kissinger 1994: 452), that is, classic geopolitical structural frameworks. Similar bipolar spectacles were apparent in the USSR, with Andrei Zhdanov's *Report on the International Situation* at the founding session of the Cominform in September 1947.

Chinese perceptions of the Chinese Revolution and of the international system

At the time, Han Suyin's insider-outsider perception in October 1949 was to point to 'the historic-minded Chinese, haunted by the past and memories of the Great White Injustice' alongside 'the patriotic Chinese, that hard core of strength in all Asiatic communism, which is ardently nationalism; my country, right or wrong, but mine' (1952: 148). Images were there, but images to change. On the one hand was that 'fatalism, inscrutability, serenity, these figments of western imagination . . . the myth of a China old enough to charm them' (146). On the other hand, times were changing and unsettling Westerners, 'they don't want the uncomfortable truths about China, its enormous and collective hunger, its exorbitant poverty, its violence, its urge towards assertion' (146).

From a Chinese Communist point of view, America had very much intervened in the Civil War. Mao's victory in 1949 was a victory over internal 'reactionaries', the Guomindang; but it was also a victory over external foes, traditional European imperialists, Japanese imperialism and the emerging post-war face of American international power. Mao's patriotism, his sense of China, increased his suspicions of the United States. Although Mao's own words in 1938, that 'Chinese communists, who form a part of the great Chinese nation and are linked to it by flesh and blood' need 'to turn Marxism into something specifically Chinese, to imbue every manifestation of it with Chinese characteristics' (1954: 2.260) represented a striking Sinified nationalistic re-working, which was mainly ignored in the West.

Instead the West, and especially the United States, was more struck with comments by the Chinese leadership on the wider potential impact for their Revolution. After all, as early as 1936, Mao was writing that the forthcoming Chinese Revolution would 'exert a far-reaching influence on the revolution in the East as well as in the whole world' (Mao 1954: 1.191), sentiments reiterated by him in December 1946 (1954: 4.158). In 1946, Liu Shaoqi, the Chinese number two, was also telling the sympathetic American journalist Anna Strong that 'Mao Tse-tung's great accomplishment has been to change Marxism from a European to an Asiatic form . . . he has created a Chinese or Asiatic form of Marxism', of significance, since 'there are similar conditions [to those in China] in other lands of Southeast Asia. The course chosen by China will influence them all' (Zagoria 1962: 14–15). This revolutionary 'beaconist' rhetoric continued in full flood as the PRC stood up in 1949. On 16 November 1949 Liu Shaoqi told the Conference of Asia and Austra-lasian Trade Unions in Beijing that 'the road that the Chinese people have followed . . . is the road that the peoples of many colonial and semi-colonial areas should traverse . . . It is the Mao Tse-tung road . . . the fundamental road for the people in similar colonial and semi-colonial areas' (1949b: 179). China could be seen as a challenge to the very stability of the, admittedly Western-dominated, international system.

Consequently, 'mutual suspicion and mistrust' perceptions (and misper-ceptions) were apparent between China and the United States, and with it 'a process of action and reaction' (Zhang Yongjin 1998: 49) which hardened positions. Mutual fears were exacerbated, whilst the zero-sum character of Cold War bipolarity meant that America's loss was Moscow's gain. Genuine threat perceptions were felt by China from the USA with IR security dilemma (Zhang Shu 1994: 289) spirals apparent, as each seemed to confirm the worst fears of the other. Both sides saw the other as already aligning against it in the couple of years before 1949.

In that setting, Mao's rhetoric in June 1949 was dismissive and antagonistic towards the West, where 'to win victory and consolidate it we must lean to one side . . . the side of imperialism or to the side of socialism . . . there is no third way . . . Internationally we belong to the side of the anti-imperialist front headed by the Soviet Union' (SAR 1972: 65–7). This was the 'two camp' *lianggezhenying* theory, China firmly aligned in a 'leaning to one side' *yibiandao* strategy (Bo Yibo 1992) with the Soviet-led camp. From America's point of view, Mao's China may have stood up but it had immediately fallen into a state of dependency as it crawled into the embrace of the USSR. From the PRC point of view, some real distrust of Soviet motives was present, but the United States presented the greatest threat. Using United Front tactics and classic IR balancing tactics, Mao's eyes turned towards more active alignment with the Soviet Union, in order to safeguard China's Revolution, and perhaps to spread its message further.

Exploratory talks in Moscow took place from June–August 1949, with a CCP delegation led by Liu Shaoqi. Liu's report to the Soviet Politburo in July 1949, whilst not public, was clear enough; 'the Soviet Communist Party is the main headquarters of the international Communist movement, while the Communist Party of China is only a single-front headquarters. The interests of a part [i.e. China] should be subordinated to international interests' (Westad 1998: 313). The consequences of this were clear for him, with Stalin in turn underlining with approval these sentences in his copy, that 'therefore, the CCP submits to decisions of the Soviet Communist Party' (313), so that 'in our policy in international relations we shall certainly be at one with the Soviet Union . . . we would like to get instructions from the Soviet Communist Party and Comrade Joseph Stalin on various foreign policy issues' (311). In turn, Shi Zhe, Mao's interpreter, recalled Stalin agreeing that a 'revolutionary situation' now existed in Asia and that, amidst a division of labour, the People's Republic of China would take care of promoting 'Eastern revolution' (Shi Zhe 1993: 84–5). With Soviet power already established in Eastern Europe, Stalin told the Chinese delegation on 11 July 1949 of 'the importance of your position . . . a historic mission of unprecedented significance' in which 'the peoples of Asia are looking to you with hope' (Goncharov et al. 1993: 71–2). Later on, when faced with the Chinese request to join the Cominform, Stalin instead suggested that China shape a union of Asian Communist parties, which the Soviet Union as an 'Asian Power' would join, but in which China could play the leading role. China could carry the revolutionary burden, and risks!

Consequently, Lui Shaoqi's 'famous speech' in November 1949, cited earlier, to the Conference of Asia and Australasian Trade Unions in Beijing was seen by many as the Asian equivalent of Zhdanov's 1947 global address to the Cominform, with the permanent liaison Bureau set up as the regional equivalent of the Cominform to spearhead Asian revolutions under China's inspiration and ultimately Moscow's control – 'The Great Asian Conspiracy' premises which were widely held in the West at the time. In a reverse mirror image of emerging Cold War perceptions in America, Liu Shaoqi's bipolar ideological analysis was that 'the world today has been divided into two mutually antagonistic camps', that is, 'on the one hand, the world imperialist camp, composed of American imperialists and their accomplices, the reactionaries of all countries of the world' and 'on the other hand, the world anti-imperialist camps, composed of the Soviet Union and the New Democracies of eastern Europe, and the national liberation movements in China,

Southeast Asia' (Liu Shaoqi 1949a: 32). The lines were stark, 'American imperialism has become the bastion of all reactionary forces in the world; while the Soviet Union has become the bastion of all progressive forces' (32).

Western perceptions of the Chinese Revolution

Various Western observers saw wide significance in the Chinese Revolution. Owen Lattimore reckoned in *The Situation in Asia* that 'in all Asia, China is the country farthest beyond control by America, Russia, or Europe, and the least likely to be brought under control' (1949: 136) by them, so that 'if they maintain their own political center of gravity in China, we shall have a decidedly different kind of world' (1949: 164). As to Soviet influence 'China's devotion to nationalism and national interests is more powerful among people than devotion to Marxism and Russian interests ... the China of the next few decades will be no puppet or pushover for the Russians' (163). China's sheer power potential was apparent, 'with a population larger than that of Russia – about twice as large – and with a victorious army of several million men', as was the independent nature of PRC leaders, 'its top political and military leadership is not Moscow-trained ... they are capable of changing the whole internal balance ... of world Communism' (167–8).

Other observers were just simply struck by China's own emergence. Jack Belden's *China Shakes the World* noted the dramatic changes for the PRC leaders who 'have now become major actors on the stage of world power ... Statesmen may fear them or wonder at them, and businessmen may try to serve them while philosophers shudder ... they cannot be wished out of existence nor can their importance be denied' (1950: 461). His image was of challenge, 'there they are, vibrant, vital and vigorous, marching across Asia with arms in hand, blood in their eyes and a song on their lips, a new force, a terrible force in an ancient world, a crumbling world' (461). Robert Payne, back in America, also looked at the future in his study of *Mao Tse-tung. Ruler of Red China*. Classic imagery was evoked, that 'one day in Fontainebleau, Napoleon was turning the globe of the world. He said: "China? There lies a sleeping giant. Let him sleep, for when he wakes he will move the world"', from which Payne reckoned 'now at last, and for the first time, the lion awoke from its long sleep, and stretched its claws' (1951: 275). Mao's position as PRC leader meant that 'from now on the destiny of the world will be intimately and perhaps violently, affected by the decisions made by him and by the people he leads' (263). Payne saw Mao as a 'portent of the future' in the East with his 'hard determination to bring Asia into its place in the sun' (271) and wondered that 'through him [Mao], Admiral Mahan's nightmare that the United States, in losing Asia, will forfeit its status as a world power, may be confirmed' (276), an interesting geopolitical reference.

American reactions to the Chinese Revolution were frequently strident. In the immediate aftermath, and in response to 'the theme of China lost'

(Acheson 1967: 355), the Chinese Revolution proved a significant factor in America's decision to rearm, creating panic waves of 'hysterical proportions' (358) in the United States and directly leading to McCarthyism (362–9). In 1949, one Congressman, particularly vehement over the loss of China, seen as thrown away by a sick President Franklin Roosevelt and soft diplomats and advisers like Owen Lattimore and John Fairbanks, was the young John Kennedy! Similarly, in Australia, 'the dominant perception of China throughout the 1950s and 1960s was decidedly negative . . . conservative opinion cast the PRC as an anti-Utopia, the embodiment of everything that was repugnant and alien to western civilisation and the human spirit itself' (Strahan 1996: 127). More specifically, from the American side, now pre-eminent in the Western bloc, China was viewed as a cipher for the USSR.

As Mao's forces were moving to take Beijing in 1949, US ambassador in Moscow, Walter Smith warned how 'the Soviet government, by a series of well-timed moves, has been able to seize control of vast new areas of Europe and Asia . . . since the war, Soviet control has been extended over . . . Northern China', where 'these conquered provinces must now be held in submission . . . foreign rule over people who are familiar with the devices of puppet government' (1950: 314). Dean Acheson lamented in the *China White Paper* that in China 'the communist leaders have forsworn their Chinese heritage and have publicly announced their subservience to a foreign power . . . in the interests of a foreign imperialism . . . the Communist regime serves not their [Chinese] interests but those of Soviet Russia . . . this foreign domination' bringing with it the further danger that 'the Communist regime [in China] lend itself to the aims of Soviet Russian imperialism and attempt to engage in aggression against China's neighbors' (1949: xvi–xvii). Consequently, NSC 48/1 felt 'the extension of Communist authority in China represents a grievous political defeat for us' (USA 1949: 259), in which 'Communist domination of China is significant to the USSR primarily because it enhances USSR capabilities of obtaining Soviet objectives in Asia' (253,256). As bluntly put by Acheson in January 1950, the Chinese Communist leadership were but 'puppets of Moscow' (1950a: 431).

Sino–Soviet Alliance and McCarthyism

As NSC 48/1 and Acheson ruminated on China, Mao had set out from Beijing on 6 December, arriving in Moscow on 16 December, for a somewhat terse and, in retrospect, problematic three months of negotiations (Goncharov *et al.* 1993: 84–129). The British ambassador in Moscow reported to Bevin that it was 'worth noting . . . on his arrival here Mao showed no excessive deference to the Soviet Union, but on the contrary gave an indication of his feeling of equality by referring repeatedly to their two "great peoples" and "the two great States"' (DBPO 2002: 438). Mao's trip to Moscow and the agreements made, could be, and were, seen in the West as yet one more sign of China slipping into the Soviet orbit; even though in reality the negotiations had been hard, drawn out, and indeed masking differences of approach, expectations and temperaments. This all resurfaced a decade later in the Sino–Soviet split, where Mao mentioned the distrustful attacks on him by Stalin, Molotov and Beria at those Moscow negotiations as one of 'problems' in Sino–Soviet relations (Westad 1998: 350). The Sino–Soviet Treaty of Friendship, Alliance and Mutual Assistance signed in Moscow by Mao in February 1950 brought Acheson's expressions of sympathy for the Chinese people, where 'it is Soviet Russia which, despite all the tawdry pretence of the treaty terms, occupies the role of empire builder at China's expense', leaving 'an unhappy status within the orbit of the Soviet Union' (1950b: 520) for China, and a hoped for eventual disillusionment and return towards an America which would retain its traditional friendly sentiments from afar! What is noteworthy is that this perception of China as a Soviet puppet reflected a power analysis where China was too weak to merit separate treatment. Differences were apparent in the Western camp between Britain and the USA (Martin 1986, Foot 1990, Kaufman 2001). Whereas Britain advocated recognition of the PRC and engagement policies, the USA stuck to non-recognition and containment.

However, whereas Stalin's Soviet Union could project and be interpreted in conservative terms as a 'Great Power' amenable to understandings over zones of influences and settled 'realism' *realpolitik*, Mao's China represented a more ideologically charged, overtly revolutionary, face of Communism. His emphasis on the 'intermediate zone' of oppressed non-Western countries (which included China) shifted the focus of the Cold War away from Europe and into Asia, namely China itself and Vietnam and Korea. Mao's emphasis on the role of 'continuous revolution', whilst immediately having domestic implications and applications, also pointed to foreign affairs, and external perceptions thereon of China.

It is no coincidence that Senator Joseph McCarthy's notorious speech on 20 February 1950, denouncing the internal Communist threat to the USA, used external Chinese-related episodes to illustrate how 'this is a time of the Cold War. This is a time when all the world is split into two vast, increasingly hostile armed camps', classic bipolar analysis in which 'today we can almost physically hear the mutterings and rumblings of an invigorated god of war. You can see it, feel it, and hear it all the way from the hills of Indochina, from the shores of Formosa' (1950). The next month, 30 March, he renewed his Senate attacks on how 'Soviet Russia conquered China and an important ally of the conquerors was this small left-wing element in our Department of State' (Tsou 1963: 544). China's arrival in the Soviet camp accounted for most of the increase/decrease in his global accounting of strength between Soviet and American camps.

In the US the 'Loss of China' became a highly emotive issue and the trigger for 'Cold War Orientalism' fears over widespread Communist infiltration of American departments where 'domestic containment policies revived latent "yellow peril" fears of a combined Chinese threat from both within and outside the nation' (Klein 2003: 34). John Flynn's *While You Slept: Our Tragedy in Asia and Who Made It* (1951) reflected this nightmare. Utley's *The China Story* bluntly talked about how the PRC's 'entire course of action, were dictated from Moscow' (1951: 19). Chinese experts, like Owen Lattimore, were smeared by Utley (1951: 188–218) and others, as Communist sympathisers. The FBI pursued Chinese family organisations that had maintained links with organisations in China; the Immigration and Naturalization Services deported 'Communist' Chinese. By this time China's image in the West and in the international system had been dramatically modified by the Korean War.

The Korean War

The eruption of the Korean War in June 1950 reinforced fears of Communist expansionism, within which China was seen as a mouthpiece for Moscow, even if in retrospect Stalin and Mao were indeed decidedly 'uncertain partners' (Goncharov *et al.* 1993). In even bigger retrospect, the tangled perceptions and misperceptions at play, allied to classic IR security dilemma dynamics, meant that perhaps in Korea 'the expansion of the Cold War into Asia could qualify for a comedy of errors if its consequences had not been so horrendously tragic' (Gaddis 1997: 75).

As American forces recovered from initial sweeping North Korean advances and pushed back into North Korea in the autumn of 1950, the USA dismissed Chinese warnings via the Indian ambassador Kavalam Panikkar about possible Chinese intervention. Instead General Douglas MacArthur, leading the military operations, ruminated on reversing the 'loss of China' through extending the war back into northern China. MacArthur, and much of the American military leadership, had rather dismissed both the capability as well as 'nerve' of China to intervene, 'ethnocentrism assumed a vital role in U.S. strategic thinking . . . trapped by its own self-image, the U.S. military hardly paid attention to the strategy and tactics of the Chinese Communist forces' (Zhang Shu 1995: 260). Meanwhile, Chinese troops had been secretly deployed through overland night marches, 'volunteers' ready to engage with American troops in late October. MacArthur launched a final drive for the Yalu river frontier with China, reached in some parts during November. However, this triumphant drive was shattered, under a massive and unexpected Chinese offensive of some 200,000, rather than 40,000 Chinese troops, who proceeded to drive American troops back into South Korea. At the time the UK Chiefs of Staff judged that war between the US and China 'would be the old story of the fight between the whale and the elephant – neither can do the other real harm', in part through China's dispersed rural size, its huge population, and an attitude holding human life 'very cheap' (DBPO 1991: 270). Eventually American military power re-asserted itself, and so the Korean War settled into a series of long, bloody, meat grinder drawn out confrontations – its 'meat grinder' phase. MacArthur's wilder escalatory schemes of direct attacks, including nuclear weapons, on China were dismissed, as was MacArthur himself in April 1951. By early 1953 the total number of Chinese troops in Korea had reached 1.35 million, including logistics units. In itself this represented a dramatic projection of China's power and presence outside her boundaries in a way not seen for over one and a half centuries since her old Middle Kingdom days.

China's intervention became the focus of Allen Whiting's early classic study *China Crosses the Yalu* (1960), which stressed the problem of mutual misperception at play in Sino–American relations over intents and capability, with both sides seemingly unable to understand the frame of reference within which the other was operating. In retrospect, Chen Jian sees the Chinese intervention as being 'to use the challenge and the threat brought about by the Korean crisis to cement Communist control of China's state and society, as well as to promote Communist China's international prestige and influence' (2001: 116; also Chen Jian 1994; Scobell 2004), rather than expansionism per se. On 20 November 1950, *Life* magazine took a simpler line with its profile *Aggressive China Becomes a Menace* where 'China's Red Army, a guerrilla rabble 20 years ago, has been built into a menacing Russianized fighting force'.

China's intervention and initial victories proved a dramatic moment, as 'a peasant army put to flight a modern western military force commanded by a world famous American general. In one bound China had become a world power' and 'the image of the Chinese ward, almost half a century in the making was shattered' with the USA facing 'this disturbing new presence on the world scene' (Stoessinger 1971: 59). As such, 'the battle in North Korea was the first great victory won by Chinese forces over a major power which had a lasting effect on the outcome of an international war since the Opium War opened the modern era in China' (Tsou 1963: 589). Psychologically, previous humiliation had been replaced by current glory in less than a decade. From 'the new configuration of power in the Far East ... the emergence of China as a powerful nation in the Far East ... added to the equation of power new political and emotional factors which otherwise would not have existed' (588).

Britain's Foreign Secretary, Ernest Bevin's initial comments in November 1950 had been to acknowledge 'of cardinal importance – they [the CCP] achieved success in their revolution despite the very great assistance given to the Nationalist Government by the United States of America' in which 'the continuing hostility of the American Press and public to the new China and the continuing sympathy shown to the Nationalist [Taiwan] Government has confirmed the Chinese in their impression of the implacable hostility of America' (DBPO 1991: 196). Amidst China's 'communist characteristics' he talked of China's likely goal of trying to 'erect a barrier ring of satellites for her own defence', where 'consciously or unconsciously, the Chinese may be seeking to reproduce the old system of a Chinese Empire and a ring of vassal states' (196–7). Esler Dening, British ambassador to India, thought in December that 'the more I ponder the more I come to the conclusion, fantastic as it may seem, that China really does believe that the U.S. intends to attack her and that her actions have been defensive rather than offensive' (DBPO 1991: 261). As he noted, 'in the introduction to the American *White Paper* of July 1949 Acheson declared the hostility of the U.S. towards the communist regime in China. Is there any reason why China should not have taken this declaration [by Acheson] at its face value?' (DBPO 1991: 261). For this diplomat, 'in 1950 the attitude of certain sections of the American press and of certain Congressmen may well have encouraged the Chinese in their suspicions of U.S. intentions', while 'the attitude of the U.S. towards the admission of the Central People's Government to the U.N. has been both provocative and hostile' (261).

One immediate result of the Chinese intervention in Korea was the speedy visit by the British Prime Minister Clement Attlee to Washington in December 1950. Amidst 'the frustrations of alliance' (Lowe 1989), Britain very consciously attempted to rein in the United States from too wide-ranging a response, rightly worried that MacArthur was edging towards general confrontation in China itself, non-nuclear or even nuclear. At their first meeting Truman told Attlee that 'they [China] are satellites of Russia and will be satellites so long as the present Peiping regime is in power . . . complete satellites . . . After Korea, it would be Indo-China, then Hong Kong, then Malaya . . . the situation looks very dark' (FRUS 1976: 1368). Acheson similarly felt that the CCP leadership were 'not looking at the matter as Chinese but as communists who are subservient to Moscow' (1367). Bevin begged to differ, telling the Commonwealth Prime Minister's meeting in 1951, that 'he himself did not regard China as a satellite of Russia' (DBPO 1991: 290).

Attlee's perspective was also a different one from Acheson. Attlee 'doubted if they [the Chinese] wanted to throw themselves completely in the hands of the Russians. They would rather feel their own strength' (FRUS 1976: 1365). Moreover, 'he had tried to look at the matter from the way the Chinese felt it . . . their attitude seems to include an element of fear, a genuine fear of the United States and of the European nations generally' (1365). Classic IR balance of power language was used by Attlee as he recognised China's emerging power across Asia, 'Chinese Communists who were emerging as a great power' (1398). Already 'Chinese expansionism in Malaya, in the East Indies and in Burma' was evident, where 'all over the East the Chinese had expanded as the dominant race. To this factor was now added their military force which gives them to a large extent the leadership in Asia' (1398). Attlee's suggestion was to 'use' China's emerging power. In a criticism of American thinking, Attlee maintained that 'it is easy to say that China is entirely in the hands of the Russians. This is a fatalistic attitude' since 'at least you can hope that if you back nationalism you can get Chinese imperialism opposed to Russian imperialism. Therefore, the UK had tried to drive a wedge between China and Russia' (1398). This divisive nationalist angle continued to surface in British circles. Oliver Franks publicly argued in the *New York Times* of 19 May 1951 that 'in the long run it is far from certain that the nationalism of China can be made to serve the interests of aggressive Russian imperialism . . . Chinese nationalism will resist the foreigners' attempts to control China as it always has in the past', at which point 'if that happens, provided the door has not finally been closed from our side, China, like Yugoslavia, might well be ready to enter into relations with the western world'.

Admittedly, some British voices were more denunciatory of Chinese perceptions and motives. Scott's analysis at the Foreign Office in February 1951 was that 'the Chinese are essentially aggressive and expansionist . . . there is no doubt they suffer from megalomania and overweening self-confidence . . . xenophobia . . . The ancient tributaries must pay tribute again . . . the new China is a menace to the peace of Asia . . . a peril which . . . upsets the world balance of power' (DBPO 1991: 349, 51). However, most British analysis brought out China's restraint and potential divisions between the USSR and the PRC. Moreover, some figures discounted China's ability to threaten the West. On coming to power, Winston Churchill's blunt assessment in September 1952 had been 'I do not regard Communist China as a formidable adversary . . . the Chinese might well be made to feel as uncomfortable as they make us . . . I doubt whether Communist China is going to be the monster some people imagine' (Dockrill 1989: 109). In retrospect though, it was significant that Atlee's hopes for driving a wedge between China and the Soviet Union were not met. Instead the United States locked itself into a much more bi-polar view of the world in which China was seen as simply a dangerous tool of the Soviet Union. American statements about China were generally much less nuanced than those of the UK.

In American military circles, China's intervention in Korea soon generated dramatic images and perceptions. China's massed formations and readiness to take high ground casualties heightened American perceptions of a 'teeming' (Kulischer 1953) Chinese threat ready to sweep across Asia, and 'set back US–Chinese relations for twenty years' (Khong 1996: 185). Robert Riggs's army report was bluntly titled *Red China's Fighting Hordes* (1951), and described 'a sadism and brutality inherent in many Asiatics . . . countless masses of uniformed robots' (1951: 19, 105). Colonel Samuel Marshall similarly emphasised the size of the 'ochre hordes', where American forces were being 'swamped by a yellow tide which moved upon it from all sides . . . it was like dealing with mass lunacy' (1953: 210). General Mark Clark's analysis was that 'the Chinese Communist army . . . combat effectiveness was limited to the tactic of the "human sea" because all it had initially was an overwhelming superiority in numbers of men . . . the enemy hurled overwhelming numbers of men at us, apparently heedless of how many he lost' (Clark 1954: 87, 101). MacArthur blazed in the *New York Times* on 20 April 1951 that PRC was a clear threat, since 'the Chinese people have thus become militarized in their concepts and in their ideals. They now constitute excellent soldiers . . . This has produced a new and dominant power in Asia which . . . has become aggressively imperialistic, with a lust for expansion' (MacArthur 1964: 367).

Analysts wrestled with China's military appearance in Korea. Hanson Baldwin's consideration of *China as a Military Power* was that 'they will fight. We have learned this, somewhat to our surprise and at a heavy cost, in Korea' (1951: 51), with their human wave tactics 'fitted, as might be expected to the horde' (59). In that setting he asked 'are we beginning to witness the transmutation into fact of that old bogey of 50 years ago – "the Yellow Peril"?' in which 'can China's vast manpower be harnessed – possibly by a virulent nationalism, possibly by a blend of the two – to a militaristic purpose object aggression?' (52). Although 'the modern Chinese soldier could be said to be a potential "world menace"' (52), constrictions were still apparent. First geopolitically 'China is still cabined and confined by the seas' (52). Second, in an era of industrialised warfare and foreshadowing Paul Kennedy's Great Power frameworks, 'victory today is more on the side of the big factories than the big powers' (52). Consequently, '"The Yellow Peril" in the sense we once used the term cannot exist until China is organized, developed and industrialized – a process that will surely require not years, but decades' (52). Three 'decades' later and the world was faced with Deng Xiaoping's 'Four Modernizations' (i.e. of the economy and of the military)!

Most official comments still subsumed China with a wider Soviet threat in the early 1950s. John Foster Dulles told the UN in November 1950 that 'China is to be amalgamated into the Soviet Communist "reserve". . . a new colonialism – Soviet style' (DAFR 1950: 523–4). US Secretary of State Dean Acheson famously dismissed the PRC in May 1951, 'Peiping may be a colonial Russian government – a Slavic Manchukuo on large scale. It is not the government of China. It does not pass the first test. It is not Chinese' (SAR 1972: 100). Externally, 'China has been driven by foreign masters into an adventure of foreign aggression' (100). Similarly, Truman told Congress that same month that 'the Kremlin has already reduced China to the status of a satellite. The Soviet rulers have turned their satellite armies loose on the Republic of Korea' (1951). From the Republican Party wing of American politics, Thomas Dewey's trip to the Far East in 1952 saw him similarly judging that 'Russian "advisers" are largely running Red China' (1952: 27). But then, China's own rhetoric could support such a linkage. Liu Shaoqi happily emphasised the closeness of Sino–Soviet links in 1953, where 'the friendship and unity between the peoples is enduring, indestructible and impervious to any attack . . . the Soviet Union is our model and leader' (1953: 259).

China's intervention in Korea was changing perceptions of her. William Stevenson, on his return from Korea in 1952 considered that 'the Chinese Communists were a new power in a world which was changing with dizzy speed' (1959: 2), with their intervention in Korea being 'shock treatment that would put the rest of the world in a sweat' (138). It was significant that it was China, not the Soviet Union, that was actually prepared to directly take on the United States in ground combat, and as such was able to hold its own. In terms of perceptions, 'the Korean conflict marked the end of America's sentimental attachment, the end of the image of the Chinese as heroic underdog and the end to a paternal interest and avuncular concern' and 'in fact the post-1950 American image of a hostile, menacing China dates from the Korean War' (Stoessinger 1971: 44). Lieutenant General Sir Sidney Rowell reckoned that 'Communist China's rise as a great military power is the major lesson of the Korean campaign' (*Daily Telegraph*, 30 June 1953). By 1954, Britain's Chiefs of Staff were advising, 'with the possible exception of atomic bombing, there was no effective military action that could be taken against China' (Short 1990: 250). One academic, Kenneth Younger, recognised that 'there can also be little doubt that the Korean fighting has raised the prestige of Communist China throughout South-east Asia. In that area it is China, and not Russia which is the great reality and the potential model for Communists' (1954: 102). As Harold Isaacs summarised, the Korean War proved a 'jolting' experience bringing with it 'these new images of the Chinese as a warrior' (1958: 227). Thus, 'before the Korean War ended, the new image of the Chinese warrior and foe became something more than a vision of vast numbers of massed barbarians akin to the Mongol hordes' for 'these were Mongol hordes with big guns and jet aircraft and a growing number among them who knew how to use these weapons with considerable skill and precision' (236). Older Yellow Peril images were being technologically updated. Commentators were struck by this Chinese drive to assert, or rather re-assert, China's international standing. In short, 'an important result of the war in Korea has been to establish Red China's reputation as a great military power' (Walker 1956: 253).

The PRC's whole power ratings were increased through the Korean war, and according to Walker 'in many respects this goal of achieving status as a great power had been realised by Mao's government after only five years' (1956: 253). The Indian ambassador Panikkar saw it as reflecting a sense of how 'China had become a Great Power and was insisting on being recognized as such', but 'the adjustments which such a recognition requires are not easy' (1955: 177–8) for the United States. American and Chinese negotiators stumbled to wind up the Korean War, with the American ambassador in Moscow, reporting 'Malenkov made some general references to the "sensibilities" of Communist China which felt that its "rights" as a great power had been ignored' (FRUS 1986: 53) by the United States.

The growing challenge of China

The PRC may have been seen in the US as an agent of Moscow, but its overt leading and visible role in the Korean War gave it a greater presence in Cold War calculations of the USA, and indeed across much of Asia. As the Korean War entered its middle period, American strategists were constructing the famous domino theory, first surfacing in NSC 124/2 *United States Objectives and Courses of Action With Respect to Southeast Asia*, warning that 'the loss of any of the countries of Southeast Asia to communist control as a consequence of overt or covert Chinese aggression would have crucial psychological, political and economic consequences' (USA 1952: 127), threatening the surrounding areas of India, the Middle East, Southeast Asia, the Pacific offshore islands and Japan.

Admittedly some left wingers and liberals saw the Chinese Revolution as a glorious step forward, as in Hewlett Johnson the 'Red Dean of Canterbury' and author of *China's New Creative Age* (1953). However China's steps forward were more often seen through Korean-affected military lenses. Generally, Western perceptions of China were fearful ones, albeit of a Chinese Yellow Peril subsumed within a wider Soviet 'Red Peril'. Werner Levi's *Modern China's Foreign Policy* viewed China through the bipolar rivalry between Moscow and Washington, where 'the Communists are trying to establish a formidable unit from the Elbe to the Pacific. Political relations are close, thanks to strict coordination with, or better, subordination to, the Soviet Union' (1953: 323). Within that overall Moscow leadership, was a regional 'bid for Asian leadership' (323) by China where 'Communist China's policy is active and aggressive' (325). Kenneth Younger contrasted 'the picture, which has been built up over the last few years in the United States, of a China bent on military conquest designed eventually to extend to Australia and to . . . India' with 'British opinion [which] has been . . . less alarmist about Chinese military expansion' (1954: 109). American perceptions of China were distorting foreign policy judgements, 'the fear of Communism has so gripped the United States' and caused 'their refusal to face the alternative of serious negotiations with China' even though 'a whole civilization is in a ferment there and will not be restored to calm by any simple formula or by the intervention of outside forces from the West . . . policies which are alien to their [Chinese] thinking' (111). The formation of SEATO 'South East Asia Treaty Organisation' in 1954, as well as the US–Japan Security Treaty in 1952, was aimed at this more alarmist image of a China threatening the West as a Soviet satellite. Eisenhower's famous 'Domino Theory' speech of 1954, '450 million of its people' threatening still more 'millions and millions and millions and millions of people' (1954: 201) set the scene with its heavy undertones of a Chinese threat to the West. NSC 5045 reiterated the domino theory logic, with 'the danger of an overt military attack against Southeast Asia is inherent in the existence of a hostile and aggressive Communist China' (USA 1954: 368).

One subtle presentation was by D. Howard, a missionary for twenty years in China, and his profile of *The Chinese Enigma*. On the threatening side was the process whereby 'a country of more than 500 million inhabitants . . . is becoming with incredible rapidity a strong military powerful nation . . .

accompanied by acute xenophobia directly particularly against the USA' (Smith 1955: 360). Yet he chose to highlight deeper 'profound psychological and historical reasons for the mistrust and suspicion' (370) of the West in China. For him, 'Chinese communism will not be understood unless it is realized that it is intensely nationalistic. A proud nation has again been humbled by the West, and has had to swallow its pride' (368), generating 'resentments which smouldered long before the communists came into power' (370). The image of the West was one of 'unwarrantable interference, and commercial and cultural aggression' (368) against China. In turn Mao's 'revolutionary government is heir to all the glory of Han, T'ang, Sung and Ming, and destined to lead China forward in an era of imperial greatness' (369). Strong words indeed.

By the time Dwight Eisenhower formed the first of his two administrations of 1953–61, a China threat was also seen with regard to French Indo-China where Ho Chi Minh had vigorously resisted France's attempts to reassert its pre-war colonial authority. American policy makers disregarded Ho's nationalist roots, and saw China as very much the power behind the throne. Admittedly, 'the Chinese Communist victory in 1949 changed the international environment for the Vietnamese revolution' in which 'the CPC leadership was willing to play an outstanding role in supporting the cause of the Communist comrade', but perhaps with Chen Jian's caveat that this was more 'for the purpose of promoting its international reputation and enhancing its southern border security' (2001: 120) than for wider expansionism. Ultimately, Chinese troops did not intervene directly within Vietnam, but substantial equipment, training and border operations were provided from China.

Why was Mao ready, and indeed eager, to help Ho Chi Minh in 1950? Personal ties were one reason. Consolidating China's own revolution was another, a directive from Liu Shaoqi in March 1950 arguing that aid was 'one of the most important methods to consolidate the victory of the Chinese revolution in the international arena' (Zhai Qiang 2000: 21). China and the international system were entwined, in the past the old international system had shackled and crippled China, whereas a new international order could support and rejuvenate China. In addition was Mao's 'international mission' (20), Mao's 'messianic' belief 'that China had a special role in the reshaping of a future revolutionary order in the world' (21; also Chen Jian 2001: 122). Images were at play, 'CCP leaders intervened in Indochina to define China's identity or self-image in the world' (Zhai Qiang 2000: 21). For the PRC 'the Indochina conflict therefore provided both a test and a validation of the PRC national identity as a champion of national liberation struggles in colonial and semi-colonial areas', it 'presented the exogenous trigger for national identity mobilization and confirmed for the national self and "others" that China could stand up for the integrity of its self-image as a supporter of national liberation movements against imperialism and colonialism' (22). Eventually Mao's 'insistence on the wisdom and centrality of the Chinese model and experience was easily perceived by the Vietnamese as arrogance, bigotry, and prejudice' (Zhai Qiang 2000: 222), but that lay in the future in the late 1970s rupture between the two communist states.

On the one hand, the PRC would support, facilitate and promote but not actually lead. The key was that it was for local Communists to actually fight for their own revolutions. On the other hand, the perception in France and America was of China pulling the strings. China had been seen as a puppet of the Soviet Union, in turn the Vietnamese were perceived as puppets of China. Eisenhower had already pithily expressed this in March 1951, when NATO Commander in Chief, as that 'even if Indochina were completely cleared of Communists, right across the border is China with inexhaustible manpower' (1981: 190). When Eisenhower asked for British assistance to block China in Indochina, Churchill demurred on the grounds 'that war with China, who would invoke the Sino–Russian pact, might mean an assault by [Soviet] Hydrogen bombs on these islands' (Gilbert 1960: 973). The upshot was that Britain did not offer support to America, who in turn did not provide it to France, who in turn faced defeat at Dien Bien Phu in May 1954, thereby pulling out of Vietnam under the Geneva Accords of July 1954. In the wake of events in Korea and Vietnam, Richard Walker talked of 'the successful creation of a world power center in China' (1956: x). There, the West should not 'allow this new Communist colossus to score further victories' (328), this new force, of 'Communist China constitutes a challenge to all the non-Communist world' (326) in which 'Communist China will, whenever expedient, continue to promote revolution, and intrigue abroad' (326). Indeed, the *Boston Herald* (25 February 1956) reported an American colonel predicting that 'the Chinese Communist Army will be the most dynamic fighting machine by 1970', and that the very survival of the USA would 'be in doubt' – interesting speculation for one and half decades later.

China was a growing regional presence in the 1950s. The Indian Prime Minister, Jawaharlal Nehru admitted in January 1951 that in Asia 'there was a growing fear of China as a great Power' (DBPO 1991: 292). The PRC loomed large in Pacific sensitivities. In Australia, China was seen as a Soviet puppet, typified in *The Bulletin* cartoon 'Branding Operation' on 8 December 1948 of a submissive Chinese dragon being branded by a domineering Stalin; a *Bulletin* that until 1961 had its masthead of 'Australia for the White Man'. Paul Keating felt that post-1945 foreign policy under fellow premier Robert Menzies aimed to 'to preserve us from the yellow peril, or the red arrows thrusting downwards' (2000: 19). Already in 1949, Arthur Fadden, leader of the County Party, had been charging in the Australian federal elections that 'a major war is already raging on the battle-fronts of China, where communist forces are thrusting their red spears towards Australia' (*Sydney Morning Herald*, 6 December). Foreign Minister Percy Spender, on coming into office, warned Parliamentary colleagues on 9 March 1950 that China might well try 'to stir up unrest and rebellion in Asia'

(Harper 1955: 204). Spender was clear enough that the 1951 ANZUS Pact between the USA, New Zealand and Australia was a way of insuring 'against any possible [Chinese] Communist aggression' (1969: 76) in the future.

Australian troops fought in Korea, something of a 'Forward Line' defense against China. External Affairs Minister Richard Casey merged old and new Yellow Peril fears together in the shape of China where 'even without the threat of Communist expansion from the north, our position as a lightly-populated country on the edge of Asia and possessing a high standard of living and a selective immigration policy, would create problems enough' (1954: 20). Scorfield's *The Red River*, shown in *The Bulletin* (16 June 1954) with massed ranks of Chinese soldiers advancing through winding Korean gorges, reiterated the older yellow peril imagery of undifferentiated Asian hordes advancing on Australia. Australia could perceive herself as threatened by Chinese hordes sweeping down onto Australia itself, as 'conventional racial stereotypes were interwoven with more recent [anti-Communist] ideological constructions' (Strahan 1996: 259). At the time 'the Korean war, the conflict in China and the growing tension over Formosa and the offshore islands confirmed the conviction [for Australia] that the major threat to security in Southeast Asia and the Pacific arose out of direct and indirect pressures from Peking' (Harper 1955: 204).

Similar fears were discernible in New Zealand. The *New Zealand Herald*, whilst welcoming the 1951 Colombo Plan, saw underlying demographic nuances behind the anti-communist rhetoric, with 'reason to fear that Communist China will seize hegemony over the whole of the Far East ... land hungry Asiatics will burst their national boundaries and overflow into these Dominions? This is our greatest danger' (Brawley 1995: 255). At the time W.F. Monk considered that 'what has happened, of course, has been the emergence of the "yellow peril" ... in a still more malignant form', with him asking 'the problem of communism has come to mean rather the question: Which way will Asia go?' (1953: 221) under the pressure from China. Immigration policies remained firm for New Zealand in the face of the 'teeming Asian millions' and the need 'to build up the country's white strength in close association with Australia and the United States' (228). This trans-Pacific concern over China lay behind Eisenhower sadly telling Churchill in March 1955 that American–British attitudes to Communist 'problems in the orient are frequently so dissimilar as to be mutually antagonistic', whereas 'in our contacts with New Zealand and Australia we have a feeling that we encounter a concern no less acute than ours' (Short 1990: 60) vis-à-vis China.

China's presence as a rising element within the international system was apparent in the wake of the 1954 Geneva Conference on Korea and Indo-China. In the West, Bevin considered that 'acknowledgement of China's position as a great power in the Far East' would be one of the 'essential features of settlement' (DBPO 1991: 238) in Korea. Admittedly at the US State Department Walter McConaughy argued instead that 'the Chinese communist regime will be present (at the Geneva Conference) only because of its aggressor role . . . far from dealing with it as a Great Power, we do not even deal with it as a legitimate government' (*Department of State Bulletin*, 15 March 1954). However this American line was impossible to maintain. Chen Jian judged that amidst skilful diplomatic positioning and public relations, 'the real winner at the conference was Zhou [Enlai]', where 'the crucial role China played in the conference implied that for the first time in modern history (since the 1839–42 Opium War) China had been accepted by the international society – friends and foe alike – as a real world power' (2001: 143), and vivid contrast to the Yalta Conference in 1945 where Chinese territory had been disposed of without any Chinese representative.

The PRC was very aware of its growing role, degree of international legitimacy and Great Power recognition achieved at the Geneva Conference. The *People's Daily* (*Renmin Ribao*), 7 August 1954, article 'Six Hundred Million' noted 'the Big Power status of China' revealed at the Geneva Conference with the warning 'imperialists, beware of knocking your heads against the "wall" built by 600,000,000 people'. With some truth the *People's Daily* editorial on 22 July 1954 announced that 'for the first time as one of the Big Powers, the People's Republic of China joined the other major powers . . . the international status of the People's Republic of China as one of the big powers has gained universal recognition' and 'its international prestige has been greatly enhanced'. Soong Qingling, Sun Yat-sen's widow, similarly considered 'for the first time in modern history we have taken up our responsibilities as one of the Great powers. When we speak, we speak not only for ourselves, but for all Asia' (*New China News Agency*, 26 October 1954).

China's own territorial sovereignty had also been completed vis-à-vis the Soviet Union. In the wake of their Korean cooperation, agreements were reached between Moscow and Beijing in 1954 for the withdrawal of Soviet forces from Port Arthur/Darien, and the liquidation of joint Soviet–Chinese companies in Sinkiang. All this took effect by 1 April 1955. China's sacrifices on the battlefield in Korea were enabling it not only to stand up taller with regard to the USA, but also with regard to the USSR.

China's prominent role in 1955 at the Afro–Asian Bandung Conference was a further sign of growing Chinese projection in the international arena. The *Guardian* writer Guy Wint considered that 'the conference turned into a full-scale analysis of the question before Asia to-day, the relationship between China and the rest of the continent . . . to grapple with the problem of China' (1955: 219). There, 'for five days the countries of Asia which feared Communism expressed their apprehensions about China's plans. A new Communist imperialism by China had replaced the old Western imperialism as a main danger in Asia' (219). However, the Chinese delegation, headed by Zhou Enlai showed 'skill and dignity . . . he breathed friendliness and reconciliation . . . Chou in fact could not hardly have been more conciliatory; he made the impression he wished and had won over some of China's critics' (Wint 1955: 220). Zhou's rhetoric stressed China's solidarity with the Third World against the West, that 'gone forever are the days when the destiny of the Asian and African peoples is manipulated at will by others' (Zhou Enlai 1955: 62); for 'suffering from the same cause and struggling for the same aim . . . the Chinese delegation has come here to seek common ground . . . we seek common ground in doing away with the sufferings and calamities under colonialism' (63), in which previously 'our voices have been suppressed, our aspirations shattered, and our destiny placed in the hands of others' (57). Although excluded from the United Nations international system, China at Bandung could project itself far and wide – in part through its racially orientated rhetoric which was all the more embarrassing (Anderson 2003, also Lauren 2003) and challenging for an America that was facing international scrutiny over its own domestic 'Black' Civil Rights movement. As William Stevenson saw it, at Bandung 'in the world of coloured people, China represented success' (1959: 228). The US *National Intelligence Estimate* acknowledged, at the start of 1956, 'as a result of its achievements and growing power, Communist China's prestige and influence in Asia have greatly increased' (FRUS 1986: 231); later that year Stevenson commented on 'the re-awakening of a China which to me now looked as if it were once again indulging in its ancient dreams of a Celestial Empire surrounded by barbarians' (1959: 14).

Nathanial Peffer's summation was extensive and finely nuanced. He felt that 'China as she stands in the mid-1950s has none of the requisites of military power', and as such 'China does not now and for a long period cannot menace American security so greatly as to constitute a major factor in the Cold War . . . China need not and should not be taken too seriously' (1956: 514). Imagery was prominent in American responses, as 'America's present preoccupation with China is out of scale in the contemporary polit-ical configuration, is altogether distorted out of perspective . . . with what seems . . . short sightedness, political immaturity or irrational obsession' (506). The PRC's 'swaggering, defiant, provocative' behaviour was not down to desire of conquest, instead 'the explanation lies rather in the psychological state produced by the experience of a hundred years', her 'defeat, humili-ation, subjection to foreign rule . . . and foreign domination', all the more galling for 'a people with a historical memory, a memory of racial and cultural grandeur' (497). Meanwhile, within the ongoing American–Chinese relationship, 'resentment has produced counter-resentment, each sharpening the asperity of the other and inflaming emotions. Each country has reasons for its psychological state; each has contributed to the exacerbation of the other's' image, and 'in that condition each confronts the other, not so much in cold hostility as in tensed, rasped nerves' (508). Classic IR security dilemma dynamics and geopsychology.

China's influence did seem to be reaching beyond the Asia–Pacific, as it exerted itself within the post-Stalin Communist crises affecting Eastern Europe. Initially China had criticised and reined in Soviet heavy handedness towards Polish communists, whilst also crucially supporting and thereby legitimising Soviet military intervention against Hungary's break away. Zhou's subsequent highly public trip to Hungary and Poland in 1957 reflected this new prominence and the potential claims of China within post-Stalin communism. In retrospect, for Chen Jian 'the crises in Poland and Hungary also enhanced Mao's and the CCP's consciousness of China's centrality in the world proletarian movement', that is, 'the Beijing leadership's perception of China's great contribution to the settlement of the Polish and Hungarian crises strengthened the belief that the CCP should occupy a more prominent position in the international Communist movement' (2001: 161). With Stalin dead, Mao was left standing as, in effect, the senior figure amongst Communist leaders. During 1954–7 China stood up alongside the Soviet Union as their 'independent equal ally' (Yahuda 1978: 64–101), in the 'most productive' (64) phase of their alliance.

Mao could also hope for economic strength to buttress China's enhanced role within a generally stronger Communist bloc. Mao proudly proclaimed in 1955 that China would overtake the USA, since 'America only has a history of 180 years. Sixty years ago it produced 4 million tons of steel. We are [therefore] only sixty years behind . . . [and] we will surely overtake it' (Zhang Shu 1998: 203). Quite specifically, in 1957 Mao boasted to other Communist leaders at Moscow that China would overtake Britain in iron, steel and other heavy industries in the next fifteen years (i.e. by 1972); and that she would also soon afterwards overtake the USA in those areas as well. By 1958 he considered China as on an upward trajectory, telling the Supreme State Conference in January that 'I see this nation of ours has a great future . . . we shall catch up with Britain in about 15 years . . . there is great hope for the future development of our nation. There are no grounds for pessimism' (Mao Zedong 1974: 91). Rich imagery was wrapped up with his geopolitical aspirations, 'our nation is waking up . . . we shall catch up with Britain within fifteen years . . . now our enthusiasm has been aroused. Ours is an ardent nation, now swept by a burning tide' (92). By April 1958, his vision was even keener, with him arguing that 'it will probably not take us as long as we have anticipated to overtake the capitalist powers in industrial and agricultural production' (Barnett 1960: 203–4). The following month, Mao told military commanders that 'we are quite sure that we will exceed Britain in seven years and overtake the U.S. in ten years' (Barnett 1960: 204). How was China to transform its economic foundations? Something different was needed, 'to reach these targets in the present situation we must have great drive' (93), which for Mao came through the attempted Great Leap Forward during 1958–60, rapid 'backyard' industrialisation and communes, a bold leap to overtake the West.

It was also an attempt to by-pass the Soviet Union. Mao's clarion call, as Party Chairman, at the Chengtu Conference in March 1958 was that 'when Chinese artists painted pictures of me together with Stalin, they always made me a little bit shorter, thus blindly knuckling under to the moral pressure exerted by the Soviet Union' (Mao Zedong 1974: 99). Moreover, 'we lacked understanding of the whole economic situation, and understood still less the economic differences between the Soviet Union and China. So all we could do was to follow blindly. Now the situation has changed' (99). For Mao the 'the situation of the Great Leap Forward inspired not only us in China, but also our Soviet comrades' (129). Social and class redistribution underpinned the internal radicalisation sought by Mao's Great Leap Forward, but the economic drive had a more basic thrust still to it, as Mao put it in September 1959 'in order that our whole nation may build a strong country' (150), able to stand firm within the international system. Mao admitted it caused destabilisation, but as he graphically put it at the Lushan Conference in July 1959, 'the chaos caused was on a grand scale' but it was necessary, for 'if you have to shit, shit! If you have to fart, fart. You will feel much better for it' (146).

In the event, the Great Leap Forward failed, mass chaos combined with poor harvests in 1959 brought widespread famine, starvation and 'extra' deaths of around 2,500,000. The 1960 harvest was around one-quarter of that of 1957, bringing over nine million 'extra' deaths to China. It was no surprise that the Great Leap Forward was abandoned in late 1960. Economic planning became more directed by moderates like Chief of State Liu Shaoqi, Premier Zhou Enlai, and CCP Secretary-General Deng Xiaoping. The Great Leap Forward had though exacerbated China's negative image to the outside world, appearing as an unpredictable radical opponent of standard economic orthodoxies.

China's woes in the Great Leap Forward were exacerbated by the economic blockade and boycott from the United States. Typical Cold War views were expressed in June 1957, with US Secretary of State John Foster Dulles's justification for America neither diplomatically recognising nor trading with a China which 'does not disguise its expansionist ambitions. It is bitterly hateful of the United States, which it considers a principal obstacle in the way of its path of conquest . . . today the political purposes of Communist China clash everywhere with our own' and generally China 'does not conform to the practices of civilized nations . . . has not been peaceful in the past and gives no evidence of being peaceful in the future' (SAR 1972: 134–42). The official US State Department view in their August 1958 Memorandum over recognition of the PRC was that 'the vast population' gave the PRC the base for 'their primary purpose . . . to extend the Communist revolution beyond their borders to the rest of Asia and thence to the rest of the world' in which 'the Chinese Communist regime has made no secret of its fundamental hostility to the United States . . . nor of its avowed intention to effect their downfall' (SAR 1972: 145). Consequently, 'today its defiance of and attacks on the non-Communist world have reached a level of intensity that has not been witnessed since the Korean War' (145). An explicit linking of old Yellow Peril and new 'Red Peril' came from one high-ranking official in the Eisenhower administration, 'I was brought up to think the Chinese couldn't handle a machine' but 'now the Chinese is flying a jet! Disturbing . . . several million of them . . . I always thought the Yellow Peril business was nonsense', but 'now I can visualize that Asiatics . . . could indeed conquer the world!' (Isaacs 1958: 226–7).

In a similar vein, Guy Wint commented that China's six hundred million people gave the PRC 'a position of great strength and one from which it hopes to lay siege to the rest of the world' (1958: 7). Similarly, Michael Croft warned of 'China . . . emerging, within a few years into a world power of the first magnitude' and moving towards 'gaining effective control over most of Asia, with catastrophic repercussions upon the Western way of life' (1959: vii). William Stevenson's *The Yellow Wind* considered that whilst Mao 'has no nuclear bombs . . . he had six hundred million people . . . more numerous than the yellow grains of sand . . . waiting be given direction and drive . . . the time-tested techniques of old China in winning control over most of Asia' (1959: 13, 14). As such, China's influence was widespread, for 'Mao is more widely worshipped and yet more elusive . . . in an age crowded with Titans' and 'looms above the clumsiest tyrants. Where Hitler ranted and raved, Mao whispers', with 'the spread of this man's influence throughout that one third of humanity living in overcrowded and backward [Third World] lands' (20).

A lengthy analysis of China's roles came from Doak Barnett at the end of the 1950s. Looking back, he conceded that 'Communist China has emerged as one of the most dynamic, disrupting, and disturbing influences on the world scene. This has probably been the most important political and strategic change in the international situation since World War II' (1960: 1). Like many he still reckoned on Sino–Soviet solidarity, 'as far as outsiders can know, in no case has there been a head-on clash between them . . . strong ties – ideological, political, military and economic – unite Peking and Moscow' (158, 381) so that 'it seems highly unrealistic to formulate policy on the expectations of a split between them' (381). Nevertheless, Barnett was perceptive enough over nuclear issues, where 'Moscow still seemed reluctant to share its nuclear arsenal. The complicated question of sharing advanced military technology may well prove to be among the most delicate issues in Sino–Soviet relations' (1960: 375). Looking ahead, 'in the long run the Chinese Communists cannot be denied the status of a large and strong power' (85). Already though, in Asia there was already 'the shadow of Communist China's great military power hanging over the region' (140), underpinned by its demographic power, 'a huge mass in motion' (10). It was also underpinned by its economic potential, where 'Communist China's economic development will steadily strengthen Peking's power base for military power, thereby improving its power position in world politics' (63), a marker for the 1990s?

3   China against the world

The 1960s saw an image of China that was different in two senses from before. First, China's ideological and military presence was achieving global undertones. Second, the PRC became locked into simultaneous quarrels with both superpowers, its 'fighting with two fists' *liangge quantou daren* strategy, in Mao's words in 1962, 'abroad, the imperialists [i.e. the USA] curse us . . . the revisionists [i.e. the USSR] curse us' (1974: 181). In addition there was a general distancing but also challenge vis-à-vis the international order. Edward Crankshaw went as far as to describe China as 'an international pariah' (1965: 162, also Zhang Yongjin 1998: 58) by the mid-1960s. Trends of the 1950s were reinforced and still more evident for Zhang Yongjin, in the 1960s, 'the alienation of China from international society . . . the anomalous position of China in that society' (1998: 17) where China could be 'regarded as a "bogy" in world politics' (17).

China's general image

At the start of the 1960s, Guy Wint began the decade with the assessment that the world should be worried as 'China is now the dangerous aggressor . . . the fires of the Chinese revolution are still burning . . . and a revolutionary simply cannot believe in coexistence, even if for a brief time he has managed to wear a mask' (1960: 71). As Allen Whiting succinctly put it 'we must expect to remain in constant struggle with the People's Republic of China over the destiny of Asia' (1960: 17). Robert North's study of *Peking's Drive for Empire: the New Expansionism* saw traditional Chinese pride and chauvinism interacting with Marxist dialectical determinism and political scapegoating needs. He thought it a 'myth that Communist China has no expansionist aims in Asia' (North 1962: 54), given their 'persistent determination to re-establish the furthermost reaches of the old [Qing] empire' (55). A Middle Kingdom geopolitical agenda was present from the past. Abraham Halpern summarised Chinese strategy as 'alteration of the world environment' (1962: 233), and infused with 'uncompromising . . . Chinese irredentism' (233) and 'the drive toward recognized great power status' (235).

Admittedly a rather different slant on American policies towards China was visible in some minority currents. Robert Newman's study on *Recognition of Communist China* perceived various problems from the past at play. He felt that American politicians generally suffered from 'partisanship' and 'inadequate information' (1961: 49), in part brought about through the 'scattering and dismissal' of China specialists in the McCarthyite purges of the early 1950s, specialists like Owen Lattimore who had not fitted into the 'the institution of the new hard line on China' (47); whose absence severely detracted from 'the credibility of State Department testimony [on China] during the Dulles period' (45). Moreover, the effectiveness of that foreign policy was itself affected by race memories, for 'the most serious American debility in the eyes of the Afro–Asian nations, and one which our current China policy inflames is the problem of race' (146). Given that every other previous Communist regime had been recognised by the USA, and that they happened all to be 'White', like the USA; then the refusal to recognise a 'Yellow' China could be seen as rank hypocrisy. Indeed the past reared its head from even further back as 'our Oriental Exclusion Acts may have been repealed, but the memory of them is not allowed to die – Russia sees to that' (147).

Alarmists or not, most commentators were struck by China's rising appeal. Tabor Mende's *China and her Shadow* considered that China's influence was spreading, 'compromising half the continent's population, she is bound to become Asia's political centre of gravity . . . a new force whose presence, interests and ambitions have begun to condition all Asia' (1961: 296). Indeed, 'China is successfully translating the potential strength of her masses into a proportionate factor in international relations . . . China is rapidly emerging as a world power' (288–9), with 'her determination to re-establish the power and influence which has been hers for two millennia' (269). As such 'we are witnessing the beginning of her bid for influence over the potential power-house of future world domination' (302). The influence came in part from her international image, her ideological appeal, where 'the massive pilgrimages . . . from every corner of the world' intertwined with China's propaganda efforts 'all over the world' (269). China was 'convinced that she has something to offer to the economically backward majority of mankind . . . her missionary aims' (270). From such a peasant, intermediate industrial focus, China's revolution could be exported throughout Africa, Asia and Latin America. The result 'China's transformation . . . into one whose influence is now felt on all continents' a 'fact becoming the central theme of contemporary world politics' (288).

Harold Isaacs's geopolitical and geopsychological ruminations in 1961 were similarly direct on China's global emergence where 'the world's largest population has been put to work to transform backward old China into one of the great new powers in the world', where it had taken 'a great leap indeed in a few years from fulfilling the world's image of it as a weakling state to become abruptly a new power casting fearsome shadows on the future . . . and is viewed with a mix of fear and respect' (1961: ix). As for that future, the PRC was 'bent upon regaining China's historic place as the true centre of the world' (ix). To achieve this, 'in the great new game of power politics, it operates on its own out to the world's farthest corner', where 'Chinese missions of various kinds' (ix) could be seen across the Third World. Such missions spanning the political, cultural, economic and military divides were conducted amidst a 'hypnotic pull' where we can observe the 'image the Chinese Communists have managed to cast throughout the world as the possessors of a magic key to the swift emergence from backwardness' (ix), in part through China's rural radical peasantry path, but also 'partly out of awe, respect, and envy for the greater totality of Chinese totalitarian power. It is also because the Chinese are nonwhite' (x).

Michael Edwardes's *Asia in the Balance* also presented 'the menace of communist China' as 'a real and frightening thing' (1962: 13). As 'the awakened Giant' (155), the 'Chinese communists are also heirs to a great *imperial* past, and they are well aware of it' (159). In short, 'the present Chinese government sees itself reassessing both the power and then influence which it believes to be its right in Asia and which it was deprived of by western imperialism' (160). In other words, Middle Kingdom prototype from before its Century of Humiliation. However, China's reach was wider than its old Middle Kingdom horizons of Asia. There was 'a much larger menace . . . by the new China, upright on its two feet, dynamic, and filled with missionary zeal . . . not only to resurrect the great glory of China as the centre of civilization', but also 'to move outwards upon a new civilizing mission . . . to spread out into the whole world' (160–1). As for future diplomacy, Edwardes saw China's readiness to apply Mao's dictums, 'to defend in order to attack, to retreat in order to advance, to take a flanking position in order to advance, and to zigzag in order to go straight', as something that 'underlies every Chinese action' (167). Because of it, 'no final solutions are possible, every compromise is essentially temporary, and no agreement is organically binding', so that 'those who see in any specific rapprochement a trend towards reasonableness, or a willingness to settle outstanding problems, are sadly mistaken. It is merely a tactical withdrawal which will inevitably be followed by a new advance' by the PRC, and in which 'on this level, the struggle for Asia will continue, perhaps indefinitely' (167).

Newsweek correspondent, Robert Elegant graphically and extensively portrayed China's role in the international system in his study *The Centre of the World*, subtitled *Communism and the Mind of China*. In it lay the figure of Mao who 'has already given China power, for which his generation yearned above all else' (1963: 22). The context was that 'Mao is the creature of an overwhelming compulsion to restore China to her rightful place among the nations – at their head . . . to force other nations to their knees in order to restore the proper order of mankind' (22). Mao's world view was one tapping into 'the semi-mystical nationalism of the Chinese . . . unique in both magnitude and intensity . . . a unique conviction of superiority – racial,

cultural, moral, and physical', and within which 'harnessed to messianic
Communism, the Chinese spirit is dedicated to creating another unique
society that will be the centre of world power, just as Imperial China was
the Central Kingdom' (23). As to China's role in the world, it was partly a
matter of intent, where 'a sense of wrongs redressed – and of great wrongs
still endured – today inspires the pathologically self-confident Communist
hierarchy to further assertion' (23). A degree of success had been reached by
China in the international system by 1963, so that 'China, for decades a
source of amusement, today *must* be counted in the scales of power' and 'for
the first time in two centuries the West does not ask: "What *will* we do
about China?" The question is: "What *can* we do about China?"' (Elegant
1963: 22–3). China represented 'a wholly new moral force in the world.
After more than a decade in power, they stand opposed to most of the
world – and frighten even their allies' (25), an interesting perspective on the
seemingly strong Sino–Soviet alliance. It was also a matter of demographics,
where 'the sheer magnitude of China makes of assertiveness a major force
in the world . . . No one can ignore a nation of 650 million persons, occupying more than 4 million square miles, when it is implacably bent upon
revenge' (23). Consequently, 'the Yellow Peril did, in truth, exist and the
Chinese might yet destroy the world by seeking to conquer the world' (359).
In short, China was 'a vengeful threat to the world's existence' (370).

American leaders, and allies, certainly maintained a robust critique of
China. The US–Japan summit, between John Kennedy and Hatato Ikeda,
recorded 'their concern over the unstable aspects of the situation in Asia . . .
of various problems relating to Communist China' (Japan–USA 1961: 57).
The 1965 US–Japan summit, minuted Lyndon Johnson's particular 'grave
concern that Communist China's militant policies and expansionist pressures against its neighbors endanger the peace of Asia' (Japan–USA 1965:
40), despite Eisaku Sato's own attempts to pursue trade openings with the
PRC (Yasutomo 1977).

Roger Hilsman, Assistant Secretary of State for the Far East, finished
1963 with his profile of the 'shadows cast by China – by the China of
history . . . that threatens all its neighbours' (1963b: 302). His comments on
America's earlier interaction with China were candid, feeling that 'our
involvement with China, while intense, was not wholly real; it was fed by
illusions as well as good will' and 'we were little aware of the depth and
fervor of Chinese nationalism in reaction to a sense of repeated humiliation
at the hands of the West' (302). Moreover, there was his revealing turn of
phrase that 'there has perhaps been more emotion about our China policy
than about our policy toward any single country since World War II . . .
stereotypes die hard, and communist China by its sheer size exercises a
fascination' (307). Fascination was entwined with suspicion over Chinese
communism's 'obsessive suspicion [and] . . . paranoid view of the world' (309);
where the PRC 'remains wedded to a fundamentalist form of Communism,
which emphasises violent revolution, even if it threatens the physical ruin of

the civilized world. It refuses to admit there are common interests which cross ideological lines' (309). She was outside international society.

Hilsman's rhetoric was specifically picked up in Beijing, with the officially-sanctioned *People's Daily* profile 'US Policy towards China is in a Blind Alley' on 19 February 1964, a classic mirror image of America's own Cold War image of China. Thus, for China 'U.S. China policy is only part of the U.S. policy of aggression in Asia. In its bid to rule the roost in Asia since the end of World War II, U.S. imperialism has been following a policy of aggression and expansion in a most truculent form' (SAR 1972: 204). However, whilst on the one hand formally rejecting the American claim that China pursues 'aggressive and lone wolf policies' and was 'an increasing threat to the rest of the world', on the other hand it could in effect confirm some American fears as well with its assertion that 'much as it desires to do so, U.S. imperialism cannot overthrow', 'contain' or 'isolate' China, where 'U.S. imperialism is running into a package of troubles in South Vietnam, Laos, Japan, Cambodia, Indonesia and Pakistan. It is, in short, surrounded by its enemies', so that 'no wonder responsible officials in Washington cry out in alarm . . . precisely because the U.S. ruling circles are confronted with the irreversible situation in China and Asia described above' (206–7).

The United States and Japan were not the only neighbours concerned with China, India also had direct reason to worry about China, amidst the emergence of the 'protracted contest' generated by 'Sino–Indian rivalry in the twentieth century' (Garver 2001a). Initial pan-Asiatic sentiments had been noticeable on the Indian side, stemming from pre-Independence days, maintained in the *Hindi-Chini-Bhai-Bhai* 'India and China are brothers' slogan of the 1950s and exemplified in the Bandung Afro–Asian Conference in 1956. However, the successful Chinese defeat of the Indian army and occupation of disputed border territory in 1962 saw a radical change in Indian perceptions of China. At the time Indian public opinion considered 'the threat appears to be China, not Communism' (Cantril 1964: 238), and the defeat was in retrospect 'a mindset-shattering event, a watershed in national psychology, a transforming divide that moved national security to the centre of India's concerns' (Nayar and Paul 2003: 150–1). 'Mis-perceptions' (Vertzberger 1984) were at the heart of their lurch into war and its consequences. Conversely, whilst commentators like Neville Maxwell (1970) have unpicked many of the actual Indian forward provocations around the border issue in the early 1960s, he also succinctly summed up the psychological effects of how 'India's distrustful animus toward China is a toxic element in world politics . . . the hostility derives, of course, from the Indian political class' wounded memory of their country's humiliation in the brief, fierce, border war of 1962' (2003: 99). Over 40 year later, Wang Jisi could from Beijing acknowledge how 'the psychological wounds left by the border war in 1962 need more time to be healed' (2004: 12). As such, 'mind-sets inured in sentiments of humiliation on one side or hurt feelings on the other'

(Ranganathan 2002: 288) became an ongoing feature of India–China relations and perceived threats.

Nehru considered that China had betrayed him and India, and in its aftermath effectively abandoned non-alignment, with India turning to the USSR in order to achieve military security vis-à-vis China (Abadi 1998). Indian fears were further increased by China's explosion of a nuclear test in 1964. Already in 1966 Harrison Salisbury was judging that 'China's bomb and China's nuclear capability had worked in deadly fashion to undermine the Indian principle of ban-the-bomb', proving to be a 'catalyst' for India to move towards 'arming herself with a [nuclear] *force de frappe* against China' (1967: 107–8). Indeed, China's nuclear capacity had become an issue for all its neighbours and in the global balance.

China's nuclear drive

China had attracted attention with Mao's dismissal of the US nuclear bomb as a 'paper tiger' in 1946 and 1957, and even more with Mao's seeming readiness at the Moscow Conference in November 1957 to contemplate life after a nuclear war (Gittings 1968: 81–2). This was based in part around demography whereby China's much greater population would enable her, with half of her population, to survive whereas capitalism's smaller numbers would mean its being unable to survive a nuclear war – a chilling message for American, and also Soviet, policy makers. This was somewhat ironical given that Mao was considering in April 1956, in the wake of the Korea War and Eisenhower's veiled threats on using nuclear weapons, that 'if we are not to be bullied in the present-day world, we cannot do without the [atomic] bomb' (Mao 1977: 288). By the 1960s, it was apparent that the PRC was close to developing its own nuclear capacity, despite Soviet reluctance to help its notional ally in such a field. One interesting piece of nuclear futurology was the 1961 CIA report *China in 1971* drawn up for the new Kennedy administration, reckoning that 'in 1971 . . . China's position as one of the major power centers of the world will have been greatly strengthened', given that 'they will be producing short-range and probably medium-range missiles, and it may be that they will have a submarine-launched missile capability', in which case 'the possibility cannot be excluded that they can produce an operational intercontinental ballistic missile system with thermonuclear warheads by 1971' (FRUS 1996b: 139).

These concerns over China's advance into the nuclear club were soon realised, when 'from the start of Kennedy's administration, government researchers and officials devoted close attention to China's weapons development and concluded that China would soon join the nuclear club' (Chang 1988: 1288). By 1960 the thrust for the US administration was over whether 'to strangle the [Chinese nuclear] baby in the cradle' (Burr and Richelson 2000–1). The Special National Intelligence Estimate *Communist China's Advanced Weapons Program* reckoned that 'possession of nuclear weapons would reinforce their [i.e. PRC] efforts to achieve Asian hegemony through political pressure . . . the Chinese feat would have a profound impact on neighboring governments and peoples. It would alter the latter's sense of the realities of power' and that 'a Chinese Communist nuclear detonation would increase the momentum of China's drive for great-power status' (USA 1963: 10–11). The PRC 'would feel much stronger, and this would undoubtedly be reflected in their approach to conflicts on the periphery' and 'thus the tone of Chinese policy would probably become more assertive . . . and embark on radical new external courses' (11). Walt Rostow recalled Kennedy telling him that 'the biggest event of the 1960s [might] well be the Chinese explosion of a nuclear weapon' (Chang 1988: 1288). Kennedy worried at a January 1963 NSC meeting on the need to 'halt or delay the development of an atomic capability by the Chinese communists' since 'we will have a difficult time protecting the free areas of Asia if China get nuclear weapons' where she 'looms as our major antagonist of the late 60s and beyond' (FRUS 1996a: 462).

Such was the prospect that Kennedy tried to use a common China threat to facilitate a closer relationship and possible joint action with the Soviet Union. This was first mooted by Kennedy to Nikita Khrushchev at their Vienna summit in June 1961. Though turned down by Khrushchev, American hopes remained alive. One 1963 Defense Department briefing paper floated the idea of 'possibly joint US-USSR use of military force' (Chang 1988: 1303) against China. Kennedy remained interested in such an idea, cabling Avril Harriman, the US ambassador in Moscow, on 15 June 1963 that 'I remain convinced that the Chinese problem is more serious than Khrushchev's comment in first meeting suggests', so that 'you should try to elicit Khrushchev's view of means of limiting or preventing Chinese nuclear development, and his willingness either to take Soviet action or to accept US action aimed in this direction' (1300). Whilst the Chinese nuclear option played its part in hastening American–Soviet agreement on the Nuclear Test Ban Treaty signed in Moscow in July 1963, the USSR was unwilling, at this stage, to agree to such action against China, despite the growing tensions between the two communist giants. The Nuclear Test Ban Treaty saw Mao 'outraged', evident Chinese 'bitterness' and 'a fierce attack against it' (Liu Yawei 1998: 195) from the Chinese government at various levels. From China's point of view the Test Ban Treaty could be, and was, fiercely denounced as representing an attempt to establish a Soviet–American nuclear monopoly. Foreign Minister Chen Yi took the lesson from that that 'atomic bombs, missiles and supersonic aircraft are reflections of the technical level of a nation's industry. China will have to solve this issue within the next several years; otherwise, it will degenerate into a second-class nation' (Liu Yawei 1998: 195).

Speculation over China's nuclear progress continued in American circles during 1963. At the end of July, the Joint Chiefs of Staff were directed to draw up contingency plans for a conventional attack on Chinese nuclear facilities. The next day at Kennedy's press conference of 1 August, when asked to 'assess the power and threat of China', he replied 'introduce into that mix, nuclear weapons', a scenario which he felt would be a 'menacing situation' on which, menacingly yet enigmatically 'we would like to take some steps now which would lessen that prospect' (SAR 1972: 200). Chinese nuclear weapons would be 'potentially a more dangerous situation than any we faced since the end of the Second World War, because the Russians pursued in most cases their ambitions with some caution' (200), unlike the perception held of the Chinese.

Kennedy's assassination in November 1963 brought a change of President in Lyndon Johnson, but continuing American considerations of pre-emptive strikes against China's nuclear programme; matched by strenuous Chinese efforts to safeguard itself against such actions through decentralising and completing plants, which seems to have helped convince the US that pre-emptive strikes would be mostly ineffective and counterproductive. This realisation was evident at a high level Presidential meeting on 15 September 1964 where it was decided not to pursue 'unprovoked unilateral US military action against Chinese nuclear installations at this time' (FRUS 1998: 94). However, two important caveats lay in the talk of exploring 'a possible agreement to cooperate in preventive military action' with the USSR against China; and with reconsidering 'appropriate military action against Chinese nuclear facilities . . . if for other reasons we should find ourselves in military hostilities at any level with the Chinese Communists' (94).

Although overshadowed to some extent by the fall of Khrushchev a few days later, perhaps in part caused by China's explosion having eroded Khrushchev's credibility, China's explosion of a nuclear device on 16 October 1964 sent a further different but equally worrying message to the West. At the time, the Chinese Government officially stated that 'the mastering of nuclear weapons by China is a great encouragement to the revolutionary peoples of the world in their struggles' (*Peking Review* 1964: iii), whilst reiterating that the American nuclear arsenal remained a 'paper tiger' (ii). In the USA, Johnson went on screen to address the nation and tell them 'no American should take this lightly. Until this week, only four powers had entered the dangerous world of nuclear explosions. Whatever their differences, all four are sober and serious states', but 'Communist China has no such experiences . . . this explosion remains a fact, sad and serious. We must not, we have not and we will not ignore it' (SAR 1972: 210; see also Bundy and Rusk 1964).

Comment and discussion and disquiet were widespread in the West over China's 'bombshell' (Inglis 1965), one with overt 'political effects' (Lall 1965), a 'threat' (Candlin 1966, Fix 1966, David 1967) to 'world peace' (McMorris 1967). Warning Indian voices were also to be heard (Nehru 1965, Masani 1965). Ralph Powell's analysis of China's bomb considered 'it opened a new and dangerous phase in the atomic era' (1965: 615), in which a 'strongly nationalistic and ambitious' state that was 'more revolutionary than that of the Soviet Union' was now better able 'to support its foreign policy object-ives' (615). A racial angle was also apparent, since 'all previous atomic testing has been carried out by industrial powers of the Occident; Com-munist China is non-Western, non-white' (615). Malcolm Mackintosh's study *Yellow Peril 1975*, in looking forward in time, brought with it a 'startling picture of China in 1975 as an aggressive military power of global propor-tions, capable of offering a serious nuclear-missile threat to Europe and America' (1965). Morton Halperin's *China and the Bomb* warned his readers that 'the world must now begin to deal with a China that will soon be capable of wreaking great destruction, at least on her neighbours', with the nuclear breakthrough 'a milestone on China's road to world power and eventual triumph over the United States' (1965: 89–90).

Lyle Goldstein argues that it was precisely concerns over China's nuclear capacity generating greater Chinese strength and prestige in the region that led the US into dramatically increasing its land involvement in Vietnam in early 1965, with the nuclear angle as 'an understudied cause of the Vietnam War . . . histories of the Vietnam War must take account of the extraordin-ary, if exaggerated, US fears precipitated by China's deployment of nuclear weapons in this period' (2003: 761). Indeed, the following months saw China continuing to push its nuclear programme forward and deploy support forces into North Vietnam, with the US ominously deploying varied naval units and 'girding itself for taking the war to China' (750). However, Chinese restraint in limiting its deployment in North Vietnam, and American uncer-tainties over escalating conflict with China saw a pulling back from 'the brink of a dangerous nuclear precipice' (751) which had been apparent in the earlier part of 1965.

Consequently, US discussions with the Taiwan regime saw a 'frank exchange of views' on 20 September 1965 between American officials and Madame Chiang Kai-shek where Madame Chiang stated that the PRC's nuclear explosion 'had a decidedly powerful influence not only on adjacent Asian states but on the entire world. As a result of this development the Chinese Communists' prestige and influence throughout the entire world had been vastly increased' (FRUS 1998: 207). Nevertheless, Madame Chiang argued that the US should 'take out the ChiComs nuclear installations now by the employment of conventional forces, to destroy now their nuclear capability before it reached dangerous proportions' (FRUS 1998: 207). How-ever, the US balked at this proposal, counter-arguing that 'the ChiCom reaction would be violent and would result essentially in the employment of their principal weapon, their enormous manpower, in offensive retaliatory operations beyond their borders' (208). Demographics were a crucial factor in measuring China's power, 'the United States had only 190 million people whereas China had over 600 million' and with it 'the impossibility of em-ployment of U.S. manpower in Asia against such odds' (208).

China's nuclear programme continued to raise alarms in the West, and in India, as it rapidly progressed through 1964–7. The initial test in October

1964 of 20 kilotons was followed in quick progression, by an air drop of 40–50 kilotons in May 1965, one of c. 200 kilotons in May 1966. By then, the *Peking Review* was asserting, with pride and some truth, that 'the first nuclear test by our country surpassed the levels attained in the initial tests of the United States, Britain and France . . . [We] dare to break a path none before has walked and dare to scale peaks others have not climbed' (1966c: 31). A guided missile nuclear strike test came later in October (*Peking Review* 1966d). A still more powerful atomic bomb, of around 400 kilotons, was exploded in December 1966, dramatically followed by China's hydrogen bomb breakthrough in June 1967.

James Thomson's National Security Council memorandum on 1 March 1966 had by then succinctly flagged the PRC's drive, '700 million people; the key to stability in Asia; the grandiose belligerent aims of Chinese Communist doctrine; Peking's development of a nuclear capability' (FRUS 1998: 262). Moreover, Johnson's Sentinel ABM programme of 1967 had been justified in terms of safeguarding against a Chinese threat whilst not involving the bigger arsenal with the USSR. For Defence Secretary Robert McNamara, 'the [Sentinel] development will foreclose any possibility of a successful Chinese nuclear attack on the United States and thereby provide assurance of our determination to support our Asian friends against Chinese nuclear blackmail' (1967: 545). The 1967 US–Japan summit meeting again identified an 'intransigent' China as a particular threat to both of those countries, given 'the fact that Communist China is developing its nuclear arsenal and agreed on the importance of creating conditions wherein Asian nations would not be susceptible to threats from Communist China' (Japan–USA 1967: 1033).

Chinese statements became stronger as its nuclear capability increased. Statements during 1964–5 had been cautious in talking about general un-specified world revolutionary encouragement; whereas by 1966 statements were identifying specific conflict situations. In such a vein in October 1966, following its successful guided missile tests, the PRC officially stated 'the possession by the Chinese people of guided missiles and nuclear weapons is a great encouragement to the heroic Vietnamese people who are waging a war of resistance against U.S. aggression and for national salvation' (*Peking Review* 1966d: ii). After the hydrogen bomb threshold had been passed in 1967 the scope of China's leverage was extended still further, in rhetoric anyhow. In part it was a general technological step up, 'the development of China's nuclear weapons into an entirely new stage' (*Peking Review* 1967a: 6). It also extended China's nuclear range, as not only being trumpeted as 'a very great encouragement and support to the Vietnamese people in their heroic war against United States aggression' but also 'for national salvation, to the Arab people in their resistance to aggression by the United States and British imperialists and their tool, Israel, and to the revolutionary peoples of the whole world' (7). This may have been rhetoric, but alongside China's nuclear programme, China's path of radical Third World revolution also concerned American policy makers.

Third World revolution in Vietnam and beyond

Under John Kennedy, China-related fears escalated, as did American involvement in Vietnam. The *Washington Daily News*, 22 September 1960, had Kennedy asserting, 'the real question is what should be done about the harsh facts that China is a powerful and aggressive nation. The dangerous situation now existing' in Southeast Asia was of smaller countries 'left to be picked off one by one at the whim of the Peiping regime'. IR security dilemma dynamics may have fed into the situation, as increased American involvement brought North Vietnamese trips to Beijing in the summer of 1962. Having advised caution in 1961, the PRC leadership now moved to more active support, giving free of charge some 90,000 rifles and guns which were able to equip 230 infantry guerrilla battalions in South Vietnam. Liu Shaoqi's visit to North Vietnam in March 1963 had him pledging, 'we are standing by your side, and if war breaks out, you can regard China as your rear' (Zhai Qiang 2000: 117). Such moves further increased American concerns over the PRC (Garver 1992). Dean Rusk, at the SEATO Council meeting of 8 April 1963 emphasised how 'the blatant aggression of communist China on the Indian border has vast and historic significance' revealing Chinese readiness 'to resort to aggression whenever its expansionist aims are thereby served' (DAFR 1964: 277). The ANZUS Council, 5–6 June 1963, Communiqué agreed by the US, Australia and New Zealand 'noted with concern the communist Chinese aggression against India' and 'the continuing statements of implacable hostility by communist Chinese leaders', which 'made it clear that the principal threat to the peace and security of South and South-East Asia and the Pacific region continues to come from the Communist powers, particularly Communist China' (DAFR 1964: 282).

The following week, Assistant Secretary for Far Eastern Affairs, Roger Hilsman, emphasised 'in Asia the greatest danger to independent nations comes from Communist China, with its 700 million people forced into the service of an aggressive Communist Party,' an analysis riddled with geopolitical and domino fears, in which 'Communist China lies in direct contact with, or very close to, a whole series of free nations ranged in an arc from Afghanistan . . . Southeast Asia; and on up through . . . to Japan and Korea' (1963a: 44). Kennedy reaffirmed his personal belief in the domino theory in September 1963, 'China is so large, looms so high just beyond the frontier, that if South Vietnam went, it would not only give them an improved geographic position for a guerrilla assault on Malaya' but 'would also give the impression that the wave of the future in Southeast Asia was China' (DAFR 1964: 282). That same month the *New York Times*, 14 September 1963, warned in its editorial of how 'Communist China has made no secret of its resolve to enter upon a Napoleonic phase of expansionism'.

As already noted, Kennedy's assassination in November 1963 brought Lyndon Johnson into power. His presidency, 1963–8, saw America's escalation of its involvement in Vietnam entwined there with 'exaggerated fears'

(Schulzinger 2001: 239) concerning China's role and its nuclear capability. Under-Secretary of State McGeorge Bundy replaced the threat of the Soviet 'Iron Curtain' with China's 'Bamboo Curtain' underpinning a Chinese model for the Third World (1964). Vietnam was perceivable as part of China's ideological onslaught on the West, where the PRC's message of peasant radicalism could find favour elsewhere in the Third World. Further up the chain, Secretary of State Dean Rusk, told the American media, and in turn the public, that 'this is the nature of the appetite proclaimed from Peiping . . . the notion of a militant world revolution' (1965). Secretary of Defense McNamara argued that America's build-up of forces in Vietnam was necessary as 'the Chinese Communists have chosen to make South Viet-Nam the test case for their particular version of the so-called "wars of national liberation"' which reflected 'their preference for violence' (1965). Consequently, 'in Viet-Nam, particularly, we see the effects of the Chinese Communists' more militant stance and their hatred of the free world' (1965). The stakes were high in Vietnam. In part it was the old domino logic that 'we have here a sort of cork in the bottle, the bottle being the great area that includes Indonesia, Burma, Thailand, all of the surrounding areas of Asia with its hundreds of millions of people' (1965). There was a still wider logic for McNamara, 'a Communist success in South Viet-Nam would be taken as positive proof that the Chinese Communists' position is correct and they will have made a giant step forward in their efforts to seize control of the world Communist movement' and that 'such a success would greatly increase the prestige of Communist China among the nonaligned nations and strengthen the position of their followers everywhere' (1965).

In Beijing a growing 'sense of insecurity' was apparent, as 'Mao worried about the increasing American involvement in Vietnam, and perceived the United States as posing a serious threat to China's security' (Zhai Qiang 2000: 140). Third Front projects were started in order to build up China's industrial capacity in remote parts of China, beyond the range of American bombers, and military chiefs provided advice on how to respond to an American attack. Yet Beijing's rhetoric, revolutionary-radical foreign policy ideology, provided an equally worrying picture for the US, especially with Defense Minister Lin Biao's 'Long Live the Victory of People's War' (1965).

Lin Biao's thesis of 'global encirclement' emphasised China's revolutionary relevance 'of outstanding and universal practical importance for the present revolutionary struggle of all oppressed nations and peoples' since 'the basic political similarity and economic conditions in many of these countries have many similarities to those that prevailed in old China' (1965: 24). This similarity was one reason why China's revolutionary peasant model could be exported elsewhere in the Third World. Indeed at the global level 'taking the entire globe, if North America can be called the "cities of the world", then Asia, Africa and Latin America constitutes "the rural areas of the world"', amidst which 'the peoples revolutionary movement in Asia, Africa, and Latin America has been growing vigorously. In a sense, the contemporary world revolution also presents a picture of the encirclement of cities [the West] by the rural [i.e. Third World] areas' (24), a revolutionary bloc inspired and in American eyes led by China.

Lin Biao's thesis was picked up across America and by the American administration. Ronald Steel (1967) considered it as 'The Yellow Peril revisited'! Scholars like Rhoads Murphey admittedly argued that Lin's tract had not been particularly alarming in itself, for 'China is not in the business of attempting to export its revolution or its sovereignty' in which it was of 'importance that he [Lin] should have stated quite flatly "Revolution cannot be imported"' (1966: 512). Indeed, Murphey stressed 'the severe limitations of Chinese military power beyond the immediate border area' (511). Admittedly, 'internally the Chinese state is probably the most powerful in the world, but its military capability falls off sharply beyond its own borders . . . its possession of an infant nuclear establishment does not change this overall situation' (511). He did judge China to be 'an undoubted great power' (512), but that meant legitimate concerns on having non-hostile neighbours in Vietnam not harbouring the forces and bases 'of an alien enemy' (512), rather than the PRC being an expansionist power per se. In this setting, he considered the Domino Theory as 'little short of fantastic' (513). Damningly he concluded, 'it is difficult, in conclusion, to find any reliable basis in fact – in past behavior, in realities of the present, or in predictable future courses – for the application of the domino theory to the Chinese role in Southeast Asia' (515). As such, 'the domino theory is not fit comparison for anyone who calls himself a thoughtful man. It is a poor substitute for rational inquiry' (515), even though 'those in high office seem to subscribe to it' (510).

Those in high office certainly, and publicly, saw Lin Biao's tract as confirmation of their fears about China. Dean Rusk warned Congress that Lin Biao's thesis showed 'Peiping's strategy of violence for achieving Communist domination of the world', where 'Peiping is prepared to train and indoctrinate the leaders of these revolutions and to support them with funds, arms and propaganda as well as politically. It is even prepared to manufacture these revolutionary movements' (Rusk 1966: 273). Although he admitted 'it is true they are more cautious in actions than in words . . . it does not follow that we should disregard their plans for the future', for 'to do so would be to repeat the catastrophic miscalculations that so many people made about the ambitions of Hitler' (Rusk 1966: 273).

Drew Middleton considered that Lin's tract 'is and will be for years to come the blueprint for Chinese policy for Asia' (Middleton 1968: 199). Consequently, he commented 'no one can complain that he has not been warned' (201), for 'there is danger: for ourselves, for our children, for our children's children' (201), since 'the Chinese challenge and Chinese ambitions are enduring' (204). Elsewhere, at the Dutch embassy in Beijing, Douwe Fokkema's judgement was that Lin's treatise had 'drafted, in greater detail than ever before a programme for Maoist world domination . . . heavily coloured by sinocentrism', a limitation 'which restricts China's possibilities of increasing her influence' (1971: 166–7).

Mutual fears were evident between the United States and China during the mid-1960s, witnessed in the ongoing US–PRC ambassadorial talks at Warsaw, in retrospect 'the dialogue of the deaf' (S. Goldstein 2001). John Cabot's record for 15 September 1965 described how he had told Wang Bingnan 'Lin Piao's article [of September 1965] looked like the blueprint for Communist aggression and that it reminded me of Hitler's Mein Kampf. This stung Wang who retorted that American actions since WW II resembled those of Hitler, Mussolini, and Japanese aggressors' (FRUS 1998: 204). Nevertheless Cabot acknowledged 'I was also impressed by Wang's evident belief that the US really was hostile and had aggressive intentions towards China' since 'he was particularly eloquent on these points during his rebuttal when he was freewheeling and not reading from his text. He appeared genuinely to believe US harbors aggressive intentions towards Communist China' (234).

Analysts frequently banged the same alarmist drum. Edward Crankshaw warned that 'the powerful and unscrupulous government of a land of 650 million operating on its own, completely untrammelled by any international obligations of any kind, however tenuous, is a disconcerting element in itself' (1965: 162). It was even more worrying when allied to China's 'leadership of a world-wide subversive movement . . . in Latin America, in Africa, in Asia . . . this is the very spectre' (162) for the West, and indeed for the Soviet Union. Drew Middleton's analysis of *America's Stake in Asia* (1968) emphasised the threat from China at the height of America's fighting in Vietnam, where the 'challenge, less immediately evident but ultimately more dangerous, is that posed by Communist China' with its 'aim at establishing communism there [South and Southeast Asia], and to gather this great, rich region into the Chinese economy', a challenge where 'no one in authority in the governments concerned doubts it will come' (1968: 14).

From the PRC's point of view America's growing involvement in South Vietnam already brought her uncomfortably close to China, a southern pincer alongside America's presence in South Korea, Japan and indeed Taiwan. This was increased by America's extension of the war, in the air into North Vietnam and towards the Chinese border. Typical of the PRC's sense of being under siege were reported US air incursions into Chinese airspace in autumn of 1966. Beijing's interpretation was that air incursions were 'by no means accidental' (*Peking Review* 1966a: 26), but that 'the Chinese people who are armed with Mao Tse-tung's thoughts fear no war threats of any kind. We are in full battle array. If you must have a test of strength, then come on', for 'the iron fists of the 700 million Chinese people will definitely crush all aggressors to pulp' (25).

Nineteenth century images of the Yellow Peril resurfaced at the popular level in America. Gallup Polls, tracking attributes associated with the Chinese, showed a dramatic increase in negative attributes from the rosier

1942 days of alliance against Japan (Isaacs 1972: xviii–xix). Instead, by 1966 the figures for 'Sly' rose from 8 per cent to 20 per cent, 'Treacherous' from 4 per cent to 19 per cent, 'Cruel' from 3 per cent to 13 per cent, 'Warlike' from 4 per cent to 23 per cent. Conversely, positive attributes had also deteriorated by 1966, that is, 'Honesty' plummeting from 52 per cent to 0 per cent, 'Brave' slumping from 48 per cent to 7 per cent.

Lyndon Johnson bluntly summed up the mid-1960s perceptions where, 'over this war – and all Asia – is another reality: the deepening shadow of Communist China. The rulers in Hanoi are urged on by Peiping' (1965: 607). The PRC was 'a nation which is helping the forces of violence in almost every continent . . . the contest in Viet-Nam is part of a wider pattern of aggressive purposes' by the PRC (607). Other high level figures within the Johnson administration were very aware of what they considered to be the high issues at stake. Bundy warned Pomona College students on 12 February 1966 that 'to accept Mainland China's domination in Asia would be to look forward to conditions of external domination and probably total-itarian control, not merely for twenty years but quite possibly for genera-tions', a speech which Stanford Lyman sees as a reiteration of the old 'Yellow Peril mystique' (2000: 714). Rusk combined traditional and ideological fears over what he perceived as China's objectives, where 'they hold that China's history, size and geographic position entitles it to great-power status', and 'they seek to overcome the humiliation of 150 years of economic, cultural and political domination by outside powers' (1966: 272). Such a power drive was related in turn to its further objectives of 'dominance within Asia and leadership of the Communist world revolution, employing Maoist tactics . . . the Chinese Communists are dedicated to a fanatical and bellicose Marxist-Leninist-Maoist doctrine of world revolution', as well as to 'restore traditional Chinese influence or domination in South, Southeast, and East Asia' (272).

Such images were why, in retrospect, Henry Kissinger described how 'for twenty years US policymakers considered China as a brooding chaotic, fanatical, and alien realm difficult to understand and difficult to sway. They had been convinced that the Vietnam war was a reflection of Chinese expansionism' (1979: 685). Such China-related Yellow Peril fears, took not only American but also around 8,000 Australian military forces to Vietnam during the 1960s.

In Australia, as in most other Western countries, 'China became the arch-villain in the drama of international relations in the 1950s and 1960s' (Strahan 1996: 134) for many Australian politicians. In 1959 Senator George Cole bluntly warned 'the greatest danger to Australia today is the com-munist hordes from China coming down through South East Asia' (131); a stance reflecting the situation whereby most people were taking 'Chinese bellicosity as a given, beyond question', a 'powerful striving belligerent Maoist China' (131). Future Labour Party PM, Gough Whitlam considered in 1963 that 'China represents a very great threat. She is potentially the most powerful country in the world and she seems prepared to run risks which Russia is unwilling to run' (Strahan 1996: 227). Behind the more overt ideological Cold War fears of a 'Communist' China, was the even deeper vaguer older image of a Chinese, i.e. Yellow, China as a distinctly alarming force woven into the fabric of Australian national attitudes. External Affairs Minister, Paul Hasluck admitted in 1964 that 'the fear of China is the dominant element in much that happens in Asia, and the fear is well founded' (Clark 1968: 54).

China's population figures were highly emotive in Australia, 'exerting an almost hypnotic effect, the vertigo of numbers . . . Australians made frightening calculations . . . like an incantation, these huge numbers seemed to mesmerise both speaker and audience' (Strahan 1996: 148–9). Denis Warner's *Hurricane from China* (1961) stressed how 'China needs living space', a *lebensraum* imperative where 'Australia may survive longer', but 'should it also fall, historians will not pause to reflect too deeply on the fate of this handful of white men who thought they could live under the shadow of the Chinese phallus and, for perhaps two centuries, succeeded' (179–80). China's strive towards a nuclear bomb was entwined with talk of its 'population bomb'. In short, Australia had something of a 'pre-occupation with China in the 1960s' (Huck 1984: 164).

A retrospective summation of Australian images was Nicholas Jose's novel *Avenue of Eternal Peace* (1989), with Australia 'in Vietnam to stop the Yellow Peril running down into Australian homes and gardens as inevitably as falling dominoes', in which 'his mother said she didn't want to break her back in a rice paddy and eat stones for bread. His father said that if the Chinese stood in a line holding hands they would ring the world' (Broinowski 1992: 120). Politicians reflected these perceptions. Robert Menzies' justification to the Australian Parliament in dispatching Australian troops to South Vietnam, as did New Zealand, was that 'the takeover of South Vietnam would be a direct military threat [by China] to Australia . . . it must be seen as part of a thrust by Communist China between the Indian and Pacific Oceans' (Australia 1965: 1060, 1061). Yellow Peril associations were easy to find for many Australian troops in Vietnam. Maurice Hor, an Australian army veteran, recalled those times in the *Sydney Morning Herald*, 25 April 2002, of being woken up in Vietnam by loudspeakers every morning blaring out information about the Yellow Peril and accusing 'evil Chinese barbarians' of taking over the country. 'There were always constant references to Asians, the enemies,' he said. 'Slant eyes and yellow people who weren't the same as "us"'.

During 1966, Australian politicians frequently linked and justified Australian participation in the Vietnam conflict in terms of China. Prime Minister Harold Holt told Parliament on 5 May 1966 that 'behind the Communists in South-East Asia, wherever their structures are to be found, is the driving force of China' (Australia 1966: 32). Demographics and ideology made a potent cocktail, 'China with a population upward of 700 million' and 'subversion and guerrilla warfare, as spelled out in the writings of Mao Tse-tung, have been directed with planned thoroughness to the villages and paddy fields of South-East Asia' (32). The stakes were high, for 'if South-East Asia is to fall under Communist control we face a future in which the security of Australia is in jeopardy' (32). The next month, 30 June, Holt told the National Press Club that 'the only major military power on the mainland of Asia is Communist China. No country in Asian Asia could feel itself secure from the threat of Communist [China] aggression' (54).

His External Affairs minister was similarly China-focused during 1966. Paul Hasluck's address to the UN General Assembly painted a picture of how 'mainland China overhangs the region with a population of 700,000,000 under a regime, which while calling itself communist, represents all that is most illiberal and backward-looking and violent in communist thought' (Clark 1968: 1). Elsewhere came Hasluck's statement to Parliament, 10 March 1966, that Vietnam was 'a war that affects the fate of all countries of South–East Asia – a war that throws into sharp relief the aim of Communist China to dominate them by force' (Australia 1966: 13). Meanwhile the Chinese hydrogen bomb detonation of 1967 was greeted by an Australian Liberal MP as showing China to be 'the juvenile delinquent of international society' (Strahan 1996: 247).

Images and feelings merged into policies. Gregory Clark's recollection was 'at the time the myth of an "expansionist" China, with heavy emphasis on the 1962 Sino–Indian dispute, was being used constantly to justify Western, including Australian, intervention in Indochina' (2002). General opinion and images were such that 'it is so much easier to invoke rather than revoke the traditional "Yellow Peril" fear' (1967). In 1969 public opinion polls had over half the Australians, 53 per cent, agreeing 'looking into the future, do you feel that Australia will have a lot to worry about in regard to Communist China' (Huck 1984: 161–2). The Morgan Polls in 1967–9 showed how China was felt to be a threat to Australia's security, at 30.9 per cent significantly more than other named countries, Russia 13.5 per cent, Vietnam 10.6 per cent, Indonesia 6.9 per cent, and Japan 5.5 per cent (163).

Some dissent from this was present. Gregory Clark resigned from the Department of External Affairs in 1965, in protest against the government's China policies. Clark's *In Fear of China* lamented 'few countries, Western or non-Western, are more hostile to China than Australia' (1968: 161). He commented on 'the "unreality" of Canberra's fear of China', and 'the failure of Australian policy-makers to approach China in a rational manner' (191), in which 'the factors mainly responsible for the intensity of Canberra's China-phobia are psychological rather than ideological', reflecting 'the traditional fear of the threat from the North – the threat to Australia as a European outpost on the edge of Asia' (188). In addition, in shades of Edward Said's *Orientalism*, 'an even more important psychological factor is the "unfamiliarity" which China holds for Australia', whereby 'as a result, China remains for most Western countries an "alien" nation whose people think, talk and act somehow differently from the rest of us' (Clark 1968: 189). This 'failure to see the Chinese in human terms' had policy implications, for 'it is a failure even to comprehend China in practical terms – as a nation with a government and policies which need to be taken into account no less than the policies of any other Government' (191). It was 'a paralysis of intellect which can only be explained in terms of the fears which have accumulated in the minds of the policy-makers' (191) in Australia, and much of the West.

China as a rogue state or revolutionary paradise

China's advancement to the nuclear front and its projection of a Third World peasant model were a potent mix. Unease over China was compounded by the eruption of the Cultural Revolution, August 1966 to July 1968. Mao Zedong's call that 'China should become the arsenal for World Revolution' (1967: 454–6) saw a PRC ready to rally world opinion against the two superpowers. On the one hand Mao enthused about 'excellent' revolutionary upsurges around Asia and much of the Third World, where '[American] imperialism and [Soviet] revisionism are more isolated than ever' (455). On the other hand, across the Third World 'people in countries realize that China's road is the only road to liberation. China is not only the political center of world revolution, it must also be the center of world revolution militarily and technically' (455). Outside the PRC, China was seen as a very different type of state, a revolutionary paradise for some, a rogue state to others.

Samuel Griffith was one of the latter. He felt that the PRC 'casts menacing shadows' (Griffith 1968: 203) around the globe, in her attempts 'to overthrow the established order and replace it with one conceived by Mao Tse-tung' (203). Various strands were coalescing in China, the past was present as 'tradition is thus manipulated or created to encourage a strident militarism, xenophobia, and chauvinism. When a messianic ideology is added to these, the inevitable result is the development of a bellicose national character and an aggressive national policy' (1968: 213). Looking ahead, especially from China's nuclear programme, Griffith concluded that 'by 1975, when the Party will celebrate the fortieth anniversary of the completion of the Long March, China will have become a power to be reckoned with on the international scene' (295), and the leadership 'will have vast power at their disposal – power, in truth, to shake "the five continents"' (296). This alarmist prognosis was mirrored in Charles Hensman's *China. Yellow Peril? Red Hope?*, and his references to the PRC's 'many-pronged assault on the independence and security of the rest of the world' (1968: 30). Griffith's reference to the five continents was because (1968: 301), all the Beijing newspapers carried on their 31 December front pages Mao's 1963 poem *On This Tiny Globe* with its conclusion 'The four seas are rising, clouds and waters raging,/ The five continents are rocking, wind and thunder roaring/ Away with all pests!/ Our force is irresistible'.

PRC sources upheld China's beaconist image. For the *Peking Review*, 'China is the mainstay of the world revolution today' (1967b: 37). On the one hand 'imperialism, modern revisionism and the reactionaries of all countries have an inveterate hatred for China. They vilify and frenziedly oppose China', whilst on the other hand 'the masses of the people in various countries want to oppose imperialism' (37). The latter 'find in China their orientation and hope and enthusiastically extol China. . . . They want to take the road of Mao Tse-tung, China's road' so that 'no blustering anti-China warrior can escape the fate of being swept away by the current of history' (37). China, under Mao, saw itself as a beacon standing up in the world against the forces of reaction, with Mao's thoughts the 'common treasure' (*Peking Review* 1966b) for the world, or rather for 'the world's revolutionary people' (1966b).

China's Red Guard 'Great Proletarian Cultural Revolution' could be viewed as violent anarchy by some in the West, with its embassies under threat in shades of the Boxer Revolt of 1900. At the Dutch embassy, Douwe Fokkema considered 'in the conflict with foreign powers . . . and her own role in the world . . . the role of the humiliated and semi-colonised, nine-teenth century . . . has not been forgotten' by China, 'the humiliation that has been inflicted on China may provide an explanation of the confusion and self-investigation of which the Cultural Revolution was' (1971: 170–1). However, such ferment was attractive for some in the West, where 'the immensity of China was a source of hope for the left. The vertigo of numbers, which evinced much queasiness in so many Australians [and others], became a dizzy source of excitement for radicals', where 'left ideology celebrated the masses as the engine of history, the force which would create a new world' (Strahan 1996: 192).

Futuristic speculation was present in 1967 with Han Suyin's *China in the Year 2001*. She painted a picture of how 'China's emergence and her importance in the world influence the immediate future and preoccupy every government; but they are still regarded as something untoward, there-fore frightening, to be exorcised or pulverised out of existence' (1967: 1–2). Various strands were coalescing in this, namely 'the psychosis of racism, the hysteria of anticommunism, the "yellow peril" complex' (231). However, there were also the real claims for inspirational leadership surrounding China and what she represented. After all, 'today, the emergence of China . . . mark this epoch as that of a universal upheaval – the epoch of world revolution'; within which 'with the development of China, the first non-white power to grow strong on her own resources and through her own efforts, and today the self-proclaimed vanguard and leader of revolutionary change, a new pattern is reshaping the world' (4). History was changing where 'the main trend of world events' was one in which 'a new pattern is taking shape, whose most conspicuous trait is the new prominence of socialist China, unmistakably advancing toward the status of world power' (5). Traditional power factors were apparent, China's 'development of nuclear power . . . China's challenge and defiance of the super-power complex and her attainment of nuclear status has broken the atomic blackmail' (243) by the USA and USSR.

Some commentators were not impressed by China's power. Jacques Marcuse, in his cutting profile of China, *The Peking Papers* considered Mao as being 'guilty of precisely that Great Power chauvinism which he so readily denounces elsewhere'. (1967: 333). Harold Hinton's analysis *Communist China in World Politics* similarly stressed 'China's size and population, its potential power' (1966: vii) underpinned 'the concept of Chinese superiority', which 'will eventually restore to China the position of preeminence in the world that it once occupied in the eyes of its own tradition' (5). Indeed, for Marcuse, Mao was symptomatic of a wider Chinese attitude whereby 'when China is, or thinks she is, top dog, there are no limits to her arrogance' with her attendant hopes that 'the day will come when universe will again pay tribute to Peking, when again the sun will never set over her Empire' (333). Ironically, whilst Marcuse considered such xenophobic attitudes and intentions as being present in China, he did not feel that China was in reality much of a threat. Instead, it was a matter of theatre, a Peking Opera discourse from a Communist China that he felt was 'now fashionable to overglamorize, overfear and generally overrate' (346).

A typical product of the period was Harrison Salisbury, Assistant Editor of the *New York Times*. His *Orbit of China* painted a dramatic image, 'China! Was it sheer atavism which sent a chill down my spine as I contemplated the implications of what Peking said and Peking did' (1967: 12)? The past beckoned for the present, as 'it was no longer fashionable to speak of the "yellow peril" . . . Yet what of the chauvinistic racism of China's appeal for unity of the peoples of yellow, of brown and of black colour? . . . Peril stalked the world' (12). Demographics was a major concern for Salisbury, 'the dynamics of China – the chart of her rising population . . . fired the flames of Chinese aggression'; which 'compelled China's leaders towards a policy of chauvinism, irredentism, and adventurism along their frontiers . . . small wonder that there was in China's posture towards the outer world a constant tone of aggression, of hysteria, of menace' (190, 193). Admittedly his projection of some 2 billion, turned out by 2005 to have been something of an overestimation with the 'One Child' policy having held the Chinese population to a lower 1.3 billion stabilising population figure. However, at the time, the force of Salisbury's projections and imagery were stark, with him forecasting that 'shortly after the start of the twenty-first century China would boast of a population of 2,000 million' and that in comparative terms 'one in three people in the world would be Chinese . . . On the day 2,000 million Chinese swarmed across the globe there would be fewer than 300 million Americans' (188). In demographic and systemic terms 'the Chinese population was growing with such rapidity that this force, taken alone, seemed quite capable of changing the world balance of power. The enormous pool of manpower would inevitably propel China into the position of No. 1 world' (189) by the early twenty-first century.

Traditional fears and concerns about China were still very evident for Robert Elegant in *Foreign Affairs*. For him, there had been 'the millennia-old obsession with imposing a Chinese-directed utopia on the world' (1967: 143), in which 'believing themselves the centre of a world, which would, in time, be brought into harmonious order under their suzerainty, the Chinese could not conceive of entering into relations of equality with other self-avowed nations' (139). In terms of strategic culture, 'implicit in the Confucians' doctrine and evident in their actions was the use of armed force when force was necessary to move mankind toward the state of unitary blessedness' towards 'a utopia spanning the whole world and with laws enforced by Chinese wisdom' (140). On top of that came Maoist ideology, with Cultural Revolution zealots proclaiming 'a messianic mission . . . to torment the world . . . remake the world . . . to found a worldwide utopia under Chinese hegemony . . . obsessed Maoists . . . [with] an absolute determination to assert China's absolute supremacy' (140–2). However, Elegant considered such an approach had become self-evidently internally and externally bankrupt where 'amidst the turmoil of the last days of the Great Proletarian Cultural Revolution, there are signs that a profound change in the Chinese approach to the outside world is now in train' (140), as 'the Chinese pragmatists are being forced toward recognition that China is not so powerful – morally or materially – that she can impose her own order on mankind . . . the essential psychological adjustment (141).

Psychological adjustments, and political climate, were also evident for the USA. This was visible in an unlikely source in October 1967, namely Richard Nixon. He had followed robust Cold War lines when Vice-President under Eisenhower, but when out of office he had been 'taking the long view' (1967: 121) in *Foreign Affairs*, alongside Robert Elegant. Nixon argued 'any American policy toward China must come urgently to grips with the reality of China . . . we simply cannot afford to leave China forever outside the family of nations', there 'to nurture its fantasies, cherish its hates and threaten its neighbors. There is no place on this small planet for a billion of its potentially most able people to live in angry isolation' (121). Racial angles were acknowledged by Nixon as he rejected how 'others urge that we eliminate the threat [posed by China] by preemptive war' and also 'that we should seek an anti-Chinese alliance with European powers, even including the Soviet Union' (122). He rejected such containment policies, 'such a course would inevitably carry connotations of Europe vs. Asia, white vs. non-white, which could have catastrophic repercussions throughout the rest of the non-white world in general and Asia in particular', for 'if our long-range aim is to pull China back into the family of nations, we must avoid the impression that the great powers or the European powers are "ganging up" . . . and must be untainted with any suspicion of racism' (122). Instead, faced with collective local Asian resistance to expansionism, China's national form of Communism might, amidst 'dynamic detoxification' then 'turn their energies inward rather than outward. And that will be the time when dialogue with mainland China can begin' (123). Though out of office, and in a private law firm, a Nixon for President Committee had already been formed in March 1967, gearing up for the forthcoming 1968 Presidential election.

Sino–Soviet divergence

Although the United States and most other Western countries had long treated the Soviet Union and China as a fairly unified monolith, with China acting as a compliant surrogate for Moscow, in reality the Sino–Soviet axis was breaking up amidst Yellow Peril undertones. As late as 1960 Stuart Kirby was dismissing China as *Russia's Largest Satellite*, emphasising 'the material and practical dependence on Russia is obvious . . . the essential satellite position of China is hardly veiled . . . Russia has control over the Chinese Communists and will steer the outcome in the direction it desires' (1960: 13, 14). Tabor Mende's *China and her Shadow* still portrayed a Sino–Soviet 'mutually advantageous alliance which is still without any alternative' (1961: 173), although 'how long that [Chinese] dependence will last or how much longer Russia can impose her moderating advice, is gradually becoming the central theme of Sino–Soviet relations' (170). The irony was that even as Mende's book manuscript was going through the printing process, Sino–Soviet relations had ruptured, when in September 1960 all 1,390 Soviet advisers were withdrawn from China, and nuclear technology transfer was halted.

Consequently, 'Western visitors to the Soviet Union report a growing Russian anxiety about Communist China and its inclinations and potentialities', including its demographic superiority in any nuclear war, where for the Russian 'man in the street . . . Communist China gives him cause for deep uneasiness' (North 1960: 51). Yellow Peril imagery became explicit as the Sino–Soviet split erupted into full view during the early 1960s. This was the context for Bernard Newman's 1962 novel, *The Blue Ants: The First Authentic Account of the Russian–Chinese War of 1970*. It came complete with Feng Fong, an atomic age Fu Manchu, and a blurb on the back reading '1970 . . . the year of the war to end all wars, the dreaded clash between the two Red Giants, Russia and China' in which, 'the Russian leader is compelled to ask the Western Powers for aid against the new Yellow Peril, or else be annihilated by the savage hordes', a demographics-ridden situation where 'in a nuclear war China could sustain 200 million casualties, and still remain China. But if Russia had 200 million casualties, then there would be no Russia left' (Newman 1962: 6). In his novel, a disintegrating Soviet state asked for American assistance, with global order only re-imposed through American nuclear bombs bringing about the collapse of the Chinese menace!

Harrison Salisbury's comments remain relevant, that it was 'one short step from the concept of "blue ants" to the concept of the Chinese colossus –

the titanic China, 800 million strong; the world's greatest mass of humanity, trained, obedient, ritualistically ready to do the bidding of their mythic leaders' (1973: 22). Its lineage was clear enough, 'it was, of course, out of this construct that the Russians had fashioned their terrifying image of China as the new Mongol horde' (22). For Salisbury, it was a simple question over this epithet, 'were the Chinese, in fact, "blue ants" or was this just one more of the pejorative epithets that foreigners had applied to China over the years?' and so 'was it, in fact, merely a color shift from "yellow peril" to "blue ant"? Were these concepts, in fact, merely two sides of a common coin' (220)? The image of Blue Ants was well known, see for example, George Paloczi-Horvath's *Mao Tse-tung. Emperor of the Blue Ants* (1963).

Amidst ideological disputes over the nature of Communism, personality clashes and territorial frictions, came very basic charges by the Chinese leaders in their *Fourth Comment on the Open Letter of the Central Committee of the CPSU*, 22 October 1963, that the Soviet leadership 'peddle the "theory of racism" . . . and cry about the "Yellow Peril"' (*Renmin Ribao* 'People's Daily' and *Hongqi* 'Red Flag' 1965: 212–6). Khrushchev's recollection of those events was of Mao wanting to reclaim earlier seized territory like Vladivostok and 'bursting with an impatient desire to rule the world . . . He [Mao] was setting his sights on the future. "Think about it", he said, "You have two hundred million people, and we have seven hundred million"' (Khrushchev 1971: 474).

Marshall Green's recollection, as US ambassador, was similarly of how 'you had a Russian fear, not just a Soviet, a Russian fear of "the yellow peril" – they talked about it openly' since 'there was always a fear that China, whose population at that time was five . . . 600 million . . . were simply going to . . . like the earlier Mongol hordes, they were going to sweep over Western Europe' (1997). Chinese leaders were well aware of these old images being raised by the Soviet leadership, coming to the surface in the negotiations of September 1960 where 'Khrushchev stated that enormous efforts were being spent in China to restore the gravesite of Genghis-khan and that this smelled of "yellow peril"' (Chervenenko 1998; also Zubok 1998).

Territorial issues had also re-emerged by the 1960s, with Mao's famous comments to Japanese socialists, 11 August 1964, that 'there are too many places occupied by the Soviet Union', a geo-political situation entwined with geo-political demographic factors where 'the Soviet Union has an area of 22 million square kilometres and its population is only 220 million' (Lawrance 1975: 144–5), with the unstated comparison being China's smaller territory yet much larger population. Such demographic imbalance was exacerbated by past history, of Chinese territory having been taken by Russia during China's Century of Humiliation where 'about a hundred years ago, the area east of [Lake] Baikal became Russian territory and since then Vladivostok, Khabarovsk, Kamchatka and other areas . . . we have not yet presented our account for this list' (145). *Pravda* immediately responded with an editorial on 2 September 1964 claiming 'we are faced with an openly expansionist program' and referred pointedly to past *lebensraum* 'living space' policies of Hitler's Nazi Germany.

Nuclear issues were also entwined with geocultural nuances and demographic undertones. In 1957, Mao's willingness to contemplate survival and indeed victory after a nuclear war, thanks to China's large population numbers, was re-released in the *Peking Review*, i.e. that 'if the worst came to the worst and half of mankind died, the other half would remain while imperialism would be razed to the ground and the whole world would become socialist' (*Peking Review* 1963: 10). Soviet leaders were appalled by this 'rabid . . . blandly . . . equanimity' by their Chinese counterparts. Moscow's view then was the Beijing leadership 'evidently suppose' that 'the Chinese people will have the best chance since they are the most populous people on the earth . . . there would remain [after a nuclear conflict], in their opinion, the epoch of world domination by people of the yellow race' (Lawrance 1975: 89). It also reflected Beijing's international drive, 'their own great power aims' (90). China could take such comments as converse indications, unwitting testimony, that the Soviet Union as an already existing 'White' Great Power, at heart was reluctant to allow another 'Non-White' Great Power to arise alongside it.

Soviet fears were expressed very clearly during 1964 by Alexei Adzhubei, Khrushchev's son-in-law and editor of *Isvestiya*, whose mission to West Germany had him 'constantly warning about the "yellow peril"' (Selvage 2001: 10) posed by China; in which 'China would be Moscow's "first front"' (11) from now on. In order to have a free hand on its Western flanks for dealing with the Chinese on its eastern flanks, Moscow sought an understanding with Bonn. Such ruminations were carried by *Der Speigel* (1964) under the title 'Kampf den Mongolen', the German rendition for 'The fight against the Mongols'. In a discussion with the arch-conservative Bavarian leader, Adzhubei put it more bluntly, 'we'd just as soon give you Germans a hundred hydrogen bombs, form a corridor through the Soviet Union, and let you mop up the Chinese' (Selvage 2001: 11). Nuclear threats were a concern for Adzhubei where 'for hundreds of years, we Russians have held the Mongolian storm against Europe in check so that Europe could move forward. China will soon have the atomic bomb. We must be alert and thus have our back free' (11) in the West to deal with China in the East. A nuclear China was a challenge not only to the USA, but also to the USSR.

The Soviet eastern flank, visited by Harrison Salisbury in the summer of 1966, was one where 'along the Amur, the China question loomed larger and darker. The China threat seems close' (1967: 147, 145) by the Russians. To evoke Edward Said's *Orientalism* framework, China was 'The Other' alien presence on these far borders of the USSR. In the eyes of Salisbury's Soviet fighter pilot patrolling the border, 'this was China . . . the dark mass of China . . . where lay the greatest danger . . . the terrible danger . . . the one that might lurk in the Chinese mountains' (145). Russians were quoted as saying 'we lack people and means to develop the land' and where 'we don't know what is happening in Peking . . . that is what is so frightening about it . . . and that, you must admit, is a very dangerous thing' (155, 153).

The Cultural Revolution further damaged Sino–Soviet relations, strengthening an image (McGuire 2001) of Chinese irrationality and danger for many in the USSR, as they heard reports of anti-Soviet demonstrations, general invective, and attacks on diplomats and diplomatic buildings by rampaging Red Guards. Vladimir Vyosky talked of a very alien China, 'the far away planet of Tau Kitai' (McGuire 2001: 8). In turn, a marked Soviet military build-up took place along China's borders during 1966–8. China was well aware of the 'Brezhnev Doctrine' which had asserted the right of the Soviet Union to intervene in countries where Socialism was under threat, and which had already been invoked in 1968 to justify the dispatch of Soviet troops to overthrow Czech reformers, and see a potential invocation of it against itself.

In this light it is not surprising that Harold Isaacs's study of *Color in World Politics* discussed at some length the Soviet Union's 'yellow peril fixation around its power conflict with China' where 'mutual fears and hostilities are fed by racial differences which serve to reinforce or to rationalize politically dictated behaviour' (1969: 244). Consequently, 'in conversations with Americans and Europeans, they [i.e. the Russians, in effect] frequently promote a common cause against the prospective Chinese threat in terms of a common "whiteness" united against Chinese "yellowness"' (244), where 'they endow the latter with strength versions of all the most negative and fearsome stereotypes, bearing on numbers, limitless energy and endurance, fiendish cleverness and cruelty, deviousness and inscrutability' (244). Significantly, 'these are all images they already hold in common with other westerners, especially Americans, who get them from the same source, indeed from the same historic experience' (244). The Yellow Peril in other words.

China's worst fears were seen as dangerously close to reality by the end of the 1960s. This build up of tension provided the framework for Salisbury's *The Coming War Between Russia and China*. Amidst ideological and territorial clashes, and heightened propaganda blasts from both sides, came Salisbury's sense of demographic pressures, where 'Chinese *lebensraum* is no figment of a Chinese Goebbels', for 'it is a basic criterion for the existence of China into the twenty-first century, when – in all probability – her population will number close to 2 billion and when one out of every three human beings will be Chinese' (1969: 135). In retrospect, his figures proved wrong. China's population has stabilized around 1.3 billion, and her population is 20–22 per cent of the world's population rather than 33 per cent. However, an ongoing factor has been the dramatic demographic imbalance between China and the 'comparably small' (134) population density of Russia's territory in the Far East and Siberia. It was also dramatic as, following rumours and discussions with Russian figures in Spring 1969, Salisbury warned 'the Sino–Soviet war . . . promises to be the world's first nuclear war' (149).

Even as his book was being published various border clashes between Soviet and Chinese military forces took place along the Manchurian and Xinjiang borders. Tension was high. Henry Kissinger recalled that the US was 'asked what the US reaction would be to a Soviet attack on Chinese nuclear facilities' (1979: 183). The USA, despite its cold public relations with China, refused to back such a Soviet surgical strike, publicly declaring that 'we could not fail to be deeply concerned, however, with an escalation of this quarrel into a massive breach of international peace and security' (Richardson 1969). This was more bluntly described in *realpolitik* terms by Kissinger as 'we could not allow China to be "smashed" . . . it would upset the global balance of power' (1979: 186). Such an American refusal was an ironical twist, given Kennedy's own earlier mooting of American strikes against China's nuclear capacity in the early 1960s, which at that time were similarly blocked by Soviet non-cooperation! China, uniquely, proved to be the only state threatened by both Cold War superpowers' nuclear intervention.

Forebodings about China were prevalent across the Soviet spectrum, where 'in the late 1960s and early 1970s the idea of a China threat had spread widely throughout educated Russian society' (Lukin 2003: 89). Alexei Arbatov's inside recollections of government thinking was that 'in the minds of both politicians and the public . . . we lived with the fear and danger of a military conflict [with China] . . . we faced a combination of real political threats and our fear and ignorance of what was going on in China' (1992: 84–5). For Medvedev, 'the danger of total war with China at the end of the 1960s and beginnings of the 1970s . . . alarmed Soviet dissidents and occupied an important part in their thinking, as well as in their letters and articles' (1986: 51; also Sakharov 1968, Amalrik 1970: 46, Solzhenitsyn 1974: 14–9). Poets were drawn into this. Yevgeni Yevtushenko, in the wake of the skirmishes between Soviet and Chinese forces along the Ussuri river in March 1969, evoked ancient Russian fears of old Asiatic invaders, in his 'On the Red Snow of the Ussuri' poem, published in the *Lituraturnaya Gazeta* on 19 March, with lines like 'You can see in the murky twilight/ The new Mongol warriors [i.e. China] with [nuclear] bombs in their quivers' (Salisbury 1969: 22). In echoes of Vladimir Solovev's *Pan-Mongolism* imagery of 1900, Naum Korzhavin's poem *Walls of China* (c. 1970) speculated 'there may come an hour/ When the walls of the motionless China/ Suddenly move on us/ . . . Unaccustomed as we are, we have to/ face an enemy with manpower/ Many times greater than we have' (Lukin 2003: 142).

From the outside, Kissinger's recollections of the period also noted population factors where 'no Soviet leader could overlook the demographic realities. Close to a billion Chinese were pressing against a frontier that their government officially did not recognize . . . confronting a mere thirty million Russians' (1982: 48). Consequently, 'I began to understand how the sense of isolation and foreboding engenders near-hysteria in Soviet leaders brooding on China' generated by the 'Chinese demographic edge . . . the fact that sometime in the next generation the disparity between Soviet and Chinese power in Asia would first narrow and then tilt the other way; from then on, Siberia's future would increasingly depend on Peking's goodwill' (1982: 48). Such Sino–Soviet divergences were to overturn the wider geo-political framework of the international system and fundamentally restructure the parameters of international relations between Powers in the 1970s.

Overview

In retrospect China's role in Cold War bi-polarity deserves re-emphasis. Whilst the United States and the USSR retained overwhelming military superiority within the system, China redefined the scope of the Cold War. As Andrew Nathan and Robert Ross pointed out, 'during the Cold War, China was the only major country that stood at the intersection of the two superpower camps, a target of influence and enmity for both' (1997: 13). After all 'with the largest population and occupying the third largest territory in the world, China was a factor which neither superpower could ignore' (Chen Jian 2001: 2).

Such Cold War settings were but the first appearance of what Jonathan Pollack later saw as China's 'swing value' in international strategic politics where 'anxieties about Chinese power compelled the United States and subsequently the Soviet Union to deploy major military forces on a second front in Asia' (1984: 174). This, indeed, may have been 'a somewhat dubious accomplishment from the perspective of Chinese security, but one that testifies to China's centrality to Soviet and American calculations about war and peace', for 'Peking's position and alignment – and the defense requirements China generated for both superpowers – have frequently had a critical influence on the polarization of the international system, and on the relative defense burden each superpower has to bear' (174). This was 'a reflection of Peking's unique position in global politics' (Pollack 1984: 174). Michael Yahuda similarly noted that 'the PRC is the only power which by its independent actions over the last three decades has been able to exercise a major influence on the strategic central balance between the two superpowers' with the somewhat unusual situation being reached also of 'the PRC is the only state to have been threatened at different times with nuclear attack by both the superpowers' (1978: 14).

Meanwhile, in its Cultural Revolution turmoil, China's simultaneous challenge to the USA and the USSR left it to plough a course of Third World solidarity and radical circumvention of the existing international order, and of its established organisations. As John Simmonds noted at the time, 'in this kaleidoscopic world the Chinese are "coloured". The oppressed masses of Asia, Africa, and Latin America are likewise of a darker pigmentation than the Europeans . . . China's success is emulatable; its experience and leadership mandatory' (1970: 207). The PRC leadership indeed continued to stress that 'China belongs to the Third World' and as such 'we are convinced that so long as the Third World countries and people strengthen their unity, ally themselves with all forces that can be allied with, and persist in a protracted struggle, they are sure to win continuous new victories' (Deng Xiaoping 1974: 11). However, though the Third World could be seen as a source of some independent support vis-à-vis the two superpowers, would that be enough? In reality China was dangerously exposed. She had antagonised all her major neighbours, the USA and the USSR, as well as Japan and India and Australia. China could well prepare for invasion in 1969, but wonder from which direction, and wonder if Third World revolutionary rhetoric really would 'shield' her.

4 China re-joins the Cold War...
against the Soviet Union

Although Simmonds saw China's Third World revolutionary policy as providing a comforting theory, in reality such Third World forces were not in themselves really able to act as a protective shield around China on its long frontiers with the Soviet Union. By the end of the 1960s China's 'standing up' had resulted not just in ongoing conflict with the United States but also increasing alienation from the Soviet Union, an extremely vulnerable position to be in, with China's revolutionary fervour seeming to pit it against the international system *in toto*. The PRC had to reach some accommodations, somewhere. Whether explained in classic IR balancing terms or in Maoist United Front realignments, the imperative was the same. This was the signal for fundamental rebalancing within the international system.

Sino–American convergence

Simmonds' previously cited 1970 script on Chinese foreign policy was being dramatically challenged by unexpected geopolitical strategic developments, even as his book was going through the print room. Despite, or perhaps because of, the closeness to decisive escalation, the Soviet Union and China backed away from full-scale war in 1969. From the Soviet side, China had probably become too strong to be readily humbled in the ways that it could have been throughout the previous decade and last century. Such was the scale of potential conflict that the aftermath of the Sino–Soviet clashes and the winding down of China's internal Cultural Revolution frenzy saw moves to détente between China and the United States, under the new administration of Richard Nixon, author of that previously cited reflective paper in *Foreign Affairs* from 1967! The logic was not necessarily friendship, more the strategic sense of each recognising the other as their enemy's (i.e. the USSR's), enemy, and thus potential partners (Talbott 1981). Sino–American rapprochement was on the cards (Chen Jian 2001: 112–31). Already this had been flagged by Secretary of State William Roger's presentation of administration objectives in Asia to the Associated Press in New York City on 21 April 1969. He officially stated that 'we know that by virtue of its size, population, and the talents of its people, mainland China is bound to play an important role in East Asian and Pacific affairs', so that 'we shall take initiatives to reestablish more normal relations with Communist China and we shall remain responsive to any indications of less hostile attitudes from their side' (FRUS 2003: 78–9).

On the American side, the 'initiatives' were actually led by Nixon's National Security Adviser, Henry Kissinger. At NSC deliberations in May 1969, Kissinger wondered 'whether we really wanted China to be a world power like the Soviet Union, competing with us, rather than their present role which is limited to aiding certain insurgencies' although 'History suggested to him that it is better to align yourself with the weaker [China], not the stronger of two antagonistic partners' (FRUS 2003: 81). China's potential strength was not to be ignored though, as in Kissinger's year-end briefing in December 1969 about China, that '800 million people representing 25 per cent of the human race are a factor that cannot be ignored. They will influence international affairs . . . we are prepared to engage in a dialogue with them' (1979: 192). Kissinger carried out secret diplomacy during 1970, with delicate attempts by both sides to reach across Cold War ideological mindsets to read each other's exploratory signals, with the State Department cut out of the loop. All of this culminated in Kissinger's undercover trip to China in July 1971 (Ali 2005: 17–41), the announcement of which hit the world like a bombshell, a dramatic meeting to be followed by Nixon's own summit trip in February 1972, the famous 'week that changed the world'.

Kissinger's initial meeting brought his geopolitical structural recognition that 'we are here today, brought together by global trends. [Geopolitical] Reality has brought us together' as well as consideration of 'what each thinks of its place in the world'; to which Zhou Enlai's opening response was to stress that 'the first question is that of equality, or in other words, the principle of reciprocity' between China and the USA (Kissinger–Zhou 1971). Kissinger's confidential briefing to Nixon stressed the immediate Soviet threat to China, 'I believe they are deeply worried about the Soviet threat to their national integrity, realistically speaking, and see in us a balancing force against the USSR' (Kissinger 1971). Conversely, Kissinger's 1972 pre-summit advice to Nixon on the PRC was ambivalent, in the longer-term 'they're just as dangerous [as the Russians], in fact they're more dangerous over an historical period . . . the Chinese are much surer of themselves because they've been a great power all their history', although in the shorter term 'for the next 15 years we have to lean toward the Chinese against the Russians. We have to play this balance of power game totally unemotionally' (FRUS 2003: 105), as 'right now, we need the Chinese to correct the Russians and to discipline the Russians' (FRUS 2003: 369; also Nixon 1978: 97, 107, 119). Shortly thereafter, Kissinger continued in this vein, where 'our concern with China right now, in my view Mr. President, is to use it as a counter-weight to Russia' (FRUS 2003: 360).

Nixon had longer-term perspectives in mind in seeking détente with China, briefing his White House Staff on 19 July 1971 about Kissinger's trip he explained about China, 'they are one-fourth of the world's population. They're not a military power now but twenty-five years from now they will be decisive. For us not to do now what we can to end this isolation would leave things very dangerous' (Ali 2005: 41). China had already become indispensable to world order in the present time, whilst her potential was set to grow even more. Nixon's logic when visiting China in 1972 was clear, 'we must cultivate China during the next few decades while it is still learning to develop its national strength and potential', for 'otherwise we will one day be confronted with the most formidable enemy that has ever existed in the history of the world' (1978: 577).

American politicians were quick to assess the new situation. Senator Mike Mansfield (1974), Majority Leader in the Senate, considered that 'with Peking as the epicentre, the pattern of international relations in Asia has undergone a series of earthquakes. The repercussions have been deep and pervading' (1974: 49). This could replace 'a China policy based on myth and self-deception [which] has been a major factor in the atmosphere of crises which we have lived since the end of World War II' (61). Such a period was one where 'we still saw the People's Republic as a reckless, belligerent, and powerful Chinese dragon', but 'all the while, it is now apparent, the Chinese people were seeing themselves as a beleaguered, underdeveloped country, beset on all sides by enemies who had been marshaled by the United States to undo the achievements of the Chinese revolution' (52). IR misperceptions, evoking Jervis, were at play in Mansfield's sense that 'it is now known that during those years of ostracism, the Chinese emphasis was not on aggression beyond their borders, but on military defense of their own territory', and that 'in retrospect, it is clear that we expended billions in Asia to deter what we believed was an aggressive China at precisely the time when Chinese energies were being redirected away from militant revolution into militant social reconstruction' (52) within China. As to the future, 'we have entered a new era of relations with China . . . an era not based on the military preeminence of any single nation, but on the mutual efforts and forbearance of all nations concerned', in which 'there is every reason to expect that the new China will join with us and others in building that kind of a peace in the Pacific' (61).

China's role in the international system may have dramatically changed, and become a real 'factor' for both superpowers (Scalapino 1974; Segal 1982; also 1980, 1980–1), but to some extent she could be 'used' by the United States; the 'China Card' referred to and played by Nixon, Kissinger and also Carter, whereby concessions could be gained from the Soviet Union through the USA threatening to move closer to China. There was also a 'Soviet Card' able to be played against China by the USA (Goh 2005). Whilst the USA pursued détente simultaneously with both China and the Soviet Union, but whilst those two remained hostile to each other, the USA was able to pivot and manoeuvre between the two. Only the USA had relatively 'good' relationship with both other points in this asymmetrical triangle, and was thereby able to play one off against the other. As Kissinger put it, 'the hostility between China and the Soviet Union served our purposes best if we maintained closer relations with each side than they did with each other. The rest could be left to the dynamic of events' (1979: 712), as 'we would have a larger series of options toward either side than they had toward each other' (65). Kissinger saw America as able 'to manage the triangle in such a way that we would be closer to each of the contenders than they were to each other, thereby maximizing our options' (1982: 140; also 54). In effect, both the PRC and the Soviet Union had no choice but to move towards the USA, whilst the USA could 'choose, or at least signal that it might choose one or the other', an 'elementary game' (Dittmer 1981; also Garrett 1979) of international power politics.

Kissinger formally downplayed the existence of any China Card, ' "The China Card" was not ours to play . . . we could not exploit that rivalry' (1979: 763) between the two Communist giants. However, in effect the China Card existed. As Kissinger went on to admit 'just as pressure is not achieved by proclaiming it, so it is not ended by denying it' (1979: 766). In more blunt terms Nixon himself had succinctly told aides on 29 July 1969 'let me sum up . . . best US stance is to play each [against the other, but] – not publicly' (FRUS 2003: 95). Within the asymmetrical triangle, due to its weaker relative power base (Waltz 1979: 180) and lack of good relations with the USSR, Kissinger played on the fact that 'China was the most vulnerable party of the strategic triangle, and Mao knew it!' (151).

Kissinger provided a clear enough explanation of his triangular diplomacy to *Time* magazine correspondents in December 1970. Given the Sino–Soviet border conflict, he explained, the Soviets had an interest in dealing with the United States so as 'to free their Western rear so that they can focus more on China' and the United States could guarantee itself a maximum amount of leverage vis-à-vis Moscow simply by putting out 'the word that we are restudying the China question' (FRUS 2003: 80). Ronald Reagan's explanation was that 'let me suggest something about the China visit that, unfortunately, the President can't say, for that matter I can't say publicly without blowing the whole diplomatic game plan', which is 'the President, knowing of this dissatisfaction between China and Russia, visits China, butters up the warlords and lets them be', so that 'Russia, therefore, has to keep its forty divisions on the Chinese border; hostility between the two is increased and we buy a little time and elbow room in a plain strategic move' (Gittings 1984: 100). Mao Zedong made similar remarks to Kissinger in November 1973 about China tying down Soviet forces, where 'we are also holding down a portion of their troops which is favorable to you in China and the Middle East. For instance, they have troops stationed in Outer Mongolia, and that had not happened as late as Khrushchev' (Kissinger 1982: 149).

On the other hand critics of the 'China Card' could be found, arguing that China was too weak a card to actually effectively pressure the USSR, and conversely that misperception and over-exaggeration of the PRC's strength was leading the USA to make too many concessions to China. Robert Downen's *The Tattered China Card* argued that the normalisation of relations and talk of closer strategic cooperation 'served during 1979–81 as a highly visible psychological setback to overall Soviet strategic planning', but that 'this largely symbolic strategic asset was of only temporary, short-term benefit, with few tangible gains for Washington over time. Once Peking abandoned its interest in a regional anti-Soviet coalition in 1982, the China Card concept was dead' (Downen 1984: 60). As such, 'the limitations of symbolism could not compensate for the failure of substance', since 'the notion of Mainland China as a credible strategic asset for the United States did not mesh with the reality of the PRC as a weak and economically under developed country' (9). Given the assertive Soviet adventurism around the Asia/Asia–Pacific region, in Afghanistan, Vietnam, and the Pacific Fleet, he considered 'playing the "China Card"' to be an 'illusionary strategy' based on 'America's psychological over-reliance on the PRC's envisioned strategic assets' with the danger that 'the United States may be lulled into a false sense of security by its new military relationship with the PRC' (51). One could of course argue that Downen's emphasis on perception and misperception shows constructivist image dynamics at play in the International System, with the practical point that even if China's actual tangible power was being overestimated, then its effective power was still great through that very misperception by the United States. China was given effective power, and the illusion became tangible in terms of outcomes and consequences.

One interested observer of Kissinger's 1971 China diplomacy was the Australian commentator Ross Terrill (1975: 153–4, 163–4), who was visiting China at the same time as Kissinger, as a member of Gough Whitlam's entourage. It was an important moment in time, 'the point is that China, so long the object of our policies and judgements, is no longer a passive but an active factor in the world' (Terrill 1975: 248) in which 'China's actions, its ideas, its bomb, have become vital motifs of world history' (15). China's opening up was 'a mutation of historic proportions' (15), in which 'the flux of 1971 may turn out to have been a watershed in the way people look at China. What we think of China will matter a little less. What China thinks of us will matter a little more' (248–9). In conversations with ordinary people he found that 'in China you feel a strength which comes from belief in oneself. The importance of China is being transmuted from symbol to actuality' (1975: 26). His conversations with Zhou Enlai had Zhou stressing China 'will not be controlled by anyone' (Terrill 1975: 27) with an attitude 'evident up and down China: deep sensitivity about China's dignity as an independent power' (27), which Terrill explicitly linked to China's experience in its Century of Humiliation. China's Cultural Revolution dogmatism had crumbled; instead, Zhou had 'a picture of the world that featured power more than ideology, fluid forces more than rigid blocs' (149).

Australian relations with China showed similar trends to that manifesting itself in the USA. In the Australian Labour Party, Gough Whitlam finally ditched the 'White Australia' immigration policies in 1971, as well as visiting China in July 1971 (Terill 1975: 189–96). Whitlam's party won the 1972 General Election. Recognition of the PRC came in December 1972, and was followed by Whitlam's further trip to China in 1973. Australian troops were withdrawn from Vietnam. Ironically the incoming Conservative government under Malcolm Fraser, elected in 1975, further expanded Sino–Australian ties, amidst 'a shifting geopolitical balance' (Strahan 1996: 295), drawn together by common perceptions of Soviet expansionism in the Indian and Pacific oceans. China could emerge as a shield against the Soviet Union, to the benefit of Australia; with Whitlam seeing Fraser reverting to the Vietnam period 'forward defense', that is, 'then the Mekong was Australia's border. Now it has shifted further north to the Amur' (295). Public opinion also shifted, 'enthusiasm for China spread' (295). In 1967–9, 30.9 per cent of Australians saw China as a threat to Australia's security, considerably more than the 13.5 per cent who considered the Soviet Union to be a threat (Huck 1984: 163). By 1980 the perceptions had dramatically shifted, 40 per cent seeing the Soviet Union as a threat considerably more than the 13.5 per cent who saw China as a threat (163). These proportions were roughly maintained in 1983, 36.6 per cent seeing the Soviet Union as the threat and 13.3 per cent seeing China as a threat.

On the Chinese side, similar perceptions about a Soviet threat and realpolitik conclusions were reached, applying Mao's 1940 logic of exploiting contradictions between otherwise enemies (Armstrong 1977) in a 'One United Front' *yitiaoxian* strategy. The famous '4 Marshals' study, by Chen Yi, Ye Jiangqing, Xu Xiangqian and Nie Rongzhen, on Sino–Soviet–US relations were 'insightful reports, providing powerful strategic justification for Beijing to improve relations with the United States' (Chen Jian and Wilson 1998: 155). They advised Mao to play an American card against the USSR, 'the Soviet revisionists are scared by the prospects we might ally ourselves with the U.S. imperialists to confront them . . . the Soviet revisionists' fears about possible Sino-American unity makes it more difficult for them to launch an all-out attack on China' (Chen Yi *et al.* 1969: 170). The Marshals were not unaware of the danger of America using China, for 'in the struggle between China, the United States, and the Soviet Union, the United States hopes to utilize China and the Soviet Union' (170). However, China's own flexibility to the United States would at least enable her to block Soviet threats, 'the U.S. imperialists have suggested resuming the Sino–American ambassadorial talks, to which we should respond positively when the timing is proper. Such tactical actions may bring about results of strategic significance' (170), of benefit to China. As Chen Yi recognised 'because of the strategic need for dealing with Soviet revisionists, Nixon hopes to win over China. It is necessary for us to . . . pursue a breakthrough in the Sino–American relations', where 'we must adopt due measures, about which I have some "wild ideas" . . . to discuss with the Americans other questions of strategic significance' (Chen Yi 1969: 171).

The Chinese leadership swung into action. Mao's sense was that 'we must win over one of the two superpowers, never fight with two fists, we can take advantage of the contradictions between the two superpowers and that is our policy' (Zhang Franklin 1998: 11). In similar terms Zhou Enlai argued for Nixon's visit by briefing colleagues in December 1971 that 'at this stage it is necessary to take full advantage of the contradiction between the U.S. and USSR and magnify it' (Zhou 1971: 138; also Garver 1982). Zhou's biggest fear, expressed to Nixon, was a China encircled on all fronts, whereby 'the worst possibility is what I told Dr. Kissinger in the record of our proceedings, that is to say the eventuality that you all would attack China – the Soviet Union comes from the north, Japan and the U.S. from the east, and India into China's Tibet' (Zhou 1972).

It was the Soviet threat that dominated Chinese strategic thinking over relations with America. Ross Terrill's trip to China in summer 1971 gained a sense that 'the Russian threat is "immediate" in a crude military sense' (1975: 149) for the PRC leadership. The Cambodian leader, Prince Sihanouk, told Terrill that 'Russia is China's biggest problem' (Terrill 1975: 189). Harrison Salisbury's trip to China in 1972 similarly picked up how 'from China's standpoint, the Russian danger was bound to be paramount in foreign policy' (Salisbury 1973: 295); even if, 'in hindsight, however, it is clear that China overestimated the [actual] threat from Soviet strategic intentions' (Wang Zhongchun 2005: 153). The nuances of the Sino–Soviet split were dramatic enough, a quarrel for Salisbury which had 'flared with such incredible ferocity' (Salisbury 1973: 241) in which 'race feelings were involved, particularly on the part of the Russians' (241) and in which 'I have not spoken to a single Russian since the crisis of 1969 who was not infused with hatred for the Chinese' (240). For him geopolitical manoeuvrings were involved, 'the immediate goal of Premier Chou's foreign policy – the establishment of a triangular relationship of China, the United States and Japan that would clearly over-balance any combination the Russians might forge against it' (297).

Chinese sensitivities were still clearly maintained over what Zhou Enlai admitted had been a 'necessary compromise' (1973: 23) with the United States; a state 'increasingly on the decline' (23) in contrast with the Soviet 'Brezhnev renegade clique' (23) expansionism with its 'ugly features as the new czar' (23) which had 'massed its troops along the Chinese border' (23). Similarly, at the UN, the PRC argued 'in bullying others, the superpower [i.e. the USSR] which flaunts the label of socialism is especially vicious. It has dispatched its armed forces to occupy its "ally" Czechoslovakia . . . it is socialism in words and imperialism in deeds' (Deng Xiaoping 1974: 6). China's logic remained clear and consistent. Zhou Enlai's internal report on the international situation identified 'the most perilous and the most real enemy, Soviet revisionist social-imperialism. This strategy was laid down by Chairman Mao. Chairman Mao said: "We must not fight on two fronts; it is better to fight on one front"' (Zhou 1976: 193), to concentrate with others against the USSR. Zou's diplomacy was not just reactive and defensive;

it was also a bold jump, a pragmatic application of IR balancing-realism, 'intended to secure a major role for China on the world stage' (Shao Kuo-kang 1996: 208).

Chinese perceptions of the international system can be tracked through the eyes of her state directed media during the 1970s. China was, or at the least could feel, encircled through the Soviet Union's links with Vietnam and India. The *Peking Review* noted Soviet 'expansion and penetration . . . for years, the Soviet social-imperialists have been scheming to secure military bases in Southeast Asia'; and where, 'motivated by their quest for sea supremacy, they have sent large numbers of warships to sail between the Pacific and the Indian Ocean in a show of force which threatens the peace and security of the Southeast Asian countries' (1975: 20) and indeed China as well. This regional threat around China was, for the *Peking Review*, part of a wider Soviet threat (1975), with the Soviet Union 'engaged in unbridled aggression and expansion abroad in contending for world hegemony' (1976a: 9). Comparisons from history were made by the *Peking Review*. One was how the Soviet 'rabid expansion of its naval forces . . . to lord it over the oceans' made the 'new tsars more ambitious than the old', where 'the scramble for maritime hegemony figures high in the global strategy of Soviet social-imperialism in its bid for world domination' (1976b: 26). Another historical comparison was that 'today, the Soviet social-imperialists are following in the footsteps of Nazi Germany. The Brezhnev clique's greed and ambition far surpass Hitler's' (1976c: 13). Amidst such sweeping rhetoric was the direct concern over the Soviet Union 'massing a million troops along the Chinese border . . . posing a serious threat to China's security' (1977a: 5). Criticism of the United States was maintained but 'of the two imperialist superpowers, the Soviet Union is the more ferocious, the more reckless, the more treacherous, and the most dangerous' (1977b: 22).

Deng Xiaoping

By this time a longer-term factor starting to affect the international system was the consolidation of Deng Xiaoping's power. During the Cultural Revolution, Deng had been disgraced as a 'capitalist roader' in 1966, but was rehabilitated in 1973. However, as Mao Zedong declined in health, the ascendancy of the ultra-leftist 'Gang of Four' saw Deng purged for a second time in Spring 1976. They had though not been able to hold onto their power after Mao's death in September 1976. Consequently, Deng was again rehabilitated in July 1977, with paramount status gained by the end of 1978. China's path for the following decade was to be shaped by Deng's vision and priorities, announced in 1978 in the shape of the 'Four Modernizations'. This set out to transform China's economy, science and technology, education and military base. It set the agenda until Deng's death in 1997, and indeed posthumously through his choice of the Third and Fourth Generation leadership (i.e. Jiang Zemin and Hu Jintao).

China's profile was rising when *Time* magazine considered that 'because of the tremendous enterprise he has launched to propel the nation into the modern world, Teng Hsiao-p'ing . . . is TIME's Man of the Year for 1978' (*Time* 1979a). Its profile of this 'visionary of a new China' immediately opened with the hoary quotation 'China? There lies a sleeping giant. Let him sleep, for when he wakes he will move the world – Napoleon Bonaparte' (1979b). *Time* considered that 'Teng's scope was huge, matching China itself where the project is vast, daring, and unique in history', for 'turning 1 billion people so sharply in their course, for leading one-quarter of mankind quick-step out of dogmatic isolation into the late twentieth century and the life of the rest of the planet' to 'become a world economic and military power' (1979a). Admittedly, uncertainties remained for China, 'they may not arrive, or arrive on time, but their setting off is an extraordinary spectacle of national ambition' (1979a). However, *Time* suggested that 'the normalization opens potentially lucrative avenues of trade and new perspectives on world politics, even though it will be a long time before Peking joins Washington and Moscow as a capital of first-rank global power' (1979a). Nevertheless, it cited an unnamed Western diplomat wondering 'if an economically and militarily powerful China by the year 2000 would be an unmitigated blessing for American interests. Would a China strong enough to threaten Russia in nuclear terms not constitute any threat to us at all?' (1979a).

Deng's perspective on China's place in the international system was to maintain its own freedom of operation within it. For him, in May 1984, 'China's foreign policy can be summed up in two sentences. First, to safeguard world peace we oppose hegemony. Second, China will always belong to the Third World' (1984–94: 3.66). However, even though Deng ideologically identified China with the Third World, his goals were to lift China from Third World socio-economic levels to those found in the First World, the West, through using Western capital and technology. A paradox arose though, in Deng's linkage in April 1987 that 'to achieve modernization and to implement the reform and the open policy we need political stability and unity at home and a peaceful international environment' (3.226). Political stability at home could, and did, become a euphemism for internal political suppression and external alienation from the West, whilst Deng's peaceful economic reforms and associated collaboration with the West was still being pursued.

China's economic needs were paramount. Deng set the tone for the decade with his directive to the Central Committee of the CCP in January 1980, where Deng argued 'the role we play in international affairs is determined by the extent of our economic growth. If our country becomes more developed and prosperous, we will be in a position to play a greater role in international affairs' (1984–94: 2.225). Deng pursued the logic of China's new settings with his call in May 1984, 'we must safeguard world peace and ensure domestic development' (1984–94: 3.66), a telling enough juxtaposition of external and internal needs.

Deng's logic was simple but determined. China would not seek confrontation with the West, but would instead keep open her doors for investment, modernisation and growth, to give her long-term modernisation programme the time it needed to be carried out and come to fruition, by the middle of the twenty-first century! The international scene fed back into China's domestic needs, so that Deng was probably genuine enough in May 1984 when saying 'we sincerely hope that no war will break out and that peace will be long-lasting, so that we can concentrate on the drive to modernize our country' (1984–94: 3.66–7). Deng's time scale was carefully nuanced, long term and in two stages. In 1984 he was telling the Central Advisory Commission of the CCP that 'we should be able to quadruple our GNP by the year 2000 . . . once we have quadrupled GNP . . . China will be truly powerful, exerting a much great influence in the world' (3.94, 96). In turn, 'we have a second target to attain within another 30 to 50 years [i.e. 2030–50] . . . in which the open door policy will remain indispensable', i.e. 'we shall approach the level of the developed countries' (3.96)). Such stages were constantly re-iterated during the 1980s, for example, on 4 July 1987 came a strategic timetable that after 2000 'it will take us another 50 years or so to reach the level of the moderately developed countries. We are therefore hoping for at least 70 years of peace. We do not want to miss this opportunity for development' (3.246).

Elsewhere, from a geopolitical point of view, Geoffrey Parker considered that 'there seems to have been almost general agreement among political geographers that the principal catalyst for the transformation of the world geopolitical scene was the emergence of China as a great power in its own right' (1985: 149). All of this could be recognised by Michel Oksenberg as Deng's 'pride in China's national heritage and . . . dedication to making China a major actor in world affairs', a 'confident nationalism . . . flexible in tactics, subtle in strategy' with a 'patient . . . confidence that over time China can regain its former greatness through economic growth . . . to lay the foundations for the eventual attainment of modern military force and international greatness' (1987: 503, 505). A 50–70 year strategy for long-term rise within the system was being laid down in Deng's China. As *Time* noted, when again awarding Deng their 'Man of the Year' title for 1985, Deng's reforms were of global significance 'if it should succeed, the transformation would have profound and enormous consequences throughout the world' (*Time* 1986). In retrospect, Michael Cox considered that Deng Xiaoping's wider economic and strategic engagement with the West was not only 'impressive', but would constitute 'one of those critical "turning-points" of the twentieth century' (1998: 226) for China, but also for the international system.

In China high level discussions had been considering the implications of shifts in the international system. Huang Xiang, Deng's national security adviser, the equivalent of Henry Kissinger, argued during 1985 that 'the two largest military powers are weakening and declining . . . militarily they are developing in the direction of multipolarization' (Pillsbury: 2005: 9), having argued the previous year that the 'old [bipolar] world order has already disintegrated and the new world order is now taking shape, but up to now it still has not yet completely formed' (10), which gave openings for China where 'China must go through a long period of hard work . . . 30 to 50 years time will make it truly powerful' (10). By 1986, Huang was more certain about the multipolarization of the international system where 'future international politics and economics are facing a new period' (10), in which 'as the world moves towards a multipolar world . . . when the United States and the Soviet Union are considering problems, they must think about the China factor' (11). There may still have been a 'transition period' envisaged, but China's future lay alongside the other established Great Powers.

Although Deng's modernisation programme was primarily based on building up the economic foundations of China, military modernisation was a fourth strand. Consequently, the PRC's power projection was becoming apparent in Asia–Pacific. Consequently, 'as China and its armed forces grow strong, this country also grows more important in international relations' (Segal 1988: 222), for 'a stronger China also affects the international balance of power' (223), in which a renewed Cold War atmosphere had replaced US–Soviet détente.

Cold War II

American relations with the USSR cooled during the late 1970s, amidst signs of growing Soviet interventionism around Africa and Asia. In such a vein, under Jimmy Carter's 1977–81 Presidency, China and America collaborated on setting up an electronic observation post in Xinjiang to track Soviet missile communications. Carter's view of China's international role was simple and clear, her 'permanence and strategic importance in international affairs were evident' (1995: 191), big enough to be a significant chip against the Soviet Union. It was interesting that he felt 'without being condescending about it, the Chinese always acted as if they still considered themselves members of the Middle Kingdom – at the center of the civilized world' and were 'prepared to wait until others accepted their position on "matters of principle"' (194). The China Card still operated: his diary entry for 31 December 1978 recorded receiving worried letters from the Soviet leadership 'paranoid about the People's Republic of China' (205). Carter's own sense of events, in his diary entry for 29 January 1979, was that 'the Chinese need a long period of peace to realize their full modernization' and that 'the Soviets will launch war eventually, but we may be able to postpone war for 22 years' (i.e. until 2001), and that 'we should coordinate our activities to constrain the Soviets' (209) in the meantime.

A new Cold War, dubbed 'Cold War II', seemed in the offing as Carter's successor Ronald Reagan talked in 1982 about the Soviet Union as the 'Empire of Evil'. China's role in the international system could, in effect, be seen as part of an anti-Soviet bloc alongside the United States and its other allies, in what Garrett saw as the 'the realities of geopolitics . . . to counter growing Soviet power' (1983: 265–6, also Ali 2005).

The United States saw an 'Arc of Crisis' generated by Soviet expansionism, running from Angola, to Mozambique, Somalia, Ethiopia, Aden and Afghanistan. China also felt directly threatened by an arc of Soviet expansionism around its own particular perimeters. India had already signed a Treaty of Friendship and Cooperation with the Soviet Union in 1971. India had its own established images of China. Shashi Bhushan was trenchant over China's *Shadow on India and Bangladesh*, warning of 'China's hegemonistic aims' (1973: 15–22) and stressing that 'we in India know the Chinese a little better than many other countries that do not have a common border . . . the Chinese have committed aggression on Indian territory and have given no end of trouble by their perfidious actions' (10). China's earlier patterns were re-asserting themselves, 'their craving to revive the past grandeur of China is making them more chauvinistic than ever' (41), for 'China wants first to dominate its immediate neighbours and then extend its domination to other countries' (41). Such images matched the later China-threat perceptions that became prominent in America during the 1990s.

In turn, Vietnam signed a Treaty of Friendship and Cooperation with the USSR and joined COMECON in 1976, threw open its Cam Rahn naval base to the Soviet Pacific Fleet, and imposed a new regime in Kampuchea in January 1979. China's responses were heavy handed punitive cross-border war incursions in February 1979 to teach her former Communist ally Vietnam a lesson, but in which China's military showed itself somewhat cumbersome and unable to achieve any clear victory. China saw Domino Theory dangers at play with regard to the Soviet Union, Vice-Premier Geng Biao warning in January 1979, of 'the Soviet Union's social imperialism manipulating Vietnam, the Cuba of the Far East, to carry out its first expansionist steps into South-east Asia: it is part of the global strategic plan of Soviet social imperialism' (Gittings 1984: 111). This was then combined with still older danger models from the 1930s, that 'if we . . . dream of getting by through appeasement, then today's Kampuchea will be tomorrow's South-east Asia and other nations of the Asian Pacific region, and yesterday's Czechoslovakia will become the image for tomorrow's Europe' (Gittings 1984: 111).

China was also directly faced with Soviet military pressure on its own flanks. On the maritime front there was the continued build-up of the Soviet Pacific Fleet at Vladivostok. On land, where fighting had been seen in 1969, it was further faced with a significant increase of Soviet troop levels along the frontiers, the longest in the world, an increase in the Soviet Far Eastern region from some 17–20 divisions to 53 divisions by 1983. China felt still further threatened as Soviet forces moved into Afghanistan in December 1979, adjoining her sensitive border region of Xinjiang (Ali 2005: 166–88). As Deng Xiaoping bluntly put it the following month, 'in international affairs . . . the 1980s will be a dangerous decade. So the task of opposing hegemony will be on our agenda. The 1980s are off to a bad start, what with the Afghanistan affair' (1984–94: 2.225). Similar sentiments were expressed by the United States as it prepared for Reagan's 1984 trip to China, the NSC recommending that 'in the area of strategic and military relations, we should strive to explore possibilities of raising the level of strategic dialogue and expanding US–PRC cooperation against the common threat posed by the USSR'; so 'we should discuss with Chinese leaders Soviet military expansion in Asia, their likely future weapons development, Soviet efforts to expand their influence throughout the world' (USA 1984).

Chinese concerns about the Soviet Union were exacerbated by the USSR's close links with India, with whom a Treaty of Friendship and Cooperation had been signed in 1971, 'in China, it was taken as an axiom that the Soviet Union and India had concluded a working partnership hostile to, and directed against, China' (Salisbury 1973: 297). Sino–Indian relations remained cool during the 1980s, with talk of 'India's second China war' (Maxwell 1987) arising as troop skirmishes took place in the disputed Sumdorong Chu valley during 1986. Nevertheless the Chinese and Indian leadership were able to reach out to each other. Exploratory talks had already been launched by Indira Gandhi on her return to power in 1980, and after eight rounds of official talks, were sealed with Rajiv Gandhi's trip to China in 1988 (Baral *et al.* 1989). Both powers had an economic as well as strategic incentive to try to normalise ongoing relations, even if underlying issues were not resolved.

Shifts in the system (the Soviet collapse and Tiananmen)

Given the extra pressure placed more directly on China by the Soviet presence around her in all directions, the PRC had a greater geopolitical imperative to reduce tension with the USSR than had the USA. The last years of Brezhnev and initial short-lived successions of Andropov and Chernenko failed to remove general Soviet rigidity. Instead, the advent of Mikhail Gorbachev (1985) brought an easing of tensions, signalled in Gorbachev's Vladivostok Speech of 1986 and trip to China in 1989. However, this was overshadowed by the still more dramatic events at the end of the 1980s, where the Soviet Union pulled out of Afghanistan in 1989, lost its grip on East Europe during 1989–90, and finally imploded in 1991. Amidst a general Soviet overstretch and internal decay, Nancy Tucker saw 'China as a factor in the collapse of the Soviet Empire' in 1990, due to 'the Chinese security threat, the economic challenge, and the Tiananmen model of political suppression' (1995–6: 502).

Within China, the challenge to the regime posed at Tiananmen Square since April 1989, ironically partly encouraged by Gorbachev's overshadowed trip to China at that moment, had not sparked regime collapse but rather witnessed harsh reassertion of central control in early June. The Tiananmen Square massacres revived widespread images in the West of a brutal but also aggressive Chinese regime. Yet whilst China's international image took a sudden battering, its national power was on the rise. Commentators had already been wondering about 'the dawn of the new age of Chinese military power . . . as China grows strong' (Segal 1988: 217) under the effects of Deng's Four Modernizations. The dramatic changes in the international system and in China's own power capabilities were to provide the crucial context for the new post-Cold War China breakthrough in terms of power and presence – an opportunity for some, a threat for others, and a challenge for all.

5 A reviving Middle Kingdom for China

China's international presence

The collapse of the Soviet Union at the start of the 1990s, together with China's continuing advancement gave the decade an increasingly China-focused feel. The stakes were high for the international system of China's rise and coming role. Goodman and Segal considered that 'in thinking strategically about modern international affairs, there is no more important challenge than to understand the nature and implications of a rising China' (1997: 1). Paradoxes abounded, since 'China is not generally well understood but the world is acutely aware of it. Indeed China itself ranks as a global preoccupation' (Dellios 1999: 4). In structural terms, Rex Li argued that, in the wake of the Soviet collapse 'the emergence of China as a great power is arguably the single most important development in the post-Cold War world' (2004: 23) of the 1990s.

In part, this heightened awareness of China in the 1990s, 'the emerging China-mania' (A. Goldstein 2005: 49), was through consideration of China's desire and ability to act on the 'global' level, an involvement which had become something of a truism by the end of the decade (Hodder 1999, Yates 1999, Yahuda 1999), with *China: a World Power Again* (Kaplan 1999), and *China as No 1. The New Superpower* (Brahm 1996, also Garver 1998). In part, it was the dramatic pace of 'China's seemingly meteoric rise toward great power status' (Christensen 1998: 4, also Harris and Klintsworth 1995, A. Goldstein 1997–8, Brown *et al.* 2000). For many analysts, the 1990s became a decade where 'China, the new "Orient Express" of the East – is *the* future and will dominate the international system of the twenty-first century in much the same way as Britain before the First World War and the United States after 1945' (Cox 1998: 226).

In part, it was the challenge of trying to discern how China was seeing the international system (Deng Yong and Wang Fei-Ling 1999), and the ambiguities surrounding its role as a threat or opportunity. China's relative wariness over engaging in multilateral structures, her 'conditional multilateralism' (Yuan 2000) also made her less familiar on the diplomatic circuit. In part, it was through concern and uncertainty about the extent to which

China was, and would be, a threat. *The Economist* cover story 'China Looming' asked 'seventy years ago, scare-mongering westerners called it "the yellow peril". Today it is called the Peoples Republic. It is certainly a world event. Is it also a reason for the world to shake in its shoes?' (1996: 13). Other commentators also talked of a 'return of the Yellow Peril' (Greenfield 1992).

Actors around its borders and beyond were all affected by this macrochange in the very structure of the international system, in which President Jacques Chirac's visit to China had him saying that China's growth would bring about the 'overthrow of the planetary balance' (*South China Morning Post*, 19 May 1997). For the first time, all the core elements of the Yellow Peril paradigm, namely economic strength and military projection based on a large population base were coalescing in reality. China's 1,319 million inhabitants in 2003 dwarfed Japan's relatively static 128 million, Russia's declining 141 million and the USA's 292 million. Some observers focused on China as a 'status-quo' or 'conservative' (Ross 1997) power, whilst others focused on various 'China Threat' scenarios. The question was frequently posed, was China a *zero-sum* threat or a *win-win* opportunity (Pastor 1999, Carpenter and Dorn 2000)? Certainly a 'colossus' (Harding 1995) had arrived on the world scene, in which 'the rise of China poses perhaps the most far-reaching challenge to the international status quo' (Segal 1997: 172) as perceived potentiality gave way to a measurable and increasingly significant realised actuality.

Economics was involved in this advance of China across the global consciousness. By the 1990s, Deng Xiaoping's Four Modernizations programme had already been in operation for over a decade. Books were appearing like *The China Miracle* (Lin *et al.* 1996). Consequently, William Overholt's *China. The Next Economic Superpower* considered that 'the current takeoff of one quarter of the human race . . . is transforming the political structures of the entire globe' (1993: 211). The OECD considered China's continuing annual economic growth rates of 10 per cent as a 'remarkable accomplishment' (1996: 7) whereby, 'in just one decade and a half, China has transformed itself from a dormant, introspective giant into a dynamic powerhouse' (7) within the international economy. China's economic power was attracting negative and positive interpretations, with Cable and Ferdinand asking the question: *China as an Economic Giant: Threat or Opportunity*? (1996). Economics underpinned China's political and military projection. In Overholt's mind his *The Rise of China* was a question of *How Economic Reform is Creating a New Superpower* (1994). Kissinger's view, in 1994, was that 'of all the great, and potentially great, powers, China is the most ascendant . . . China, however, with economic growth rates approaching 10 per cent annually, a strong sense of national cohesion, and an ever more muscular military, will show the greatest relative increase in stature among the major powers (1994: 829).

Speculation on China's military capacity was noticeable (Waldron 1998). The OECD argued that 'a rapidly growing China will find it easier to raise military expenditures, but will be under far less pressure actually to do so'

(1996: 35). Some still saw PRC military forces as 'bloated' (*Economist* 2000: 17), more appropriate for a struggling developing state rather than a great power (Karmel 2000). However, others were struck by China's readiness to strengthen her military forces, Taeho Kim's 'reality check' (1998; also Hirschfield 1999, Wortzel 1999), as the world's biggest military force started to implement Deng's modernisation programme. Add to this an expanding maritime reach, with an ocean going 'blue water navy' (Ji You 1997), able to project 'strategic seapower in the nuclear age' (Lewis and Litai 1994), and to achieve 'China's ambitions to be a regional naval superpower' (Khanna 1999).

Uncertainties remained apparent. Joseph Nye, in a sceptical frame of mind, asked rhetorically 'as China rises, must others bow' (1998)? Indeed, Gerald Segal's discussion of *Does China Matter?* attracted attention with his assertion that China's geopolitical significance had been exaggerated, advocating a 'China . . . cut down to size in Western imagination' (1999: 36). He considered China 'overrated as a market, a power, and a source of ideas', a 'second-rank middle power that has mastered the art of diplomatic theatre: it has us willingly suspending our disbelief in its strength. In fact China is best understood as a theoretical power' (24). Yet, theoretical or not, the PRC was attracting the world's attention, in which 'China still has a hold on the imagination of CEO's' (36), *The China Dream: The Quest for the Last Great Untapped Market on Earth* (Studwell 2002). One could argue that even if China was relatively weak, IR constructivism-wise, if the world perceived China as stronger than what she was, then she was already influencing the system.

China's perspectives on the international system

Chinese security thinking was dominated by the changes in China's strategic situation. At one level, Gorbachev's force reductions of 1989–90, followed by the Soviet collapse in 1991, meant that China's northern situation was dramatically transformed in her favour. For China, the collapse of the Soviet Union represented an 'immense shift in the regional balance of power in its favour', freeing it from conventional continental land threats, and instead giving it significant 'strategic latitude in dealing with maritime East Asia' (Yahuda 1999b: 655), in ways that could be seen as too assertive and threatening.

Potential conflict with other Powers was something to be avoided, particularly as China sought to build up its longer-term strength. Deng Xiaoping's seminal advice on handling the new emerging world affairs of the 1990s was his famous 24 Chinese-character maxim, to 'observe calmly; secure our position; cope with affairs calmly; hide our capacities and bide our time; be good at maintaining a low profile; and never claim leadership' (1991, also Wang Jisi 1994: 29). Crucially this was an immediate tactic with long-term strategy in mind, as China continued its modernisation programme.

China saw opportunities for herself from this collapse of the old bipolar Soviet–American duopoly. During the 1990s, China's view of its place in the world reflected a 'world multipolarity' *shijie duojihua* strategy. Deng Xiaoping was already telling leading members of the Central Committee in 1990 that 'the situation in which the United States and the Soviet Union dominated all international affairs is changing . . . in future when the world becomes three-polar, four-polar or five-polar . . . in the so called multi-polar world China will be counted as a pole' (1984–94: 3.341). The PRC leadership continued to use this analysis. Jiang Zemin considered that 'the world is moving towards multipolarity, a hall mark of the present day international situation . . . the relations between and among big powers are in constant shifts and a multitude of power centers is now taking shape' (1997c: 9). In other words, 'world multipolarization is an inevitable trend' (Jiang Zemin 1999: 7). Foreign Minister Tang Jiaxuan argued that 'in today's world, there is an accelerated movement towards multi-polarity' (1999b: 10). Chinese military figures reckoned on a multipolar order in the offing, Major General Yu Qifen welcoming 'the rapid development of multipolarity' (1995: 70; also Chi Haotian 1996: 62, Wang Naiming 1997: 39). In the *Beijing Review* Yang Xiyue welcomed 'the increasing multi-polarization trend of the present times, which has especially been sponsored by China' (1999: 6).

The language was still carefully nuanced, a process of arriving, rather than a state that had been reached. Deng Xiaoping warned in 1990 'the old [bipolar] pattern is changing but has not yet come to an end, and the new one is yet to take shape' (1984–94: 3.341). If multipolarity was a coming process rather than a reached situation, how long would this transition process take? Lieutenant General Li Jijun, thought 'it probably will not take another 40 years before a world structure of multipolar coexistence comes into being. It might take 10 or 20 years to take shape. During this transitional period the world situation might be very unstable' (1994: 222).

Some post-Cold War trends pointed to increasing American power and a unipolar situation, rather than China's hopes for multipolarity. American power projection and technological expertise in the Gulf War of 1991, and operations against Serbia in 1999, provided salutary lessons for the PRC. Jiang Zemin admitted 'the Gulf war makes us further see the functions of science and technology' (Godwin 1996: 473). For military figures like Senior Colonel Wang Naiming 'the recent Gulf War has shown that high tech weapons have played the main role' (1997: 41). For outside observers like Paul Godwin 'the devastating display of military technology during the 1991 Gulf War had a profound influence on the Chinese military leaders', as 'following that war, China's military strategists placed even greater emphasis on technology . . . the Gulf War quickly became the reference point for the PLA's modernization programmes' (1996: 473; also Jencks 1992).

The lessons were disquieting for China. American assertiveness and mastery for this new type of warfare was juxtaposed with Chinese deficiencies. China's leading military figure, Admiral Liu Huaqing, felt that the current PLA 'fails to meet the needs of modern warfare' (Godwin 1996: 473), i.e. there was a need 'to improve our weapons and technology as soon as possible . . . using science . . . with an emphasis on electronic technology' (Shambaugh 1996c: 281). Although American strength was evident here, Chinese strategists could look for 'military dialectics . . . the ways and methods to defeat a powerful opponent with a weak force in a high tech war' (Shen Kuiguan 1994: 218). For Senior Colonels Wang Baocun and Li Fei, 'the Gulf War . . . enabled us to determine certain innate features of information warfare' centred on 'the digitized battlefield' (1995: 332), in which 'the key 21st century weapon will be the computer' (330), a mechanism giving China the opportunity to conduct 'computer virus warfare' (330), and which 'will expand the limits of war into outerspace' (337). Cyberspace and outer space were to be domains where Chinese advances were to become noticeable in the next decade.

Other developments heightened China's profile in the international system, where Samuel Kim considered that 'one of the most remarkable and potentially dangerous developments in the post-Cold war era' was the concept of *haiyangguoto gua* (sea as national territory), which would feed 'China's *lebensraum* in the coming years' and take China's naval projection 'progressively further away from coastal waters' (1996: 9). Chinese strategists talked of necessary *hengcun kongjian* 'survival space' (9) as not only extending on land around its traditional perimeters but also into the Indian Ocean, the South China and East China Seas and indeed vertically into space. The development of the Chinese fleet was noticeable in the 1990s, the more so when juxtaposed with the decay of the Soviet Pacific Fleet. Admiral Liu Huaqing, the leading advocate of Chinese maritime expansion, argued that 'the strategic importance of the oceans has increased day by day . . . we must understand the ocean from a strategic point of view and its importance . . . China should build a powerful navy' (1994: 118). Advocates of China's blue-water long-range oceanic capability talked of it as not just protecting specific shipping lanes, fishing grounds and other specific fields but also for increasing China's *quo wei* (national awesomeness). *Jinhai fangyu* (coastal defence) was to be extended to *jinyang fangyu* (offshore defence), the defence perimeter extended from coastal waters to 200–400 nautical miles offshore, an offshore 'green water' capable navy was to be ready for 2000, and a long range *yuanyang haijun* (blue water) navy by 2050.

Underneath and around these military security perceptions was the economic drive, initiated in 1978 and moving into full force in the 1990s, a decade for which Deng Xiaoping had outlined in 1990 the imperative to 'develop the economy without delay . . . and quadruple the GNP by the end of this century. I am afraid that for at least ten years this question will keep us awake at night', for 'if China is to withstand the pressures of hegemonism and power politics . . . it is crucial for us to achieve rapid economic growth and to carry out our development strategy' (1984–94: 3.342–3) of the Four Modernizations. Within that, Deng reckoned 'China's prospects for the next century are excellent . . . it will not be long before the Republic of China, which is already a political power, becomes an economic power as well' (3.342–3). Of interest was Deng's sense of a *dazhonghua* 'Greater China' (Harding 1993, Shambaugh 1995) beyond the PRC, i.e. 'the mainland has developed a solid economic foundation. Besides, we have tens of millions of overseas compatriots, and they want to see China strong and prosperous' (Deng Xiaoping 1984–94: 3.345). By the end of the decade, Zheng Yongnian accurately judged that "the Chinese feel that with increasing economic wealth, their country is for the first time in modern history capable of pursuing power in the international system' (1999: 138).

Pursuing international power reflected 'China's quest for Great Power Identity' (Rozman 1999), both in terms of actual and perceived power and respect. This was 'a product of images of other great powers and the balance among them', in which 'inspired by the goal of catching up and ending their victimization at the hands of "imperialists". . . Chinese leaders and analysts are fixated on the balance of great powers' (384–5). Consequently, 'of all the contenders in the quest for national identity in the 1990s, the notion of China as a Great Power (*daguo*) has gained a clear cut victory' (385; also Shih 2005: 758–70).

The hard power element was entwined with soft power respect, as in Wang Jisi's *Da guo de zunyan* (The dignity of a Great Power) (2001). IR constructivist elements of image perception were apparent in the way in which criticism and steam soon appeared in China over Segal's 1999 down-playing of China's significance, with Gu Ping writing in the *People's Daily* about Segal 'belittling China' (1999; also Sutter 2003–4). Some perception of actual or potential loss of international 'face' would seem to have been at play in such Chinese outrage.

The China Threat image was quickly and strongly perceived in China. At one level, 'the response from the ordinary Chinese citizen to the issue has been largely emotional. Indeed the issue has aroused a strong wave of nationalistic feelings among a significant portion of the Chinese population' and 'helped to change their views of the world and especially of the United States' (Ong 2002: 161). At another level, Chinese analysts were frequently to be found, trying to rebut in various forums 'often . . . in a rather vehe-ment manner' (161) *Zhongguo weixie lun*, the 'China Threat theory'. Such China Threat rebuttals 'sharply rose' (Yee and Feng 2002: 22) in 1995–6, in parallel with increasing American talk of such a China Threat. Typical of this were the spate of articles in the state-approved *Beijing Review* like Hu Ping's, 'China constitutes no military threat' (1994), Ge Yang's 'China's rise: threat or not?' (1995), Ren Xin's '"China threat" theory untenable' (1996), Da Jun's 'True threat comes from those trumpeting "China Threat"' (1996), and Wang Zhongren's '"China Threat" theory groundless' (1997).

The government concentrated on showing China in a non-threatening light, in part through emphasising China's own earlier humiliations. Evoca-tion of China's previous national humiliation featured widely in Chinese 'patriotic education' campaigns during the 1990s, given the green light by Deng's own post-Tiananmen comments. This was first seen with the publication of *The Indignation of National Humiliation*, coming out on the eve of the one hundred and fiftieth anniversary of the Opium War, and able to divert attention away from the first anniversary of the Beijing Spring that had led up to Tiananmen Square. Consequently, in his own trips to China, Callahan found then, 'the more I looked for national humiliation discourse, the more I found it' (2004b: 199). For him, 'national humiliation unproblematically dots texts (in both Chinese and English) about Chinese identity and politics . . . the master narrative of modern Chinese history is the discourse of the century of national humiliation' (2004b: 204; also P. Cohen 2002). This went beyond just state propaganda. On the one hand 'while it is true that patriotic education [the national humiliation material] started out as a state-driven propaganda campaign, by the mid-1990s national humiliation discourse had spread beyond official control as the Chinese popular media were opened up to market forces' (Callahan 2006: 187). On the other hand 'this security/insecurity discourse went beyond school textbooks and educational journals to a multimedia campaign in museums, film, literature, television, popular magazines, and newspapers' (187). Boundaries were crossed. What had started off as 'cultural governance' from the top had become 'nationalist performance in international space' (187) from the bottom. Ironies were present here, as it was noticeable how the state was deliberately invoking China's previous humiliations, even though China itself was very much on the rise.

In part, this could be seen as a way to deflect China Threat images that were becoming noticeable in the West and Japan. In part, it was a question of the state re-inventing itself, of regaining political legitimacy in a post-Maoist ideological vacuum, of responding to growing popular nationalism and anti-Westernism, through '*containing* the nation' (Callahan 2006: 179) and its nationalism. In part, it was also an evocation to the future, for China never again to be humiliated. In short, for Deng Yong, 'through an exclusive and continuous nationalist discourse, China's collective recollection of "one hundred years of suffering and humiliations" in a Social Darwinian world has become ingrained in the national psyche . . . To redeem past grievance China must be strong and vigilant' now (2000: 47).

Another response was to directly denounce, 'vociferous rebuttal' (Callahan 2005: 707), China Threat arguments whenever they appeared. The official media and politicians were prominent in this. Qian Qichen, foreign minister, thought that 'those people crying "China Threat" don't bother to study either history or reality . . . these views could not be more wrong' (1997: 8, 7). Chinese Premier Li Peng kept on specifically denying the China Threat argument throughout the decade at various times, that 'even if China is well developed in the future, China will not pose a threat to any other nation, nor will it invade or oppress other countries' (1996: 9; also Xinhua 1994, *People's Daily* 2000). A similar thrust was maintained by Jiang Zemin, that 'we will never impose upon others the kind of sufferings we once experienced. A developing and progressing China does not pose a threat to anyone. China will never seek hegemony' (1997b). For Jiang, 'a developed China will play a positive role in maintaining world peace and stability and will by no means constitute a threat to anybody' (2000). Military figures sang the same song, for General Chi Haotian 'there are still some people around the world who keep spreading the fallacy of the 'China threat' (1996: 64). The end of the decade saw Li Zhaoxing, the Chinese ambassador in Washington, similarly dismissing China Threat stories as 'Cold War mentality' fabrications (Li Yan 2000). However, on its own such sustained PRC rebuttal rhetoric was impressive, yet ultimately was 'public relations' (A. Goldstein 2005: 114–15) but not necessarily public policy, which could be seen as 'cheap talk' (115) and which 'failed to reassure regional and global actors' (115).

Again though, one is presented with varied levels of interpretation. At times specific China Threat theory appearances triggered specific China Threat rebuttals. The focus for such PRC rebuttals was on 'foreign' misunderstanding of China, but Callahan argues that China rebuttal material was not just aimed at external audiences, but was also, at times primarily so, directed at 'China's domestic audience to construct identity' (Callahan 2005: 708), where 'this negative discourse mirrors the glories of China and serves to differentiate and estrange China as a unique entity in an increasingly globalised world' (713). Yet, the PRC's vociferous responses, at times labelling China Threat views as mere malevolence and madness on the part of foreign observers, ignored the genuine rational grounds for concern about China: PRC rebuttals 'end up policing what Chinese and foreigners can *rationally* say' on the rise of China, so that 'China Threat theory [rebuttal] texts vigorously reproduce the dangers of the very threat they seek to deny' (712).

Samuel Huntington's *Clash of Civilizations* identification of China as the leading state threat to the West, and to the United States in particular, was quickly picked up in China, for Wang Jisi 'une question sensible en Chine depuis un siecle' (1995: 107). Chinese nationalism may have been flattered in some sense for China to be identified as a strongly emerging rival for pre-eminence. However, most Chinese commentators saw it as providing a threat in turn to China, 'Huntington's theory suggests a sense of frustration and anxiety among many Westerners toward the rise of Asia . . . Huntington hopes his theory will line up the different fractions of American society, and even the whole West, to fight an imaginary enemy' (Wang Jisi and Zou Sicheng 1996: 11; also Xiang 1998). Chinese circles argued there was a political agenda, where 'in a sense Huntington's thesis is more a political essay than an academic report, given that he has written it to advise the US government' (Wang Jisi and Zou Sicheng 1996: 11). Chinese sources considered that Huntington 'offers nothing new. What he advises the government to do has already been undertaken by the United States . . . maintaining relations with Russia and Japan; containing militarily China' (11); although 'it will be dangerous if the clash theory finds its way into policy making. The recently bandied notion of a "China threat" is based on assumptions similar to Huntington's', where 'it is misleading and dangerous to magnify such [civilizational] frictions ['between civilizations'] into world political clashes and wars' (12).

China's ongoing growth, when combined with a more immediate American pre-eminence in the wake of the Soviet collapse, and dangers posed by China Threat perceptions and IR security dilemma spirals meant that 'by 1996 a rough consensus on a basic foreign policy line began to emerge among China's top leaders', reflecting 'a de facto grand strategy guiding the country's rise to great power status within the constraints of a unipolar international system that the United States dominates' (A. Goldsmith 2005: 12). Any hegemonic or indeed counter-hegemonic balancing against the United States seemed pointless. Instead the Chinese consensus was to pursue with vigour Deng's economic modernisation programme, in effect 'a strategy of transition' (38), strengthening China from an economics base upwards, but in a way that would not be too alarmist for others and thus not counter-productive to China. The last thing the PRC wanted was either American intervention against her, or balancing against her by her neighbours. Consequently a two-fold approach was pursued in the later 1990s, a road of practical 'reassurance' (119–130) manifested in greater, albeit somewhat reluctant, multilateralism and currency cooperation, alongside 'Great Power diplomacy: partnerships and linkages' (130–5).

Ambiguities continued to surround the PRC. Her 1998 *Defence White Paper* talked of China seeking to 'lead a peaceful, stable, prosperous world into the new century'; with the reassuring phrases of 'peaceful, stable' coupled with the more worryingly (Mosher 2000: 9–10) ambiguous prefix of hoping to 'lead' (PRC 1998). Whilst China's multilateral work with the Shanghai group, founded September 1996 by China, Russia, Kazakhstan, Kyrgyzstan, Tajikistan, was used by China as a rebuttal of the 'China threat theory', for others it could be a further sign of Chinese sphere expanding, of Chinese nationalism asserting itself in an assertive fashion outside China. By the end of the decade, for the *Economist* all this was 'a blustering, touchy, Sinocentric form of diplomacy abroad, and a whipped up nationalism and sense of grievance at home' (*Economist* 2000: 18).

Perceptions, and perhaps Jervis-like misperceptions, abound here as 'many Chinese, including China's leaders find it difficult to understand and cannot accept Western ideas of a China threat; they are confused and annoyed, if not outraged', for 'the average Chinese feels that the West wants to "demonise" China, while Chinese leaders interpret the China threat as a threat *to* China: a Western creation . . . in the post-Cold War era when a real enemy does not exist' (Yee and Zhu 2002: 33). Consequently, 'in fact, the so-called "China threat" has backfired and become a motivating force for the development of a radical Chinese nationalism or chauvinism' (1).

Chinese nationalism

Even as China argued against posing any China Threat externally, domestic nationalism had become more evident, indeed 'scholarly debate on Chinese nationalism in the West reached a fever pitch in the 1990s' amidst a 'flood of publications on the phenomenon' (Lei Guang 2005: 492). This was part of the general interest, and concerns, about China that had become so noticeable in the 1990s.

Western impressions of Chinese nationalism were generally negative. For Nicholas Kristof this 'nationalist tide' was a 'booming, aggrieved, chip-on-the-shoulder nationalism among many ordinary people' (2002). Some aspects of Chinese nationalism seemed racially tinged, Frank Dikotter commenting on how 'signs of an elemental form of racial nationalism . . . are already reappearing in the post-Tiananmen era' (1992: 198). Internal and external directions could overlap, where 'if the racial nationalist ideology being promoted today continues its inflationary trend, it is highly unlikely that China will retain the characteristics of a quasi-status-quo power' (Sautman 1997: 78). All in all, linkage between nationalism, capability and intent in foreign policy was typified in David Shambaugh's comment that 'as China has grown economically more powerful in recent years, nationalism has increased exponentially', with an increased Chinese strength something that 'is likely to result in increased defensiveness and assertiveness' (1996a: 205; also Gries 2004) on the part of the PRC.

Nationalism, never far removed from the surface, became more overt in PRC political, academic (Zhao Suisheng 1997) and media circles, 'the dominant ideology' (Cao 2005; also Zheng Yongnian 1999) during the 1990s. In China, living with the world and engaging with it was a problematic issue. Given the American political and cultural sway, Modernisation could be seen as Westernisation and in turn Americanisation. Deng Xiaoping's pithy phrase could be utilised, that 'when you open the windows, flies and mosquitoes come in'. The 'self-abasement nationalism' (Men Jing 2003: 26) of the 1980s was typified by the TV series 'River Elegy' *Heshang*, a fairly uncritical optimistic acceptance of Western modes, 'sentimental nationalism' (Liu Toming 2001). This was increasingly rejected as 'reverse nationalism' (*nixiang minzuzhuyi*) in the 1990s. This 1990s 'wounded national pride and the resentment to foreign interference' (Men Jing 2003: 28) became noticeable in many avenues of the PRC. In Xu Guangqiu's analysis 'anti-Western nationalism increased in China in the 1990s. From official media to the frontiers of popular culture, from Beijing to Guangzhou, there was a mixture of rising pride and lingering insecurity' (2001: 151), an interesting juxtaposition. Past images continued to lurk in the Chinese collective subconscious, 'many Chinese believed that they were reclaiming their rightful place as an international powerhouse in the world, a position they had lost decades before'; and 'as part of the return to prominence, nationalists were explaining the profound sense of humiliation among Chinese who suffered at the hands of Western powers during the nineteenth and twentieth centuries. They increasingly criticised U.S.-led Western countries' (151).

This rising wave of nationalism was strongly evident in the *China Can Say No* literature of the 1990s (Liu Toming 2001, Hughes 2006: 104–6). This had been sparked by Zhang Xiabo and Song Qiang's collection *Zhongguo keyi shuo bu* (i.e. *China Can Say No*) (1996; also Zhang Xudong 1998: 11–11) complete with contributions like 'Burn down Hollywood', 'I won't get on a Boeing 777' and 'Prepare for war'. Its subtitle *The Political and Emotional Choice in the Post-Cold War Era* was telling enough in its coupling of geopolitics and geopsychology. Elsewhere, the editors explained bluntly that 'at the end of the 20th century, China has once again become a world power in its own right. It need not play second fiddle to anyone', for 'the next generation coming to power in China is prepared to say no and won't hesitate to do so when it is in our interests' (Zhang Xiabo and Song Qiang 1996: 56). Geoculture was involved in this since they feel that 'a generation of Chinese has totally and uncritically absorbed Western, particularly American, values', but 'lately however, the tide has begun to turn. More and more people in China are looking East instead of West to find a future' (55). Geoeconomics came into the picture alongside geoculture, as 'because of the growth of the Chinese economy and the legacy of China's rich cultural traditions, many of us maintain that China should aspire to take its place as a world power, instead of lamely emulating Western society' (55). Their attacks were maintained in their Chinese sequel, later that year, *China Can Still Say No*. Similar sentiments were apparent with mainstream commentators like Wang Jisi who argued that 'in fact engagement . . . is not a friendly gesture but rather an attempt to pervade China with US economic, political, cultural and ideological influences. Eventually, the United States hopes China will accept Western-led international norms' (1996: 7).

Reactions within China were mixed to the *China Can Say No* genre. At the *Beijing Review*, Si Chen thought its 'emotive' nature was a fair enough response to the 'misrepresentations and slanderous reports about China coming from the United States' and was a 'strong Chinese voice opposing US power politics and hegemony' (1996). However the very forcefulness and heatedness of their analysis were to some extent embarrassing to the government and condemned by Chinese commentators like Wang Fei-Ling as reflecting 'ignorance, arrogance and radical nationalism' (1997; also Li Hongshan 1997, Garver 1998). On the other hand, they set something of a trend with other related Chinese language publications quickly appearing (Garver 2001b), like Song Qiang's *Why China Says No*, Jia Qingguo's *China Should Not Just Say No*; Qin Xiaoying's *China is Still Capable of Saying No*, Zhang Xueli's *How China Can Say No* and Peng Qian's *Why Does China Say No?* (Cordingley and Hsieh 1997). Such writings were ones that Wang Fei-Ling saw as entwining 'self-image and strategic intention', albeit 'filled with nationalistic rhetoric and even xenophobic writings' (1999: 34).

All in all, John Fitzgerald considered that 'thymotic [i.e. "desire for recognition"] resentment' is at play with this material, where 'the resentment that surfaces in the Say No literature is grounded in deeply etched personal experiences of national humiliation' (1999: 51). The authors, Zhang Xiabo and Song Qiang, argued that it was only in terms of this strongly perceived national humiliation lingering from the past that 'we can understand why China's writers have been crying out to the heavens for a hundred years now: "when will China become great and powerful" to which the answer is only when China finds the courage to stand-up to the outside [Western-dominated] world to stand firm and say "No"' (1996: 55), another deliberate invoking of Mao's standing up phrase.

Chinese–American scholars, on both sides of the Pacific, noted this turn to nationalism by the PRC, this 'state-led nationalism' (Zhao Suisheng 1998a). Samuel Kim pointed out how 'the regime has turned with greater urgency to hyper nationalism based on a new amalgam of ethnonational appeals to the ancient Confucian past and greatness of Chinese civilization and people' (1996: 2) as 'necessary compensatory-searching behaviour, the function of a regime with weak legitimacy trying hard to bring about national reunification and restore what Chinese of every ideological coloration believe to be their natural and inalienable right to great power status' (2). Increasingly bereft of charismatic and ideological authority his picture was of a regime seeking 'legitimacy grounded in the national identity enacting mission of restoring China's great-power status . . . hyper-militarism, hyper-nationalism . . . synergistically linked' (24). Ironically then, for Kim 'the PRC today [1996] is a *weak state pretending and trying desperately to be a strong state*' (1996: 24; also Nathan and Ross's *The Great Wall and the Empty Fortress*, 1997: xii, 25). In terms of domestic politics, Kim reckoned that 'as China becomes more insecure and fragmented at home, it feels more compelled to demonstrate its toughness abroad' (24). For Maria Hsia Chang it was a question of 'China's wounded nationalism' (2001), of great 'hypersensitivity' during the 1990s, of a 'collective insecurity' (186) used by the state in terms of 'patriotic nationalism' (177–98), and of wider concern since 'more than being reactive and xenophobic, Chinese patriotic nationalism also has a profoundly irredentist dimension' (198). In reconstructing previous boundaries and spheres 'how they conceive the historical Middle Kingdom has troubling implications for the Asia–Pacific region' (206), given the wide-ranging nature of such claims from the past for the present and future. Deng Yong also noted how 'China's democratic values, socio-economic interdependence, and multilateralism remain weak, inchoate, and submerged under the hyper-nationalist, hard core realpolitik paradigm' where 'from the perspective of the established great powers, China holds an international identity that is overall periphery, sometimes illegitimate, and often anachronistic' (2000: 43).

Of relevance here was Peter Gries's focus on China's 'face [*mianzi*] nationalism', a concept which 'is culturally specific' and 'captures both the emotional and instrumental motivations of China's nationalists' (1999: 63).

Images abound in this, where 'the vital issue is not what China's international status actually was, but rather what contemporary Chinese think it was and how they feel about it', that 'to get at the goals of contemporary Chinese nationalists, their feelings are more important than historical evidence' (64). Amidst feelings of deep national humiliation from the past, 'face nationalism' is deeply concerned with image (i.e. regaining respect). However 'because face is located in other people's minds, however, it cannot be easily manipulated' (69) by the PRC. The argument over 'face' was that 'treating China as an equal . . . the Chinese people will feel that China has gained face in international society. That will foster both a healthy Chinese nationalism and a commitment to international norms and institutions' (71).

Zhao Suisheng's profile of *Chinese Nationalism and its International Orientations* pinpointed various strands and linkages arising during the 1990s. Between the extremes of confrontational xenophobic nativism and cooperative welcoming antitraditionalism lay a dominant 'pragmatic nationalism . . . asserting China's national interests by both reacting to and absorbing from the outside world' (2000: 10). It is significant that for Zhao 'pragmatic nationalism is reactive. It tends to become strong in response to perceived foreign pressures that are said to erode, corrode, or endanger the national interests of China' (21). Where Chinese national interests are perceived to be at stake, then China was seen by Zhao as likely to prove determined in its resistance, but not necessarily with any wider expansionist, global, aggressive agenda. Shambaugh's 'defensive nationalism . . . assertive [and at times prickly] in form, but reactive in essence' (1996b: 205) comes to mind. A related assessment was Wang Fei-Ling's discernment of how 'the PRC government in Beijing had demonstrated a profound concern bordering on a strong sense of insecurity – a siege mentality if you will' (1999: 22). Though nationalism could be used by the PRC leadership, it had its 'limits', there was a 'contrast between China's nationalist rhetoric and its restrained international behaviour', so that 'when forced to choose, Chinese leaders pursued economic development at the expense of nationalist goals' (Downs and Saunders 1998–9: 117). To some extent this may well have been a question of horizons and time scales since 'the Chinese government is confident that economic growth and improvements in China's technological and military capabilities will eventually increase its relative power and reduce its economic dependence', so that 'by deferring the resolution of territorial and border conflicts [during the 1990s] until China's position improves, the leadership hopes eventually to be able to dictate settlements on Chinese terms. Chinese political leaders make tactical shifts', or in other words are 'waiting until the country becomes powerful enough to achieve their nationalist objectives' (122).

Military figures frequently evoked the past, where the ' "century of shame and humiliation" remains the emotive referent for an assertive nationalism underlying PLA pronouncements on perceived threats to territorial integrity'

(Whiting 1996: 600). In such a vein, General Chi Haotian emphasised 'the deep scars that agonizing chapter has left on the hearts and minds of our people', who 'saw its territories ceded and its people's subjected to foreign aggression, plunder and enslavement in more than one century from the Opium War in 1840 to the founding of the Peoples Republic of China in 1949 (1996: 64–5). Similarly, his colleague Lieutenant-General Li Jijun reiterated how 'over the last 150 years, however, China has been the victim of repeated aggression and pillages . . . 1.8 million square kilometres were also taken away from Chinese territory. This was a period of humiliation that the Chinese people can never forget' (1997: 2–3). This had become deeply engrained 'this is why the people [and government] of China show such strong emotions in matters concerning our national independence, unity, integrity of territory, and sovereignty' (3).

Such recourse to the image of the past to shape the present became all the more prominent in the 1990s, as the CCP wrapped itself in a cloak of nationalism to replace its previous revolutionary Marxist–Maoist line. Consequently, ' "do not forget" – *wuwang* – became the mantra of the *guochi* [Humiliation] writing of this decade' (P. Cohen 2002: 2; also Callahan 2004a). In 1994 the Propaganda Department of the Central Committee of the Chinese Communist Youth League published its Patriotic Education Poster Set, including its poster *Women Zen Neng Wangdiao* 'How Can We Forget' (Landsberger 2004). Shots of the Imperial Yuanming Yuan summer palace deliberately sacked by British troops in 1860 were enclosed by corner representations of the Century of Humiliation – the 'Opium War' of 1839–42, the varied 'Unequal Treaties' imposed during the nineteenth century, the multinational outside intervention to crush the Boxer Uprising of 1900, and the Nanjing Massacre carried out by Japan in 1938. Its accompanying text read, 'Why the descendants of the dragon [were] reduced to the "Sick Man of the East" and subjected to endless bullying and humiliation'. The lesson was 'the hundred years of humiliation have told us that when you are backwards, you come under attack'.

Chinese 'strategic culture' was, though, picked up as an important, though unclear issue in the mid-1990s, the past pointing to the present and future. The paradigm most frequently posited by Chinese figures (e.g. Li Jijun 1997) was peacefully orientated. This led to Wang Qingxin's call 'for more scholarly attention to the impact of Chinese cultural norms as a source of foreign policy', norms for which 'the Confucian emphasis on moral conduct and rules of propriety, pragmatism, the aversions to use of force and the preference for defense over offence that had important bearings on international relations' (2000: 164).

A rather different strand was highlighted in the 1990s in Alastair Johnston's *Cultural Realism. Strategic Culture and Grand Strategy in Chinese History*, with his focus on a harsher more coercive violent approach (1995: 250; also Warren Cohen 1997: 105); a dominant 'parabellum paradigm' that ran alongside and when circumstances permitted displaced the more restrained defensive Confucian–Mencian paradigm, in earlier times 'defined in essentially racialist zero-sum terms' (Johnston 1995: 250). China's application of force in Korea 1950–4, Quemoy–Matsu 1954–5, Ussuri border 1969 and Vietnam 1979, suggested to him that 'post-1949 China's use of force in a crisis appears to have been related to improved relative capabilities, again consistent with a [offensive] parabellum strategic culture', whereby *'when in a crisis* China tended to act in a more conflictual manner as it grew relatively stronger' (Johnston 1995: 256; also Johnston 1996). China Threat analysts naturally stressed the relevance of these earlier dominant parabellum elements. As Michael Cox put it, the implications were that from such 'ancient . . . realpolitik . . . they [Chinese leaders] could call for flexibility; but only as an expedient until China could be sure of prevailing. Moreover, though negotiations were not unimportant, they were basically a cover for delaying action until the moment was ripe to destroy the enemy' (1998: 239). Thomas Christensen also discerned the prominence of 'Chinese Realpolitik' (1997) in its conduct of foreign affairs. As China sought a 'new role in world affairs', Wang Jisi emphasised how 'China's leading political analysts . . . tend to see the world as increasingly chaotic and assertive nationalism and fierce economic competition as the main features of international relations. In their eyes world politics continues to involve a zero-sum game', where 'a hierarchy of power inevitably exists within which the more powerful nations dominate the weaker' (1994: 29), though perhaps subject to change.

However Christensen saw such IR realpolitik realism as being the agent of its own breakdown. He argued that 'Chinese realism is deep rooted and stubborn . . . the Hobbesian view of international politics' (1999b: 240). However, he could then immediately go on that 'ironically . . . China's realpolitik quest to restore its place among internationally recognized great powers might actually be the most important force pushing China into international institutions and agreements that could, in the long run, transform Chinese thinking about international politics' (240) and facilitate IR liberalism-functionalism tendencies? Whilst Deng Yong still thought, 'Chinese decision-makers continue to view the world as essentially conflict-prone, interstate relations as zero-sum power struggles . . . of atomistic nation-states locked in a perpetual struggle for power' (1999: 52, 53); nevertheless his research during the 1990s found that IR 'liberal values do exist and are expanding their space in China's discourse on international relations . . . facilitating at least "tactical" if not "cognitive" learning' (54, 55; also A. Johnston 2004b). As such, 'there are signs that the liberal considerations are having some impact in [IR] policy, as China is noticeably more susceptible to ideas and policies of interdependence, multilateralism, and collective security' (64). Wang Jianwei saw similar trends in the 1990s, 'multilateralism and collective security have increased in legitimacy and weight in China's post-Cold war foreign policy thinking and behaviour' (1999: 91). However in terms of perceptions it is perhaps significant that even IR 'Chinese liberals have in fact started to question the sincerity of the

United States in encouraging the rise of a liberal and *strong* China' (Deng Yong 1999: 59).

Chinese perceptions were that strength was needed in an often hostile world, but was also something that China could aspire to in the 1990s, given her underlying land, size, population and increasingly realised economic resources. Jiang Zemin's strategy, like Deng's, remained centred on 'economic strategies which face the future and taking it as a task of primary importance to increase their overall national strength so as [for China] to take up their proper places in the world in the next century' (Jiang Zemin 1995). In conversation with Jiang Zemin in 1997, Wen Jieming had hoped, and indeed expected that 'a rising China will never be a nation that is satisfied with only food and shelter . . . our nation used to be a crucial player on the playground [or perhaps battlefield] of international politics' and now 'its enhancing economic capabilities, and its status of being a major nuclear power and a permanent member of the UN Security Council, will give our nation a larger and larger role in world affairs' (Wang Fei-Ling 1999: 24). Consequently, Yu Bin reckoned by the end of the 1990s that 'China's historical ascendance cannot be contained or reversed now' (1999: 197). By then China's 'omni-directional diplomacy' (Hsuing 1995) had become noticeable, with the Fifteenth Party Congress in 1997 stressing 'managing relations among great powers' *chuli daguo guanxi*, of which China saw itself as one (Shih 2005). As China sought to shape its environment and its rise, such a rise impinged on all of China's neighbours, to whom we can now turn.

6 A reviving Middle Kingdom for China's neighbours

The preceding chapter concerned China at the general 'systemic' level. Within the international system, China particularly impacted on other significant actors in various ways during the 1990s. The United States is dealt with within the following chapter, given China's key global and regional relationship with it, but already *Growing Strong: China's Challenge to Asian Security* was a process isolated by Shambaugh (1994a). China may have had its drive for 'traditional Great-Power status' (Wortzel 1994; also Khalilzad 1999: 137), but it was 'an irredentist China with a boulder rather than just a chip on its shoulder' (Segal 1996: 110). As such there was a regional re-ordering in the offing, a 'Chinese hegemony' emerging in East Asia for Huntington (1997: 229–38), a *Hegemon on the Horizon? China's Threat to East Asian Security* (D. Roy 1994), with perhaps *Chinese Hegemony over East Asia by 2015?* (Shambaugh 1997b). As China stood ever more strongly up in the world its impact on its neighbours were all the more noticeable (i.e. Russia, Southeast Asia and Australasia, India and Japan).

China–Russia relations in the 1990s

One major power greatly affected by the rise of China was Russia, a Russia trying to reshape and recover its position amidst the rubble of the disintegration and disappearance of the USSR. Structurally the relationship between China and Boris Yeltsin's new Russia was deeply affected by China's simultaneous rise and Russia's simultaneous decline across a whole measurement of indicators. As the USSR gave way to a re-emerging Russia, swathes of populated territory had been lost in Central Asia, the Caucasus and Eastern Europe (i.e. the Ukraine, Byelorussia and the Baltic States). Inheriting around 80 per cent of the territory of the Soviet Union, Russia was left with less than half of its population and GDP. The Soviet economy had been bigger than China's at the start of the 1990s, but by 2001 Russia's GNP was only 22 per cent, less than one-quarter, of China's burgeoning economy (Weede 2003: 344). Thus, looking at the two states 'in the 1990s Russian weakness was met with Chinese ascendance . . . in short, Russia was a descending power and China an ascendant power' (Wilson 2004: 196, 143), or as Nolan put it in *China's Rise, Russia's Fall* (1995) with regard to their economic fortunes. As Russia floundered in its first years of post-Soviet survival, her Deputy Foreign Minister rightly recognised China's growing strength, 'our common border stretches for 4,300 km. China is a major power . . . China boasts an impressive military potential', and unlike Russia 'China has scored some impressive economic successes' (Karasin 1996).

Generally the 1990s saw a complex multifaceted Sino–Russian relationship developing, in which central geopolitical strategic convergence went alongside regional geocultural divergence and perceptions of a China Threat, inherited but if anything strengthened since the 1960s and hearkening back to much earlier Yellow Peril motifs.

At the central level some degree of shared strategic concerns over American hegemonism was apparent for Russia (Shlapentokh 1995, Gelbars 1997, Voskreseenski 1997, Rozman 1998, Lukin 1999, Wishnick 2001) and for the PRC. Initial Sino–Russian border agreements of 1991 and a cooperation agreement in 1992 led the Russian leadership to hold that 'it is urgent to consolidate the breakthrough achieved in relations with China – from our standpoint – the region's most important state in geopolitical and economic terms' (Yeltsin 1993). The 1994 'Agreement on Mutual Non-targeting of Missiles', in effect a nuclear non-aggression pact, was complemented by the troop reduction border agreement of 1997. All this reduced general tension although to some extent also giving China more decisive potential future military leverage. A 'constructive partnership' in 1994 was deepened into a 'strategic partnership' in 1996, alongside initial frontier border agreements during 1998/99.

Some trade was of military significance, as with the sale of 72 of Russia's state of the art SU-30 fighter bombers to China in June 1999, with IR constructivism and balance of power considerations apparent (Donaldson 2003). However, apart from their weapons exports, the Russians had little high tech economic materials to offer China in trade during the 1990s, whilst the Russian Far East (RFE) market was not very big from a Chinese point of view. In the Maritime Krai, testimony to the region's further economic weakness was the way trade with China had peaked at $413 billion, 58 per cent of the region's overall foreign trade in 1992 before slumping to $237 million by 1996, approximately 12 per cent of the region's overall trade. Moreover, in the Russian Far East, economic perspectives made Japan, South Korea and the USA rather than China seem the more economically attractive partners.

Economics was interlaced with other concerns, with 'China viewed as a threat to Russia's economic independence. Such views were not entirely unfounded. By the early 2000s, China had emerged as an economic colossus, with a GNP that greatly surpassed that of the Russian Federation' (Wilson 2004: 91). Economics were also closely related to demographic perceptions, where, 'although residents of the Russian Far East depended on border trade with China for necessary goods, they soon began to fear geo-economic consequences of an influx of Chinese migrants to the once closed provinces' (296). From a Russian point of view there were two 'root causes of unease about China in the Far East – economic decline and outmigration' (300) of Russians in the face of Chinese economic and demographic expansion.

At the centre Russian figures expressed demographic unease over China throughout the 1990s. Minister of Defence, Pavel Grachev warned in 1995 that 'Chinese citizens are peacefully conquering Russia's Far East' (Lukin 2003: 124), as did other political figures from across the political spectrum like Stanislav Govorukhin (Lukin 2003: 237), Yegor Gaydar (Lukin 2003: 99), General Lev Rokhin (Lukin 2002: 100), Alexander Dugan (Lukin 2002: 100), and Alexander Yakovlev (Vitkovskaya *et al.* 2000: 348). Whilst these concerns in Moscow were overlaid with official government support for its strategic relationship with Beijing, officials in the RFE had 'a much more jaundiced view of the Chinese' (Thornton and Ziegler 2002: 21; also Wishnick 1998). Viktor Larin, Director of the Vladivostok Institute of History, saw the '"*Yellow Peril*" again' (1995), and counted more than 150 articles in the local and national press that raised the spectre of Yellow Peril Chinese migration into the Far East (Alexseev 2002: 319; Wishnick 2002), 'filled with highly speculative and often grossly alarmist estimations . . . routinely exaggerated in the Russian press and in political debate' (Vitkovskaya *et al.* 2000: 347, 350). Identity and perceptions were at issue. As such, there was 'geoculturally . . . the identity crisis in the RFE, which exists as an outpost amid Asian civilizations' in which 'fears abound of living in a sparsely settled and little subsidized periphery' while Chinese 'neighbors amass resources capable of overwhelming a dwindling residue of citizens' (Rozman 2000: 180). Indeed, 'for Russians, it did not take a book by Samuel Huntington to demonstrate that the RFE stands as the frontline in a clash of civilizations' (Rozman 2000: 180). Local opinion considered that Chinese 'migration was bringing a Yellow Peril into the RFE cities' (188). Such emotive perceptions reflected the anti-Chinese 'frontier demonology' (Stephan 1994: 284; also Minakir 1996: 85; Lukin 1998; Troyakova 2000: 214, 224) at play in the Russian Far East. All in all, power and population continued to intertwine in the 1990s, 'popular perception, laced with racial overtones that China poses an immediate demographic threat' (Menon and Ziegler 2002: 47).

In some ways the question of demographic expansion, which was played out across the region, was partly an image of Jervis-type misperception (Lomanov 2001: 12) on actual numbers. The numbers of Chinese in the Russian Far East probably peaked at c. 50–60,000 in 1992–3, decreasing after restrictions of 1994, and nowhere near the 10–12 per cent of the population in 1910 nor even the 4 per cent in the late 1920s (Portiakov 1996). However rising migration and mortality was reducing the Russian population by around 10 per cent, leaving a mere 5 million thinly spread over the RFE's 3 million-odd sq. km, with Russian demographers projecting a likely further 25 per cent population fall by 2020. By contrast (Trenin 1999: 410), the three Chinese provinces across the river border from the Russian Far

East numbered around 120 million – only 10 per cent of China's total, but vastly outnumbering Russia's RFE population. Such trends 'have deepened China's demographic footprint over the last decade' (Menon 2003: 102) in the Russian Far East. Russian analysts looked at such population trends and felt 'their message is an inevitable and irresistible spread of the Chinese into the demographic vacuum across the border' and that 'few knowledgeable observers would dispute that the differences in "demographic potential" on the two sides of the border are an important geopolitical factor' (Vitkovskaya *et al.* 2000: 350), witnessing 'the combination of geostrategic alarm and geocultural clashes' (Rozman 2000: 179).

The readiness of regional administrations in the East to use the China Threat issue was noteworthy. Viktor Ishaev, Governor of Khabarovsk Territory, argued in 1994 that 'today a covert Chinese expansion in the RFE is being perpetuated and it hurts and humiliates Russians' (Lukin 2002: 94); and warned the Prime Minister Sergei Stepashin in 1999 that 'the peaceful capture of the Far East is under way . . . a mass influx of Chinese . . . all this is strictly planned. As we all know, China has some official program in this connection' (Wilson 2004: 127). Meanwhile, the Maritime Krai administration at Vladivostok implemented a policy 'to ignite anti-Chinese feeling' (Lukin 2003: 171) during the 1990s. Unilateral border closures were soon followed by more restrictive legislation at central and local levels during 1993–4. The Maritime Krai governor, Yevgeni Nazdratenko, restricted external trade agreements and gave support to various vociferous publications – of which 'the most notorious of them' (Lukin 2003: 171, also Troyakova 2000: 220) was Boris Dyachenko's 1996 blast *Zheltaya Opasnost* 'The Yellow Peril'. Having 'demonised China' (Kuchins 1999: 32), Nazdratenko ran for re-election in 1999 and won. Such was this late 1990s furore that even tighter cross-border procedures were agreed between Russia and China in February 2000 – all of which reduced population flows, but also general trade levels!

A final factor in Sino–Russian relations in the 1990s was the military dynamics. On the one hand their strategic cooperation enabled both sides to reduce troop levels and military burdens along their long border, witnessed in the 1996 Shanghai Agreement on frontier military confidence-building measures and the Moscow 1997 Agreement on mutual cuts in the armed forces deployed along the frontier. However, this did not result in a balanced military equilibrium. The continuing collapse of Russian military morale, equipment, and logistics reduced its forces to an increasing shadow of its former might in the region, amidst an 'unravelling of Russia's Far Eastern power' (Chang: 1999). As with the United States, much military analysis continued in Russian circles over how far China's capabilities and intentions represented a threat to Russia, in its post-Soviet setting. Here though, one can note, Blank's perception of how 'the military has adopted a visibly racist attitude toward Japan and China' (1994: 2). As the Soviet nuclear arsenal degraded and that of China increased, Vadim Marenko fused demographic and nuclear concerns in 1993, when arguing that 'for Russia, moreover, with its sparsely populated Siberia and Far East, and its sharply decreasing capacities for maintaining large conventional armed forces, guarantees of nuclear security [vis-à-vis China] are becoming vitally necessary' (Blank 1994: 5).

For Trenin a 'doomsday scenario' lay in how such immigration issues 'may easily lead to violent clashes between the local Russians and Chinese immigrants, which in turn could escalate to inter-state conflict between Russia and China. Such a conflict may result in a resumption of the Russian–Chinese military standoff, but this time on terms much less advantageous for Moscow' given that 'both the Russian military forces and [demographic] presence in Asia are decreasing' (1999: 41). Even if war did not break out, for Trenin, the 1990s showed signs of a 'dangerous . . . "quiet", gradual withdrawal of Russia from the Far East and Siberia', manifested in the form of reduced interest in the region' by Moscow, 'the exodus of the remaining population, growth of separatist trends in the territories and republics, and their re-orientation toward Asian power centers, above all to Beijing' (40). Trenin felt that such trends meant 'Russia could become economically and politically dependent on China to such an extent that Moscow would lose the freedom of manoeuvring in foreign policy and to a certain extent in domestic policy as well' (40). Such musings represented a dramatic change from earlier decades of a strong Russian Empire/Soviet Union facing a weaker subordinatory China. Positions had been reversed, and China's presence was being increasingly felt along Russia's long and increasingly weakened frontier, as it was elsewhere in the Asia–Pacific.

China–Southeast Asia and Australasia relations in the 1990s

China's presence was also further felt to its south in the 1990s, with the PRC able to 'cast a shadow over the states of Southeast Asia because of its huge size, enormous population, close geographic proximity and considerable economic potential' (Leifer 1997: 157), a fundamentally asymmetrical situation. A 'hegemonic ascension' by the PRC continued to accelerate so that 'living with the China "colossus"' (Deng Yong 1988; Storey 1999–2000) became a key issue for the region in the 1990s.

China's presence was magnified by her creeping but sweeping irredentist agenda in the South China Sea (Shee 1998, Studeman 1998). In the north this focused around the Paracels, where PRC forces had already evicted South Vietnamese units in 1974. Bigger claims were asserted by the PRC much further south in the Spratlys, against overlapping claims by Vietnam, the Philippines, Malaysia, Brunei and Indonesia. Having suffered the punitive, though not very effective, PRC land campaign against it during 1989, 'to teach it a lesson', it was not surprising that Vietnam viewed China with concern during the 1990s. The Vietnamese Foreign Minster, Nguyen Manh Cam told his National Assembly in 1992 that 'China desires to become one of the pivotal countries in the future . . . to become a superpower in the

Asian–Pacific by taking advantage of economic, military, scientific and technical weakness in the region' (Thayer 2002: 274). The setting up of the ASEAN Regional Forum (ARF), in 1994 was partly to diffuse China's threat through constructively engaging with China, and thereby restraining her.

Chinese occupation of the disputed Mischief Reef in 1995 triggered immediate protests by the Philippines. American–Filipino relations were re-strengthened, with Senate President Bas Ople commenting that 'in our part of the world, East Asia, the Chinese colossus has awakened . . . this giant has not only awakened but is belching forth a stream of fire' (Pablo-Baviera 2002: 259). Across ASEAN there was 'an over-arching concern about China, its growing military power, and its . . . maritime claims' (Wortzel 1996: 19) manifest at the 1995 ARF meeting. The Singapore Prime Minister, Goh could thus go to Beijing in 1995 and warn the Chinese leadership that 'in Asia, China's rising power and arms build-up has stirred anxiety . . . this underlying sense of discomfort, and even insecurity' (*Reuter's News Service*, 14 May 1995; also Storey 2002). All this triggered institutional changes in the region. The decision to allow Vietnam membership of ASEAN in 1995 could also be seen as 'a hedge against China' (Wortzel 1996: 17). The inclusion of India in the ARF in 1996 could also be seen as 'another move to check Chinese maritime influence' (20). From China's perspective, South China Sea consolidation was a question of asserting her territorial integrity, a key feature of China's outlook; from the point of view of others this was ominous expansionism in an area of key strategic location and economic resources.

Whereas in Southeast Asia China could increasingly hope to exert decisive hegemony through its own strength and the relative smallness of the states/ economies facing it in the area, in the wider Pacific region its own 'threat' was itself giving rise to corresponding actions against itself by larger actors, which in a different light could then be seen as threatening to China (Shambaugh 1994b). Samuel Kim talked of 'the "rise of the China threat" debate in the Asia–Pacific region', as 'Beijing uses its new military strength', using a familiar metaphor that 'China has cast a long shadow over the strategic landscape of the Asia–Pacific region' (1996: 1). An irony here for Avery Goldstein was that in the mid-1990s, 'although China was increasing its capabilities, as others reacted to what Beijing believed were simple necessary steps to ensure its own interests, greater capabilities were not clearly enhancing the country's security' (2001: 839). In IR terms, 'China's leaders were caught in the familiar dynamic of the security dilemma' and as 'is so often the case in such circumstances, they focused less on their own role in provoking concern and more on what they saw as other's unwarranted and threatening hostility' (2001: 839). Hostility was present around China's perimeters and periphery.

China's growing presence in Southeast Asia reverberated in Australia. There, the 'Asianisation' policies of Paul Keating's administration were controversial for many in politics and the media (McAllister and Ravenhill 1998). Keating's 1994 logic was 'that China' is likely to be 'the strongest country in Asia' and central to the region's security so that Australia should 'help China find a place for itself' (Strahan 1996: 319), and thereby draw China into APEC and regional security dialogue. However Australia's 1995 Security Agreement with Indonesia was also 'the sine qua non of any regional resistance to China' (Lim 1998: 99), with the two states recognising that their 'mutual [anti-China] strategic interests outweigh the cultural and political issues that divide them' (100).

Distrust of China was evident in various Australian media quarters. Older images came in Cameron Stewart's warning that 'Napoleon believed that when China awoke, the whole world would shake. Two centuries later China is finally starting to stir, and its emerging military might is sending a shiver through the region' (*Australian*, 1 July 1993). Similarly, in the wake of Keating's comments, Bartholomew Santamaria resurrected old images of 'the strategic reach of China's traditional policy', seen where 'the Chinese interest in southern Asia and the Indian Ocean goes back to the thirteenth century when a Mongol-led armada sailed to Borneo and Java in search of trade and conquest' (*Australian*, 24 September 1994). China's size and population worried Santamaria, with large PRC military budgets juxtaposed with Australia's relative emptiness, all of which was likely to lead to China at a future date eventually demanding Australia's empty spaces for its own millions. Explicit old perceptions of the Yellow Peril were evident from the anonymous (1995) author of *The Ballad of the Bleeding Heart Liberal*, that 'in the future, when the Asian hordes/ follow their brothers' call:/ They'll outnumber Aussies ten to one/ ("We're all human", after all)'.

The fall of the Keating government in early 1996 and its replacement by the more conservative John Howard government brought into question the previous government's Asia focus. Economic imperatives remained noticeable, with its White Paper *In the National Interest* noting how 'China's economic growth, with attendant confidence and enhanced influence, will be the most important strategic development of the next fifteen years', as 'China manages its economic growth and pursues its international objectives' (Australia 1997: 27). However military-security issues were a different matter. Bilateral links were quickly strengthened with the USA. The July 1996 *Sydney Declaration* (i.e. the *Relations of Strategic Partners of the 21st Century Between Australia and the United States*), increased the level of Australian–American military cooperation, with it being noted that 'the clear logic of maintaining U.S. power in the Asia–Pacific is that it balances the highly predictable power of China' (*Australian Financial Review* 1996). The agreement included forward deployment in Australia of American forces and moves towards building a ballistic missile defence system in Australia. The following year, around 17,000 Australian and US troops conducted joint military exercises in Queensland.

Australasian concern about China was in part because of China's increased presence in the Pacific, or more particularly the southern and western reaches closer to Australasia. Conversely, China's presence in the Pacific basin, fostered through vigorous aid diplomacy, military training support to various governments, was encapsulated in the space tracking facilities set up in Kiribati in 1997. New Zealand upgraded its Waihopai spy station in 1997 to monitor China and replace Hong Kong, which was reverting to China's jurisdiction in 1997. Meanwhile Japan and Australia expanded their own bilateral defence ties during 1997, with China again being a common perceived threat. All of this was considered, accurately enough, by Beijing as being directed against China. With talk by US Defence Secretary William Perry that Australia was one of two 'anchors' in the Asia–Pacific region, Beijing raised fears about an antagonistic 'triangular security framework in the Asia–Pacific region' (A. Goldstein 2001: 839) knitting together the USA, Japan and Australia. Such a stance was criticised by China as being an American-led attempt to contain China through its two 'crab claws' of Australia and Japan. Australia not only rejected such Chinese comments as being counter-productive, but also was the only country in the region to openly applaud the US dispatch of aircraft carriers to face down China during the Taiwan missile crisis of 1995–6. Cross-bracing and common concerns over China were also seen within the region between Australia and Japan, with annual summits inaugurated in 1997. Such cross bracing also emerged between Japan and India.

China–India relations in the 1990s

Although some easing of tensions in the post-Mao years was achieved, 'continuing rivalry' (J. Malik 1995; also Mitra 1996, Mattoo and Kanti 2000) was still clear in the 1990s between China and India. Gary Klintworth foresaw that India was a state for China 'with whom it may eventually have to have a day of reckoning' (1992: 96). For Gurmeet Kanwal, 'China's long march to world power status' was becoming a 'strategic challenge for India' (1999). India, like others, was 'in China's shadow' amidst the PRC's 'emerging power' and more assertive 'military role' (Dutta 1998) around the South Asian region. An 'Asian balance of power' was at stake between China and India (Nathan 1999).

On the one hand some normalisation had been achieved following Rajiv Gandhi's trip to China in 1988. However, Indian analysts acknowledged 'the fact of the potential rivalry for regional dominance between the "giants" of Asia could not be wished away' (Baral *et al.* 1989: 257). Typical of underlying Indian unease was their reaction to Sino–Soviet normalisation, which 'created some problems for India' with the withdrawal of around 80,000 Chinese troops from the Soviet border. The problem was where they might go, 'even if these troops are not deployed on the Sino–Indian borders, the possibility of their availability in the south at any time should cause intense concern to India' (Baral *et al.* 1989: 269–70).

Strategic encirclement by China became a rising concern for India during the 1990s. China was perceived as a threat, in part through its innate power, but also because of China's multi-directional 'pincer movement' (Nair 2001; also Ranganathan 1998). To India's north came China's hold on Tibet and the Himalayan heights. China's continuing ethnic programme of mass Chinese (i.e. 'Han'), settlement threatened to change the previous light demographic nature of Tibet for India (Norbu 1997). China's own naval outreach into the Indian Ocean, to India's south, further exacerbated Indian concerns (Kreisberg 1996). To India's west, China's established links with Pakistan were maintained and strengthened during the 1990s. To India's east, Myanmar also become a worry for India in the mid-1990s, as it offered China military port facilities, and with it Chinese access to the Bay of Bengal and India's eastern coastlines, with potential disruption of India's lines of communication with South East Asia (Selth 1996, Banerjee 1996, Singh 1997).

For India, nuclear concerns arise not just with regard to Pakistan, helped in such matters by China, but also with China itself (Rappai 1999). Indeed, as India was setting up its nuclear tests at Pokhran, the Indian Defence Minister George Fernandes bluntly warned that 'China is potential threat number one . . . China is and is likely to remain the primary security challenge to India in the medium and long-term' and that 'the potential threat from China is greater than that from Pakistan and any person who is concerned about India's security must agree with that' (1998; also *Financial Times* 1998, *New York Times* 1998). Such concerns were stressed by Prime Minister Atal Vajpayee, explaining to US President Clinton, that India's nuclear tests were necessary since 'we have an overt nuclear state on our borders, a state that committed armed aggression against India in 1962' with whom 'an atmosphere of distrust persists' (1998) (i.e. China). Foreign Minister Jaswant Singh similarly argued that the rise of China was a critical new threatening factor for Indian security, for which India's nuclear option was needed (1998; also Richard Hu 1999). In retrospect Waldron argues that 'India's development of an all-round military capability, including nuclear weapons, is a direct product of Indian concerns about China's growing strength' (2005: 723), already evident in the 1990s.

As can be seen, China's challenge to India in the 1990s was becoming not just overland from its Tibetan heights and land links with Pakistan. It had also become a challenge at sea. Plans for a blue-water oceanic going naval capacity were bringing the PRC not just into America's Pacific but also into India's Indian Ocean. Long-range Chinese naval vessels started appearing in the Indian Ocean during the 1990s, paying high profile courtesy calls around the littoral. This was already apparent in 1993 with the concept of 'high sea defence', with Zhao Nanqi, PRC General Staff, arguing, 'we can no longer accept the Indian Ocean as only an ocean of the Indians' (Nanda 2002). Such comments had been quickly picked up in India. As Defence Minister Fernandes noted 'China's senior officials have said the Indian Ocean is not India's ocean . . . There is no doubt in my mind China's fast-expanding Navy will be getting into the Indian Ocean fairly soon' (1998).

Faced with China's increased presence in the Indian Ocean and around India, India's response was in part to go out and meet China's challenge in China's own backyard of Southeast Asia and East Asia. India's *Look East* policy, initiated in the 1990s, was partly an attempt to match China's intrusion into India's Indian Ocean with an Indian presence in the South China Sea and East China Sea, in which 'it is quite apparent that strategic competition with China is an undeclared element of India's Look East strategy . . . a new balancing game' (Batabyal 2006: 179). In doing so, closer links with other threatened powers like Japan emerged in the latter 1990s (Jain 1997), with Indian–Japanese naval cooperation initiated in 1998 (Basu 1998), and taking place in the Indian Ocean and East Asian waters. This takes us to the China–Japan relationship during the 1990s.

China–Japan relations in the 1990s

India was able to find a ready listener in Japan to her concerns about China. Indeed the one constant during the twentieth century in the shifting constellation of International Relations has been a generally negative Chinese–Japanese relationship as the rule, and war as a recurring option by Japan in 1894–5 and 1935–45. China's geopolitical re-emergence posed a particularly acute 'challenge' (Mendl 1979) to Japan in terms of its relationship, and importance to the USA, and in term of Japan's own regional presence – a challenge that had got even stronger during the 1990s (Deng Yong 1997).

Economic opportunities were widely mooted, expressed in Shaokui's analogy of the 'double locomotive model' (Deng Yong 1997: 384), with Japan pulling and China pushing the regional economic drives in a mutually beneficial 'economic partnership' (Taylor 1996) based on 'economic interdependence' (Howe 1996). Expanding economic links meant that Japan had overtaken the US as China's largest trading partner by 1995. However the 'normalisation' announced by the 1978 Sino–Japanese *Treaty of Peace and Friendship* was a 'fragile entente' (Bedeski 1983), a limited 'political partnership' (Wang Qingxin 1994) aimed against the Soviet Union. In military-security terms, the 1990s consequently saw renewed frictions in Sino–Japanese relations as the collapse of the Soviet Union left China as the remaining local power able and perhaps likely to threaten Japan. The PRC during the 1990s had become a powerful neighbour on Japan's very doorstep, starting to flex maritime forces, improving her conventional and nuclear capabilities, with unresolved territorial disputes able to feed off an extremely entrenched historical unease between the two powers. By the mid-1990s the ambiguities were apparent, between these 'rivals for pre-eminence' (Shambaugh 1996b), locked in 'strategic rivalry' (Park and Taeho 1998), and with highly negative images from history well established in their collective memories.

Relations between Japan and China generally deteriorated during the 1990s. Territorial disputes over continental shelf demarcation lines and the

Diaoyu/Senkaku isles were raised and the subject of rising nationalist furore (Downs and Saunders 1998–9). Moreover, Japan's economy went into something of a slump in the 1990s, whilst China's economy continued to boom. Japan's model of the flying V-shaped goose formation of Asian economies, with itself leading from the front was overtaken by events and different models in the neighbourhood. By 1997, PRC scholars were recognising that 'the unprecedented economic integration of China, Taiwan and Hong Kong in the 1990s has triggered concern among some Japanese about the possible Chinese dominance in the region', whereby 'Japan is understandably concerned about the possible emergence of "the Greater Chinese economic empire"' (Deng Yong 1997: 389). China's re-absorption of Hong Kong in 1997 heightened PRC economic strength vis-à-vis Japan, and Japanese concerns. Conversely, overlaps between economic, military and cultural images – the mainstays of the Yellow Peril motifs earlier in the century in the West – can be seen where 'China's basic distrust of Japan has been transferred to the economic realm. Japanese business people are often described as unreliable, selfish and slimy (*youhua*)' (Christensen 1999a: 54) in Chinese circles.

Military issues became noticeable areas of tension between these two regional giants. It was no coincidence that Japan's 1995 *National Defence Program Outline* argued that a strengthened link with the USA was 'indispensable for safeguarding our country's security, considering there is a large military power with nuclear capabilities in our countries surrounding area' (Jiang Wenran 2002: 159) (i.e. China). This focus echoed Vajpayee's nuclear concerns about China in 1998, and prompted Japan's alignment with India, in effect against China. Similarly, China's assertiveness in the 1995–6 Taiwan Straits crisis had prompted the dispatch of two American aircraft carrier battle groups, including one based in Japan, to patrol those waters. In its wake came the Clinton–Hashimoto *Joint Security Declaration*, April 1996, subtitled 'Alliance for the 21st Century'. A more active role for both countries in the security area was pointed to, whereby 'both governments will continue to consult closely on defense policies and military postures' (Japan–USA 1996), prompting 'Chinese apprehensions about the revitalization of the U.S. Japan Alliance' (Garrett and Glaser 1997; also Yang Bojiang 1996). The subsequent revised *Guidelines for U.S.–Japan Defense Cooperation* were released in September 1997 (Japan–USA 1997, Cronin 1997). Its enabling legislation, amidst rising Chinese concerns about it, was passed by the Japanese Diet in April–May 1999. Michael Green's analysis of the process was that 'throughout this process China was a constant factor in alliance managers' thinking' (2001: 78) in which China's verbal denunciations meant 'China was inevitably an actor – though more of a Greek chorus' (82). The underlying dynamics in these shifts were summed up in Bernstein and Munro's argument that 'the growth of Chinese power' meant that 'a strong Japan, in genuine partnership with the United States, is vital to a new balance of power in Asia', since 'a weak Japan benefits only

China, which wants no stabilizing balance of power but Chinese hegemony, under which Japan would be little more than Beijing's most useful tributary state' (1997a: 31).

IR security dilemma dynamics were soon apparent. Beijing sought assurances that the *Guidelines* new 'situational areas' did not cover Taiwanese waters, which the PRC considered as its own territory, assurances that Japan pointedly refrained from providing. Chinese fears were apparent. Ni Feng, in the *Beijing Review*, immediately saw any 'enhanced' US–Japan Security Alliance as a direct 'cause for concern' (1997) to the PRC. For Yu Bin, 'many in China view the newly secured alliance with grave concerns . . . perhaps most disturbing for Chinese defense planners is the implicit but unambiguous indication that China has replaced the Soviet Union as the major target' (1999: 201) for Japan.

China and Japan's military signals continued to be perceived as threatening by the one and defensive by the other. Here, for Shambaugh the 'anti-Japanese sentiment one encounters among the PLA [the military] is palpable. Distrust of Japan runs deep, transcends generations, and is virulent' (1999–2000: 69). Indeed, 'although at present Chinese analysts fear U.S. power much more than Japanese power' it was the case that 'in terms of national intentions, Chinese analysts view Japan with much less trust, and, in many cases, with a loathing rarely found in their attitudes about the United States' (Christensen 1999a: 52; also Tsang 1999).

By the end of the 1990s Sino–Japanese relations were in a downwards spiral, 'public distrust was growing out of control' (Rozman 2003: 10), and were evident in the 'the palpable tensions' (Shambaugh 1999–2000) present in 1998 around the first visit to Japan by a Chinese Head of State, Jiang Zemin. Emotive images 'based on historical legacies and national perceptions' (Christensen 1999a: 52) continually affected analysis and response between the two countries. Gut level racial undertones were present, for Thomas Christensen 'severe spirals of tension based on the security dilemma . . . a Chinese/Japanese spiral portends to be particularly powerful . . . because it is fuelled by racial animosity and visceral distrust' (1998: 28,29), that is, 'ethnic hatred exacerbates the security dilemma in Sino–Japanese relations' (1999a: 26).

Perceptions and lack of perceptions had then become noticeable in the Chinese–Japanese relationships during the 1990s. These two Asian neighbours, in many ways 'The East' and with ancient shared Confucian and Buddhist roots, were able so easily to blunder over the other, and to be genuinely blinkered. Thus, 'while many Chinese analysts can imagine some states as legitimately worried about China and can picture Japan legitimately worried about other states' (Christensen 1999a: 69–70), it was 'harder to find those who believe that Japan's military security policy could be driven by fears about specific policies in China' (70). Japanese concerns over Chinese weapons development, or provocative Chinese behavior around Taiwan and in the South China Sea during the 1990s could be dismissed by

Chinese analysts as 'mere "excuses" (*jiekou*) designed to facilitate Japanese hawks' predetermined plans for military buildups' (70). That Japanese actions could be threatening for China was also often unnoticed in Japan. Instead, such was Japan's concerns over China that it strengthened links with other potential anti-China partners, in IR terms balancing with other concerned states like India and bandwagoning with the United States, to which we now turn.

7   Up against the hegemon, the USA

Despite the significance, in various ways, of the preceding immediate Asian neighbours, it was the Sino–American relationship in the Asia–Pacific that became ever more significant during the post-Cold War 1990s. With the collapse of the Soviet Union, China was left with a remaining hegemonic threat from the United States, whilst the United States saw China as a competitor with whom there was no common anti-Soviet glue to keep them together. As an academic issue, China still remained an enigma in the 1990s. According to Jonathan Spence 'China . . . now provides endless ground for armchair speculation' in which 'we do not understand China and so we constantly invent it' through images, perceptions and misperceptions, in which 'China's opacity is what draws people, along with the remoteness and the size' (1990: 110). However, China was no mere academic issue. Her relationship with the United States was becoming the most important bilateral relationship on the globe. William Overholt commented, 'these two great civilizations must now engage each other – for better or for worse – to a degree that has never before occurred', since 'much of the future of humanity will hinge on whether both sides can approach this engagement with appropriate gravity and earnest efforts to understand one another's real motives' (1994: 416). China could not be ignored; 'living with China' (Vogel 1997) had become a central issue for the USA.

However, US–China relations were frequently problematic during the 1990s, as 'a thick-skinned Washington and a thin-skinned Beijing' (Gries 1999: 73) faced each other. It was a 'painful, decade-long process' in which 'at the same time that they recognized the need to cooperate, each nation became increasingly concerned about how the other would use its growing power. And herein lies the management challenge for the twenty-first century' (Lampton 2001: 15; Wang Jianwei 2000). 'Dramatic fluctuations' (Huang Xiaoming 2000: 269) were the pattern for the 1990s. Both China and America were becoming more assertive. Yu Bin simply called it *China's Syndrome* of 'rising nationalism and the conflict with the West' (1996). American policy was torn between 'containment or engagement' (Wang Jisi 1996) of China, 'increasingly notable for a lack of consistency and clarity' with 'confusion and stereotypes' (Carpenter and Dorn 2000: 69) at play during the Clinton administration of 1992–2000. Both sides had their own distinct hopes and fears, 'our nations have substantially different dreams. This has provided the dynamic of the first decade of post-Cold War US–China relations and will continue to do so well into the twenty-first century' (Lampton 2001: ix). Chinese images of the USA during the 1990s, a perception or perhaps misperception, were simultaneously one of America being a power past its peak but which was antagonistic towards China, 'dangerous but declining' (Pillsbury 2001a: 5). American perceptions were similar yet different, of China as dangerous and ascending.

The Tiananmen crack down in 1989 resulted in a chill in relations between the two states, casting an immediate and enduring cloud over George H.W. Bush's one-term administration 1989–92. In the US Senate, Jesse Helms warned of the 'growing military threat posed by Communist China . . . the same political elite which came to power in Communist China in 1949 is still running the country. This same group has directed border wars against all their neighbors for the last 40 years' (1992). China's image in the West went into nose-dive. Its Tiananmen impact coincided with geopolitical changes, for Lampton 'the grand bargain of the 1970s and 1980s became the humpty-dumpty of the 1990s' (2001: 5). The common US–China interest in restraining the Soviet threat, which in the 1970s and 1980s had dampened down otherwise friction points like Taiwan and Japan, became redundant when the Soviet Union collapsed in 1991, leading to points of divergence to re-emerge with greater vigour between China and the USA during the 1990s. In addition to the more obvious Tiananmen and Soviet factors, 'other developments' made the US–China relationship 'so difficult to manage' (Lampton 2001: 3) in the 1990s; namely China's quicker than expected modernisation programme, the growth of independence sentiments in Taiwan, the growth of domestic centres of influence on foreign policy formulation, the impact of globalisation and economic relationships, the information revolution shaping views on ever more rapid scale, and the revolution in military affairs which in its high-tech application seemed to provide the USA with still greater power advantages and China with renewed apprehensions.

China's previous assumptions of a continental land war against a Soviet foe had been scrapped by Deng Xiaoping in 1985 and replaced in the 1990s by a more fluid 'strategic frontier' including and projecting into the oceans and outer space. Both areas were ones likely to bring it into conflict with the USA, the dominant Pacific and space power. Direct military confrontation loomed in the wake of the 1995–6 Missile Crisis, with two US aircraft carrier groups sent to interpose themselves in the Taiwan Straits in February 1996. Some voices in the West warned of China's weakness, the PLA as a 'bloated . . . woefully inadequate force', in which 'China's modernization risks falling behind [America]. No large country, therefore, fears American "hegemony" more than China does' (*Economist* 2000: 17). Yet perceptions often went the other way, of an increasing Chinese challenge.

Admittedly, there was some talk of building a 'constructive strategic partnership' during the US–China Clinton–Jiang summits of 1997 and 1998, but in which scepticism could be seen, 'for its part, China had no intention of abandoning its aspiration for increased international influence, even if that conflicted with an American interest in preserving its primacy', for 'instead, strategic partnership with the U.S. was designed to better enable China to cope with the potentially dangerous constraints of American hegemony during China's rise to great-power status' (A. Goldstein 2003: 77). In other words, Lampton's classic *Same Bed Different Dreams* (2001) image of the relationship.

Building such a strategic partnership was overshadowed by the 'accidental' American bombing of the China embassy in May 1999 and resultant Chinese nationalist outrage and 'tears of rage' (Gries: 2001). For China 'the bombing became a symbol of a perceived hidden agenda in how the U.S. was handling relations with China' (Huang Xiaoming 2000: 274). The uncertainties between China and the USA were mired in negative attitudinal dynamics, distrust was endemic, 'fundamentally, mutual fears colors every aspect of U.S.–China interaction . . . bilateral relations are mired in this vortex of fear and suspicion' (Anderson 1999: 1, 5). In the wake of nuclear espionage scares of 1999–2000, Warren Cohen prefaced his updated edition of *America's Response to China* by warning 'in the closing months of the twentieth century, Chinese–American relations are dangerously close to degenerating into a new Cold War' with him hoping that any next edition 'does not tell a sad story of how two nations . . . stumbled into war' (2000: ix). The *Economist* reckoned that 'as a power, China simply cannot remotely be described as satisfied. The debate in the West about "containment" versus "engagement" is simply a debate about how to respond to that fact' (2000: 16).

Here it may be important to reiterate the application of IR constructivism theory. At the US Army War College, Susan Puska argued 'the profound perceptual gap between the United States and China . . . has helped give the boom-bust paradigm a life of its own in state-to-state relations between the United States and China' (1998: 2). States of mind, 'the psychological impact of China's presumed rise adds a volatile dimension to the U.S.-China state relations' (4). On the one hand, 'for China, the possibility of this change in power relations presents an intoxicating opportunity, which has eluded China for well over a century, to gain a dominant position within the Asia–Pacific region and the world' (4). On the other hand 'for the United States, such a change in the power relationship with China raises an uncertain, if not fearsome, specter of major change, even loss, in terms of international influence, prestige, and possibly way of life' (4). Consequently, 'this psychological dimension, I think, is at the heart of the current China threat and U.S. threat arguments in each country' (4). That such a bastion of hard-nosed realpolitik perspectives could discern such soft emotive psychological factors is revealing. Understanding the dynamics of Sino–American relations was not just of academic interest, it was all the more important given the structural importance for the international system of their relationship.

Structural importance of the China–US relationship

The importance of Sino–American relations became manifest during the 1990s. At the bilateral level, with the collapse of the Soviet Union, each state became the single most important state actor to whom the other had to relate. In turn, their military and economic importance to the other coloured their participation and projection in other bilateral relationships and multilateral forums. At a general level some commentators were arguing that the US's post-Soviet advantages were 'unipolar illusion' since 'new Great Powers will rise' (Layne 1993) as 'a structurally driven phenomenon' (Waltz 1993) in the international system. China was the power seen in that light, and so rapidly became the focus for post-Soviet strategic reviews in the USA, which focused on avoiding the re-emergence of any new rival (Posen and Ross 1996–7, Byman *et al.* 1999). Whereas the 'Chinese military during the 1970s and 1980s was generally judged either inconsequential or marginally beneficial to American security interests', the post-Cold War period saw 'heightened interest among analysts and . . . among defence planners . . . over the course of the 1990s, attention to the consequences of the growth of Chinese power has increased measurably' (Pollack 2002a: 43, 44, 50).

The then Secretary of Defense William Perry (1994) succinctly summed up China's growing presence as one where 'China is fast becoming the world's largest economic power, and that combined with its UN PermFive status, its political clout, its nuclear weapons and a modernizing military, make China a player with which the United States must work together' (1994). Previous images came up, as he later wondered and compared 'what if China, early in the next century, were to go the way of Japan in the 1930s, and a Pacific conflict were to rise because of that? There is a great debate in our country today as to what our policy to China should be' (1998). By the end of the decade, 'the challenge presented by a rising China was the principal issue facing American foreign policy' (Betts and Christensen 2000/01: 17). Moreover, not only did many see China itself as a threat, but also its proliferation policies, through its 'strategic proxies' (Bernier 2003) had created American anxieties over North Korea, Iran, Libya, Syria and indeed Iraq. Alternatives were present, at the immediate but also longer-term structural level, of 'containment or engagement' (Shambaugh 1996a, Wang Jisi 1996) on America's part towards China, reflecting their 'cooperation or confrontation' (Shambaugh 1997a). For many it was explicitly a worrying 'threat' (Gordon 1997, Aubin 1998, Schultz 1998). For others it was something to be 'managed' (Johnston and Ross 1999). This uncertainty went all the way up to the Presidency, with Clinton warning, in 8 April 1999, about 'the potential challenge that a strong China could present to the United States in the future' as well as 'the risks of a weak China, beset by internal conflicts, social dislocation and criminal activity, becoming a vast zone of instability in Asia' (Gurtov 2002: 130; also Shinn 1996: 5–6).

'China Threat' literature and images in the USA

Although China Threat perceptions were evident around the Asia–Pacific in the 1990s, their appearance in the United States were the most noticeable and most maintained. In the literary arena, it was perhaps no coincidence that the first of David Wingrove's epic 7-volume series *Chung Kuo* appeared in 1990, describing the world as a new Middle Kingdom dominated by China. Set in 2190, its preface read how under Mao and his successors there 'grew a giant of a nation, capable of competing with the West and its own Eastern rivals, Japan and Korea, from a position of incomparable strength' (Wingrove 1990: preface). Emma Broomfield's analysis of *Perceptions of Danger: the China Threat Theory* concludes that such China Threat perceptions, though strongly felt in some quarters had been 'grossly exaggerated' (2003: 278). Daniel Burstein and Arne de Keijzer may have argued that 'the "Chinese Threat" is overblown' (1998b), but the majority of analysis during the 1990s tended to emphasise such a 'China Threat' (D. Roy 1996). Thirty-three years after penning the previously cited *The Centre of the World. Communism and the Mind of China* (1963), long-time observer Robert Elegant reckoned that engagement policies were an 'illusion' and 'kowtows' towards a regime that was driven by antagonistic premises, 'the chief impetus of Beijing's foreign policy . . . will be the compulsion to punish and humiliate foreign countries, particularly former imperial powers like the United States, Britain and France, to pay them back for what they did to China in the past' and 'a closely related purpose will continue to be the expansion of Chinese influence in Asia and other parts of the world. China's foreign policy will remain in the service of the regime's passion for revenge and for power' (1996).

Part of the China Threat paradigm was over analogous perceptions. Comparisons and images were rife in the mid-1990s between China and pre-1914 Wilhemine imperial Germany (e.g. Kristof 1993: 71–2, Waldron 1995, Pye 1996, Garver 1996, Friedman 1997), in terms of an unsettling rising power model. For Fareed Zakaria, 'like Germany in the late 19th century, China is also growing rapidly into a global system in which it feels it deserves more attention and honor' (1996), with a similarly strong military elite and a shaky authoritarian political regime sitting on top of unleashed socio-economic forces. One particularly interesting figure to have used the 'obvious and disturbing analogy' of 1914 Germany was Paul Wolfowitz, whose *Bridging Centuries: Fin de Siecle all Over Again* characterised China as a country that also felt it had been denied its 'place in the sun', with 'real sense of grievance at mistreatment by the European powers in the last century' (1997: 7), and was determined to gain its rightful place through nationalistic assertiveness, which could lead to another world war. Wolfowitz' own rise was significant with the coming of the Republican administration in 2000, where he became deputy Defence Secretary, and was a prominent member of the BLUE team arguing for a tougher line with China (Waller 2001). Other 'rising powers' parallels were drawn by Wolfowitz with pre-1939 Imperial Japan and Nazi Germany as well as post-1945 Soviet Union.

Some American commentators dissented from such comparisons. Chas Freeman argued that 'China is not Germany, Japan, the USSR, or even the United States', since 'China does not seek lebensraum; is not pursuing its manifest destiny; does not want to incorporate additional non-Han peoples into its territory; has no ideology to export; and is certainly not a colonizer and does not station any troops overseas' (1998: 123–4; similarly A. Goldstein 2001: 862, 2003, 2005: 204–12). One could question his non-incorporation of non-Han peoples, given Chinese sway over Tibet and Xinjiang. One variant was Richard Bett's and Thomas Christensen's (2000–1) suggestion that the worrying parallel for China's neighbours was not Germany, but rather the pattern of overt and frequent American interventionism during the twentieth century throughout its own regional backyard, Mexico, the Caribbean, and Central America. A further variant came from Bryce Marland's concern that 'the more talk there is of "containing", the greater the danger of the Chinese as becoming as paranoid as the Germans were before 1914 when they feared "encirclement". If China is frustrated and baited, it could become aggressive' (1996).

However, in America there was more and more talk of the China Threat during the 1990s, where Ross's article in *Foreign Affairs*, 'China II: Beijing as a conservative power' (1997) was overshadowed by Richard Bernstein and Ross Munro's preceding article 'China: the coming conflict with America' (1997a). For worried 'neo-cons' like Kagan (1997a, 1997b, 1999a, 1999b; also Krauthammer 1995) engagement with China was to be replaced by her containment through diplomatic, political and military means. Such 'China Threat' concerns were exemplified not just amongst politicians but also by a continuing vein of serious yet best-selling for books by commentators and journalists. This 'spectre of rising Chinese power' became a 'new cottage industry' (Lampton 2001: 75) of sensationalist best sellers, most notably typified in *The Coming Conflict With China* (Bernstein and Munro 1997b), *Red Dragon Rising. Communist China's Military Threat to America* (Timperlake and Triplett 1999), *The China Threat. How the People's Republic Targets America* (Gertz 2000) and *Hegemon. China's Plan to Dominate Asia and the World* (Mosher 2000).

Such writings had been preceded by Samuel Huntington's arguments first broached in his article in *Foreign Affairs* (1993) and then elaborated in his book *Clash of Civilizations* (1997). He pinpointed China, as well as Islam, as the leading challenge to the West, where 'centrally important to the development of counter-West military capabilities is the sustained expansion of China's military power and its means to create military power', since 'buoyed by spectacular economic development, China is rapidly increasing its military spending and vigorously moving forward with the modernization of its armed forces' (1997: 147). From such a build-up of 'capability' capacity came Huntington's dramatic scenario for a 'civilizational war' between China and the USA (313–16) breaking out in 2010, a scenario with obvious similarities to 'invasion scare' literature that has surrounded Yellow Peril fears for much of the past one hundred and fifty years. Structurally, alongside his comments on a rift line between Islam and the West, Huntington saw China as 'the' State challenge to the international system; 'a more dangerous source of a global intercivilizational war is the shifting balance of power among civilizations and their core states' in which 'the rise of China and the increasing assertiveness of this "biggest player in the history of man" will place tremendous stress on international stability in the early twenty-first century' (312). The West's military, economic and financial position of primacy was being eroded where 'the most significant increases in power are accruing to Asian civilizations, with China gradually emerging as the society most likely to challenge the West for global influence' (83).

Bernstein and Munro's *The Coming Conflict With China* was widely noticed in the PRC circles, it 'reflects the imbalanced psychology of some Americans towards the rise of China' (Zhang Ming 1999b: 146), with Bernstein seen as having joined the ranks of the 'master demonizers' (Zhang Xudong 1998: 109), and reflecting a 'post-Cold War frenzy of China bashing in the American media' (109). Liu Ji saw the book as 'irrational, wrong' (2004: 243). Criticisms were also heard in the US. James Lilley criticised its 'provocative' language as 'reviving old fears about the "Yellow peril"' through evoking 'the "Fu Manchu" problem' (1997). Karl Zinsmeister also saw the book as typical of how 'today, attacking China is a cause celebre . . . a herd running in today's campaign to isolate China . . . painting the Dragon as a Godzilla of the twenty-first century . . . Darth Vader in a Mao suit' (1998: 4, 1, 3) – a striking topical image to have conjured up! An irony here is that amidst the wave of criticisms of Chinese foreign policy, Bernstein eventually distanced himself from some of the China-attacks materialising in America. As Bernstein put it, he and Munro had found themselves outflanked by still more strident voices, who 'see China, incorrectly in our view, as a new incarnation of the old Soviet expansionist menace that must be contained at all costs', for 'China does not entertain any ambition to dominate the world; nor does it have the resources to entertain such an ambition' (1997).

Michael Swaine's warning at the time was 'don't demonize China' through misleading analysis which 'routinely employ distortions, half-truths and, in some cases falsehoods' (1997). Zbigniew Brzezinski, no soft-hearted liberal and a former NSC adviser to Carter, reckoned 'our fashion is to have the enemy of the year. China is big, it's large on the map, it's yellow, so there is an under-the-surface racist element, and it fits very nicely an obsessive state of mind . . . because China is big enough to sustain this obsession' (Erlanger 1997). For Karl Zinsmeister, 'these alarms will prove false' from 'today's

Sinophobes' and their 'mistakes' (1988: 1). In the immediate-term there was an overestimation of Chinese strength and an underestimation of American reactions, but also in the longer-term was the crucial process of economic transformation taking place. To be successfully completed it would need fundamental political democratisation and decentralisation and with it a China that would be stronger but 'nicer', a 'non-noxious state' (6). Thus, behind the alarmist 'hubbub of current headlines . . . my guess is that today's "China threat" will mostly solve itself' (1,6). John O'Sullivan acknowledged, but also dissented from, the way in which 'in recent years, China has become the focus of conservative discontents in foreign policy' and the 'excesses of the new anti-China lobby'. He concluded 'A Yellow Peril? No' (2000: 28)!

In 1999, several high profile issues emerged between the US and China. It kicked off with allegations of dubious Chinese money being laundered into the Democratic Party campaign. Behind that, for Palumbo-Lui, were much more charged undertones whereby 'the furore . . . discloses an anxiety over U.S. sovereignty, particularly with regard to America's imagined relation to Eastasia' where amidst notoriously loose and wide-ranging fund contributions within the American political process, particular sensitivity was shown on this issue where 'Chinese money is most significantly read as Chinese money, that is as particularly raced and nationalized. This could not have happened if the U.S. did not already have in its ideological repertoire the image of China as the Evil Empire' (1998).

The year continued with spying allegations, China's WTO membership negotiations, Taiwan, and the bombing of the Chinese embassy in Belgrade. As such Owen Harries considered it very much 'a year of debating China' in which 'the chances of a cool, sensible American reaction' were absent, given that 'over the years Americans have had great difficulty thinking rationally about China. They have tended to oscillate violently between romanticizing and demonizing the country and its people', entrapped as they were by various stereotypical images of China; as 'Treasure', 'Paragon', 'Sick Patient' and 'and of course, China as Threat' (1999–2000: 141). Amidst his own pinpointing of double standards at play came Owen Harries's mention 'of the awkward fact that in recent years China has used force in the pursuit of its foreign policy much less frequently than has the United States itself' (141). Nevertheless, this was not stopping a conversely negative image of China where 'it is now widely believed that the most serious challenge to America's primacy will come from China . . . belief in the virtual inevitability of a clash is widespread' (141, 142). A 'demonizing of China by some in Congress' based on 'superficial and often caricatured images of China' was a feature in 1999–2000 (Lubman 2004: 562, 565). Huang Yasheng lamented that 'these days it is a nightmare to be a Chinese national living in the United States. Newspapers and TV are saturated with coverage of the Los Alamos case' and asked 'are we guilty by ethnic association . . . China bashing is in vogue. Many Americans now believe that China will be the enemy of the United States in the 21st century . . . fears of the Yellow Peril are magnified by yellow journalism' (1999; cf. Moore 1999).

In the meantime emotive comments and passions had been generated and were picked up in the *Luce Report* surveys carried out in June 1999. In perceptual terms it was significant that it found 'a majority of Americans look at China nervously, as primarily a threat' (Watts 1999: 4). Indeed, 'one of the most significant patterns to emerge from our new survey is the extent to which the People's Republic of China (PRC) commands increased – and generally negative – attention', where 'the historical American fascination with the world's most populous nation' was dominated by a clearly perceived Chinese peril. When asked 'How do you look upon China's growth and emergence as a global power?' some 51 per cent thought that 'China is primarily a threat and challenge to American security interests and needs to be contained', with 40 per cent disagreeing. In addition though, 'on the economic front, China has surpassed Japan as the country most Americans see as "unfair" in its trading practices, and whose exports to the United States represent a "serious threat" to American jobs' – testimony to how 'China's rise to the top on both these issues has been remarkably swift' (3).

Specifically, in the wake of the *Cox Report* and the Wen Ho Lee case, the Chinese–American 'Committee of 100' commissioned an in-depth survey during January–March 2001 of American attitudes amongst various focus groups and poll surveys. The organisers 'were startled. We thought that the findings would indicate some prejudice and identify some stereotypes, but the findings reflect highly negative attitudes and stereotypes among a significant group of Americans' (Committee of 100: 2001a: 6, also 2001b). Apart from evidence on domestic attitudes, it also found that with regard to foreign affairs, the focus group participants 'believed the military and/or economic power of China is a looming future threat to U.S. security . . . the focus group participants saw the Chinese leaders as wilful adversaries: any future tension will not be accidental', and 'several expressed the belief that a serious showdown between the U.S. and China was inevitable' (12). Around this general unease vis-à-vis China, in the polling surveys, 68 per cent of participants agreed with the proposition that 'China will be a future threat to the U.S'. With regard to the question that 'Chinese Americans passing on secret information to China is a problem in the U.S', 46 per cent thought it was true and 16 per cent were unsure. As to the question whether Chinese–Americans 'are more loyal to China than to the USA', 32 per cent thought they were, and 20 per cent were not sure.

Chinese perceptions of America's 'China Threat' imagery

The PRC was particularly sensitive to *China Threat* perceptions in the United States, as something that might shape its single most important bilateral relationship. The media, America's Fourth Estate, was seen as crucial in that 'the US media work to demonize China' (Dai Xiaohua 1997). In China the public had been 'gripped' (Hughes 2006: 104) by the publication of Li Xiguang's best seller, *Yaomo hua Zhongguo de beihou* ('Behind the Demoniza-tion of China') (Li Xiguang 1998–9), with Li arguing that 'US media [is] behind the demonization of China' (1996). Chinese scholars were given full rein in the PRC official media to counteract such American-held images. For Wang Jisi 'wantonly attacking China has become the vogue' (1996: 9) in America. According to Yan Xuetong, Bernstein and Munro's book *The Coming Conflict With China* was Cold War rhetoric, reflecting 'a new wave of anti-China sentiment reminiscent of McCarthyism in the 1950s' (1997: 7). Wang Jisi, Shi Yinhong and Zhang Baijia argued that Burstein and Munro's book, and general China Threat sentiments, were erroneously based on various factors, ranging from 'racial sentiment, cultural psychology to geopolitics' (1997: 10–11).

The American media was seen as extremely political, with an agenda that was detrimental to China's own goals. Invoking Gramsci's hegemony theory on the role of the media in advancing the dominant ideology in capitalist societies, Wang Mei-ling lamented how 'these days, reports about China or Chinese-related issues in the American media are likely to be negative, voicing a fear of the rise of China or a Gargantuan-like evil empire', that 'China-bashing is gaining more space and attention in the Western media ... created a virtual [i.e. media construct] evil empire, an enemy whose image is looming larger and larger in the minds of the American public. The creation of a virtual enemy' (1998: 73–4). For him, this 'cast a dark shadow over the American psyche' in which 'the American mass media have engaged in ideological mobilization to shape the public's opinion ... a virtual enemy ... China ... has been created in the minds of the American public ... However, cross-cultural/international relations constructed in a virtual world are likely to create a real war' (97). A worrying scenario indeed!

Chinese politicians were keen to counteract such criticism in America. PRC foreign minister Qian Qichen thought that 'some people in the United States are spreading the "China Threat" theory ... these views could not be more wrong' (1997: 7). Zhu Rongji's visit to Washington in 1999 saw him telling American business leaders that, 'China is the biggest market, not the biggest threat to the U.S. The China-threat theory should be the China-opportunity theory' (Gilley and Crispin 1999); and telling Secretary of State Albright that 'one of the purposes of my current visit to the United States is try to cool some Americans down' (Zhu Rongji 1999b), whilst telling President Clinton and the Press that 'the current political atmosphere in the United States is so anti-China' (Zhu Rongji 1999a). Qian's successor as foreign minister, Tang Jiaxuan, was also concerned about how 'anti-China elements within the United States are going all-out to interfere with and obstruct the normal development of China–U.S. relations' (1999a) through their emphasis on the China Threat paradigm. Conversely, China could in effect point out an 'America Threat' in its 1998 White Paper *China's National Defense*, where American 'hegemonism and power politics remain the main source of threats to world peace and stability . . . Some countries [i.e. the USA], by relying on their military advantages, pose military threats to other countries, even resorting to armed intervention' (PRC 1998). Deng Yong saw the USA as a 'hegemon on the offensive' (2001: 359).

America's high-tech multi-service integrated RMA (Revolution in Military Affairs), demonstrated in offensive operation during America's Gulf War 'Operation Desert Storm' of 1991 and Serbia 1999 campaigns, proved highly disquieting for Chinese strategists. This was perceived as an area where America's lead had, if anything, increased vis-à-vis China, spurring the latter, in turn, to make determined efforts to catch up. The massive, highly centralised technology-driven area of nuclear weapons and ballistic missiles technologies was one area where China made the greatest strides, though still being some 30–35 years behind America in terms of force and capability in its RMA endeavours. However across the range of RMA possibilities, the more flexible areas of coordination and processes have come up against subtle cultural inertia factors stemming from both a Confucian and Communist heritage of rigidity. Be that as it may, some observers (Henley 1996) were concluding it would still take China some 10–20 years (i.e. c. 2005–15), to get to the stage reached by American forces in 1990. That still left it some 15–25 years behind the USA. On the other hand, it is perhaps of significance that Bates Gill, whilst pointing out the limitations in China's attempts to catch up with the American wave of RMA still acknowledged that 'it is possible that the concentrated effort of China's greatest resource, its people, could result once again in significant advances within the current RMA' (1996: 29). Here, the 1980/90s RMA was already giving way in the late 1990s to an emerging twenty-first century 'digital battlefield' in which Information Warfare, or cyber-space disruption was being picked up inside and outside China, as a way for PRC to compensate for its deficiencies vis-à-vis American military superiority in other fields (Yoshihara 2001).

This imbalance was the spur for the appearance in China during 1999 of *Unrestricted Warfare* by Qiao Liang and Wang Xiangsui, dealing with possibilities of 'asymmetrical' warfare. When reprinted by Pan American Publishing Company in 2002 it was given the extra damning subtitle *China's Master Plan to Destroy America*, complete with a dustcover photograph of the Twin Towers on September 11, thereby conflating the fears of the Yellow Peril with those of international terrorism in the wake of 9/11. Thomas's *Seeds of Fire: China and the Story Behind the Attack on America* (2001), painted similar linkages between Osama bin Laden, nuclear espionage, and CIA briefing papers on China launching an all-out nuclear attack against America 'before 2015'! With regard to asymmetrical warfare, Chinese used past frameworks to coin phrases like developing 'Assassin's Mace' *shashaujian* weapons to back up the doctrine of 'the inferior defeats the superior', using sensitive high-tech system fragilities, in effect techno-military 'acupuncture points' (Pillsbury 2001b: 9), 'its major tool for conducting asymmetric warfare to defeat the US' (Corpus 2006).

Indeed, American worries over China could be heightened by the clear signs of readiness in PLA circles to take on the USA. Thus, in the wake of Chinese outrage over the American bombs dropped on its Belgrade embassy in Serbia and signs of Taiwan moving towards declaring independence, Garver noticed how 'in early 2000, a spate of fire-breathing popular magazines appeared in China's interior provinces' (2003b: 575) where 'what *is* new . . . is their open contemplation of war between the United States and China over Taiwan' (576). Whether their hopes of likely Vietnam-style American war-weariness were correct or not is not the point, what is significant were their close links to the PLA. Admittedly the PRC leadership curbed such literature in February 2000, amidst worries of it triggering American reactions and complicating China's diplomatic image; but it could still be seen as 'examples of a muscular nationalism in contemporary China . . . indicative of the popular appeal of the notion that China can fight and win a war against the United States over Taiwan' (575).

US responses to the PRC

American political and military circles reflected these tangled China concerns, under the Clinton administration of 1992–2000, with the President making the point that 'we have argued about China with competing caricatures'. Is China 'a country to be engaged or isolated? Is this a country beyond our power to influence or a country that is ours to gain and ours to lose? Now we hear that China is a country to be feared' (Clinton 1999).

At the Defense Department, the volatile nature of images and consequences were present in Assistant Secretary of Defense Nye's arguments for 'deep engagement' with China where 'it is wrong to portray China as an enemy. Nor is there reason to believe China must be an enemy in the future . . . enmity would become self-fulfilling prophecy' (1995: 94). His chief, Secretary of Defense William Perry similarly argued that containment was the wrong option, alienating China and damaging America's own security interests. Instead, the US should 'engage China, not contain it . . . We believe that engagement is the best strategy to ensure that as China increases its power, it does so as a responsible member of the international community' (1995).

At the State Department, Secretary of State, Madeleine Albright similarly talked of how 'no nation will play a larger role in shaping the course of 21st century Asia than China. With its huge population and vast territory, China's emergence as a modern, growing economic and military power is a major historical event' (1997). As such, a containment policy for China would be a mistake, 'would, in fact, guarantee an outcome contrary to American interests. A policy of containment would divide our Asian allies and encourage China to withdraw into narrow nationalism and militarism' (1997). Instead, in a rebuttal of Samuel Huntington, she held that 'what we see in Asia today is not a clash of civilizations, but a test of civilization' (Albright

1997) and 'that test is whether we can seize the opportunity for mutually beneficial cooperation that now exists' (1997) with the PRC. Admittedly, 'we are not yet where we want to be, nor has China evolved as rapidly or thoroughly as some have hoped, but the direction we must go is clear; greater interaction based on China's acceptance of international norms' (1997).

Some defence caution over China was apparent in the Pentagon's report *The United States Security Strategy for the East Asia–Pacific Region 1998*, 'China's rise as a major power presents an array of potential challenges', given 'China's growing defense expenditures and modernization of the People's Liberation Army' (USA 1998) indicated by their development and acquisition of advanced fighter aircraft, programs to develop mobile ballistic missile systems, land-attack and anti-ship cruise missiles, advanced surface-to-air missiles, and a range of power projection platforms. Nevertheless, 'comprehensive engagement' (section 2.5) was still felt to be the answer. Some awareness of the importance of images of the 'other' was apparent in the document, the need 'to ensure that both countries have a clear appreciation of one another's regional security interests. Dialogue and exchanges can reduce misperceptions between our two countries', so as to 'increase our understanding of Chinese security concerns, and build confidence between our two defense establishments to avoid military accidents and miscalculations' (USA 1998). The agreement not to target strategic nuclear weapons at one another, reached during President Clinton's June 1998 visit to China, was seen as an important reassuring symbolic action. The need for such reassurances was itself testimony to the perceptual divides between the two powers, where 'although the United States and China have a long history of interaction, missing from this contact over much of the past two centuries has been continuity, balance and a sober dialogue concerning mutual interests and strategic visions (USA 1998: section 6.2).

Competition rather than cooperation seemed more apparent, as the Congressional *Cox Report*, January 1999, highlighted Chinese nuclear espionage discovered at the Department of Energy, where 'PRC penetration of our weapons laboratories spans at least the past several decades and almost certainly continues today' (House Select Committee 1999; also Johnston 1999, Pollack 1999). Some considered it disturbing confirmation of the China Threat thesis, 'shocking findings' from a 'stunning document' (Timperlake and Triplett 1999: 12). With emotions raised and the whole Chinese American community seen as potential or actual fifth columnists, Franklin Ng (1998) and Lars-Erik Nelson (1999) saw it as an irresponsible "Yellow Peril' tract. Stanford Lyman considered it was 'the capstone thus far on the current revival of yellow peril Sinophobia' (2000: 719).

In turn, the Chinese government released a detailed rebuttal, denouncing the *Cox Report* as 'demagoguery' designed to 'fan anti-China feelings' through 'sensational lies . . . fabrication . . . clumsy distortion . . . absurd logic . . . running counter to historical trends' (PRC 1999). For Zhao Qizheng, Minister of Information Office of the State Council, it was a 'a farce . . . a great slander against the Chinese nation and is typical racial prejudice' (1999). His grounds for the perception of racial prejudice were indicative of China's own sensitivities, that 'China is a large country with a long history of civiliza- tion. The Chinese nation is an industrious and ingenious nation. China has always relied on its own efforts to handle its own affairs' so 'nor does it at present, nor will it in the future, base its development of the sophisticated national defense technology related to national security and interests on the "theft" of technology from other countries' (1999).

What of the *Cox Report* itself? Its claims were dramatic, its 'Overview' drawing attention to long-term secret sleeper agents over the decades, con- cluding that 'the PRC thefts from our National laboratories began at least as early as the late 1970s. Significant secrets are known to have been stolen' (House Select Committee 1999: iii), which was 'the result of a 20-year intel- ligence collection programme [by China] to develop modern thermonuclear weapons, continuing to this very day' (iv). The results were that 'with the stolen U.S. technology the PRC has leaped in a handful of years, from 1950s-era strategic nuclear capabilities to the more modern thermonuclear weapons designs' (vi), that is, 'the stolen U.S. nuclear secrets give the PRC design information on thermonuclear weapons on a par with our own' (v). Such estimation of China's hard power tangible gains was entwined with estimations of China's intentions, over what she was likely to do with such enhanced, albeit 'stolen' nuclear capabilities. In his 'Foreword' to the *Cox Report*, former Secretary of Defense Caspar Weinberger considered that 'the PRC in the past twelve to fifteen years has changed' from its 1970s/80s setting of 'being a friend that is anxious to have our support in its attempt to wield a strong defense against the Soviets' to now 'being a power that has made a conscious effort to replace the former Soviet Union as a superpower rival of the United States . . . to displace American influence in Asia and the Pacific region' (1999) through using whatever means. As for Kenneth Degraffenreid, his 'Editor's Introduction' to the *Cox Report* concluded that 'the American people should be in no doubt about this – in important ways Communist China might pose a more dangerous threat to the United States than did the Soviet Union' (1999).

Two months after the *Cox Report*, such perceptions of China and emotive imagery from earlier times surrounded the arrest on charges of nuclear espionage of a Chinese–American, Lee Wen Ho (2002) in March 1999. Zhang Ming was not swept away by the furore, asserting that 'the Chinese nuclear arsenal has always been far behind the United States, not only in quantity but also in quality. No amount of spying, if it occurred, will dramatically change' and 'the U.S.–China nuclear relationship will continue to be vastly asymmetrical' (1999a: 7). Yet the dangers of perceptions and misperceptions were there. Thus 'if the United States adopts a Cold War- style containment policy as many advocate, China could eventually pose a threat' (57) through possibly withdrawing from the various nuclear interna- tional agreements (e.g. Nuclear Non-Proliferation treaty, the Comprehensive

Test Ban treaty) and divert resources from economic development into military spending. Consequently, 'in the end, the nightmare of a China threat could be made a reality by an anti-China fantasy promoted in the United States . . . treating China as a nuclear enemy would be unwise' as it would, in all likelihood, become 'a self-fulfilling prophesy' (57), a point also made by Nye (1995).

Nevertheless, the *Cox Report* and the Lee Wen Ho case ensured that China remained highly visible in American perceptions, as did the bombing of the Chinese embassy at Belgrade. Kissinger warned of 'storm clouds gathering' (1999), indeed that in the USA 'some are fatalistic about this drift toward confrontation . . . that since a showdown is foreordained, better now, when China is still relatively weak' (1999). Other American commentators picked up on the images being circulated. Unfortunately though, both the *Cox Report* and the Lee Wen Ho allegations showed for Maurice Meisner 'a habit of distrust . . . only the latest in a long succession of ruptures in the relationship between China and the United States' where 'mutual racism and arrogance . . . in recent years has been accompanied by a revival of old racial stereotypes. From this ugly pottage – an indiscriminate mix of fact, fiction, and conjecture – opportunistic American politicians now portray Chinese in stereotypical fashion' (Meisner 1999). The stereotype was of Yellow Peril provenance, 'the increasingly dominant images are of nineteenth century vintage: Chinese are crafty, deceitful, villainous and half-crazed automatons manipulated by evil rulers' (1999). Constructivist IR theory, with its focus on image, and Jervis with his focus on the role of misperceptions in IR come to mind. However, it was precisely such stereotypical images that had been bandied about in the furore of reporting and commentaries, and with it the prestigious Committee of 100 'fears that the anti-Chinese hysteria . . . which led to Dr. Lee's indictment and prosecution may reappear wherever tensions or disagreements arise between China and the United States'; a case that Robert Scheer had considered a 'revival of the Yellow Peril . . . in search of an enemy' (2004; see also Wang Ling-chi 1999).

Ironically, the court resolution of the Lee Wen Ho case in September 2000, which involved some nine months in solitary confinement, saw all but one of the original 59 charges dropped, with apologies to Lee and rebukes to the government by US District Judge James Parker. Indeed June 2006 saw a $1.65 million dollar settlement of the suit for invasion of his privacy! Gertz' own comments in *The China Threat*, in the light of this court resolution, and having previously emphasised Lee's involvement with Beijing, was to instead highlight Lee's possible links with Taiwan, rather than Communist China, a setting that did nothing to dent his continuing concerns over the structural threat to the international system from Beijing.

Already the early Clinton talk of engagement and strategic partnership was giving way to containment and China as a strategic competitor (Shambaugh 2000). As the Clinton administration was approaching its end, the Pentagon's *Asia 2025* summer study report in 2000 highlighted the general significance attached to China, and specific worries over her intents for American strategists (Kaiser 2000). Various scenarios were outlined, but China was seen as a threat regardless. On the one hand, a stable powerful China would challenge the status quo in Asia, whilst an unstable weak China might lead its leadership into trying to bolster their power with foreign military adventures. Gershman, who was more concerned about US unilateralism and militarisation in the Asia–Pacific, worriedly warned that its message could be summed up as 'we have seen the enemy and it is China' (2001). The advice from *Asia 2025* was for the US to curb China through extending its range of allies, like India, and to plan for a future where China would be an enemy – regardless of whether China had become democratic or had successfully managed its transition to a market economy.

Elsewhere the CIA National Intelligence Council's *Global Trends for 2015* released in December 2000 warned that in Asia–Pacific major power realignments and the more fluid post-Cold War security environment in the region were raising serious questions about how regional leaders would handle nascent great-power rivalries (US–China, China–Japan, China–India), related regional 'hot spots' (Taiwan, Korea, South China Sea), the future of challenged political regimes (Indonesia, North Korea absent unification, China), and communal tensions and minority issues (in China, Indonesia, the Philippines, and Malaysia). All of these were China-related, where 'on balance, the number and range of rivalries and potential flashpoints suggest a better-than-even chance that episodes of military confrontation and conflict will erupt over the next 15 years' and where 'the rise of China as an economic and increasingly capable regional military power – even as the influence of Communism and authoritarianism weakens – pose the greatest uncertainty in the area' (NIC 2000). Uncertainties cut both ways though, for the 1990s had left a troubled legacy, 'a new equilibrium, one of deep, mutual ambivalence, if not mounting distrust' (Lampton 2001: 16) between the two states.

Zbigniew Brzezinski's concerns in 2000 with American–Chinese relations form an interesting conclusion for the 1990s, with this hard-bitten politician reckoning that 'allegedly informed writings regarding China often tend to be quite muddled, occasionally even verging toward the hysterical extremes' (2000: 6). Brzezinski pinpointed paradoxes, 'an obvious but fundamental reality: China is too big to be ignored, too old to be slighted, too weak to be appeased, and too ambitious to be taken for granted' (6). She was 'driven simultaneously by a sense of national grievance over perceived (and in many cases, real) humiliations over the past two centuries, but also by growing and even arrogant self-confidence' (6). He felt there were 'some important parallels between China's current situation and imperial Germany's circa 1890', that is, they both had 'a resentment of a perceived lack of recognition and respect' by others, they both had 'fears of encirclement by a confining and increasingly antagonistic coalition', they both had 'rising ambitions on the part of a predominantly young population', and they both had a 'desire to precipitate a significant rearrangement in the global pecking order' (11). Uncertainties were still evident as 'one cannot be certain about which direction China will head over the next quarter of a century' (11). This points to the coming century, which even as Brzezinski spoke was starting to be talked about as China's Century.

8 China and the world in the twenty-first century

In the twenty-first century, China looms large. The events of 9/11 may have put Islamic *jihadist* groups on the world map in 2001, and shaped America's War on Terrorism, but at the state level, and within the global economy, China is the big question for the coming century, 'this time China's rise is different . . . the sheer scale . . . considerably overshadows anything in the past' (Waldron 2005: 715). James Kynge sees a 'tipping point' (2005: 4) in Spring 2004, when 'quite suddenly, or so it seemed, China became an issue of daily international importance' (6). It has remained that way ever since. The past turns into the present, and with it thoughts for the future.

Towards a 'China's Century'?

Talk of the twenty-first century as being China's Century became commonplace: within one week of the century opening, John Lloyd was asking 'Will this be the Chinese century?', in which 'China is this new century's wildest card . . . for those who look for a new 21st century hegemon, the signs are here' (2000: 15). Robert Skidelsky talks of *The Chinese Shadow* in which 'China has suddenly become the all-absorbing topic for those professionally concerned with the future of the planet. Will the twenty-first century be the Chinese century, and, if so, in what sense?' (2005). For Emad Mekay it is 'The dawn of the Chinese century', 'if the last century was America's, this one looks to be the Chinese century' (2005), and for William Rees-Mogg, 'this is the Chinese century' (2005). *Newsweek* devoted an entire issue to 'China's Century' in May 2005, including an extended and frequently cited profile by Fareed Zakaria 'Does the future belong to China'? (2005).

China's continuing economic surge underpins this identification, as in Laurence Brahm's *China's Century. The Awakening of the Next Economic Powerhouse* (2001), George Gu's 'How Should We Understand a Chinese Century?' (2004), Ian Campbell's 'The Chinese Century Begins' (2004), Oded Shenkar's *The Chinese Century. The Rising Chinese Economy and Its Impact on the Global Economy, the Balance of Power, and Your Job.* (2005), and William Pesek's 'Welcome to the Chinese century?' (2005). Rees-Mogg emphasises 'the economic maturity of the new China . . . for the future of what is beginning to look like the Chinese century' (2005). Gordon Chang is certain, despite his speculation on China's political instability (2002), that 'one thing we do know: the People's Republic will profoundly affect the shape of tomorrow', as an 'economic powerhouse . . . there could be a decidedly China-centric look to the developing world. Not just Asians tell us this is "China's Century"' (2003). Ted Fishman's widely read and cited profile 'Will the 21st century become the Chinese century?' highlights the role of demographics, that 'behind China's rapid economic ascendancy over the last 25 (and especially last 10) years is the basic fact of China's huge population,' that is, 'China's people must be regarded as the critical mass in a new world order. The productive might . . . have turned China's people into probably the greatest natural resource on the planet' (2004). Consequently, 'how the Chinese (and the rest of the world) use that resource will shape our economy (and every other economy in the world)' (2004; also Fishman 2005).

Within China awareness of China's possibilities are growing. On the streets of Beijing, Pepe Escobar noticed general Chinese perceptions, 'they feel in the air what is beginning to look like the Chinese century' (2005). Talk of the twenty-first century as *China's Century* meets with some Chinese pride, but also some unease over its impact on others' perceptions and actions towards the PRC. In the *Beijing Review*, Lii Haibo's 'Whose century is it?' argues 'there will be no so-called China century . . . nor has this country had any desire for a China century or China-era, or something similar' (Lii Haibo 2004: 32). In part, this was a normative judgement as 'that term conveys to some extent a chauvinistic tinge' (32). In part, it was also the judgement that 'pursuing that kind of object will result in a state of isolation . . . crowning itself with the China century or being an aggressive superpower, it [China] would lose its friends and other countries would feel uncomfortable' (32), a practical and perhaps crucial consideration, affecting language used if not actual hopes.

China's presence in the twenty-first century

The twenty-first century is then increasingly envisaged as a century in which China will be a particularly significant actor. Suggestions by academics in the 1990s (Kristof 1993: 74, 59; Huntington 1997: 231; Burstein and Keijzer 1998a: 308, 336, 341) and politicians (Clinton 1997) have become assumptions for commentators and diplomats as the century actually started to unfold. Rex Li argues that 'the profound effects of China's growing process cannot be underestimated' (2004: 23) for the international system. In a similar vein, Thomas Kane suggests 'as the People's Republic of China assumes greater prominence in world affairs, the question of how its government will approach key issues in international politics becomes increasingly critical' (2004: 101) for the world. Henry Kissinger, politician turned observer, recognises that 'the rise of China . . . will, over the next decades, bring about a substantial reordering of the international system. The center of gravity of world affairs is shifting' (2005). Australia's ambassador to China, Alan Thomas, considers that 'China's rise . . . is one of the top global developments of the present time' (2004). America's former ambassador at Beijing, James Stapleton Roy, similarly feels that 'never before in history has a country risen as rapidly as China is now doing' (2005: 15).

Nevertheless, perceptions continue to affect reality, as with 'the fact that Chinese tend to see themselves as currently weaker than outsiders do has important consequences' (Lampton 2001: 78). The Japanese and even more so the American government made an issue of transparency in 2005–6, yet David Lampton's caution at the start of the decade remains relevant, that 'transparency is a very different matter for the strong than for the relatively weak' (2001: 79), since any transparency would reveal any inferiority. In classic IR security dilemma fashion, such secrecy tends to still exacerbate China Threat fears by others. The envisaged future affects the present, China 'as a rising power, where it will be in the future rather than where it is today is what influences policy making in most countries' (Harris: 2002: 23). It is still the situation that 'China successfully plays on expectations about its future capability in order to enhance its status in the present . . . Expectations of China's rapid rise to great power status . . . remains strong' (Buzan 2004: 148), and 'the tendency of the rest of the world to believe in the inexorability of China's rise to power will help its status' (149). Within this, there is Beijing's 'particularly heightened sensitivity to status' (Deng Yong 2005: 53), to see 'international status' as in some ways 'better than power' (51).

However China's rise is based on very tangible assets. Its continuingly high economic growth, noticeable throughout the 1990s and maintained at around 10 per cent in the face of the Asian meltdown elsewhere in East Asia during 1997–8, has continued. The first few years of the twenty-first century saw China's economy continuing to pass others, overtaking the UK in 2005–6 to become the fourth biggest economy, and set to overtake Germany and Japan in the near future. Indeed in terms of PPP (Purchasing Power Parity), China is already the second largest economy. Gerald Segal's minimal estimation of China's economic capability in 'Does China Matter?' (1999) has been overtaken by Robert Sutter's 'Why Does China Matter?' holding that 'China exerts worldwide economic influence' (2003–4: 87; also Harris 2003: 23). David and Lyric Hale's 'China Takes Off' reckons that 'there is no question, therefore, that China's emergence as a great economic power will rank as one of the major issues confronting world leaders in the next few decades' (2003: 36). In relative terms, the American ambassador, Roy considers that 'in the broader sweep of history, however, the challenge of terrorism will prove to be of lesser significance than the stunning surge of Chinese economic growth over the last two decades' (2005: 14; also A. Thomas 2004).

China's economic advancement continued to help its wider political and ultimately strategic position. In the case of Australia, China's economic surge was becoming all the more pivotal, 'a new vision of Asia with China at its centre is now the focus of Australia's international agenda' in which 'it has accepted Beijing's requirement that a country that wants to benefit from China's unique economic opportunities must recognise China's growing weight as well, and take careful account of China's political and strategic interests' (White 2005: 470). Such economic growth by the PRC had wide-ranging implications for the international system, 'its emergence as a major economic power with global reach cannot but evoke the spectre of hegemonic transition and its political fallout' (Laliberté 2005: 17). Chinese figures have been quick to recognise this power knock-on effect, 'as China's economic strength grows, no one, not even the Chinese ourselves, can prevent China's influence from spreading into politics, values and ideology' (Xiang Lanxin 2006).

Metaphors abounded around China's economic surge, 'the workshop of the world' (Watts 2005; also David Zweig and Bi Jianhai 2005: 2, 5), a crucial 'engine of growth' (George Gu 2004; also Hoge 2004: 3; Zheng Bijian 2005: 18). Economic strength gives financial strength, 'it is in the realm of remunerative power growth that China's ascent has been most marked' (Lampton 2005: 308). All in all, 'the past two or three years have marked a new moment in the global perception of China', for 'there is suddenly a new awareness that encompasses both a recognition of China's economic transformation and an understanding that, because of its huge size and cohesive character, it will have a profound impact on the rest of the world' in which 'China has arrived and will increasingly shape our future, not just its own' (Jacques 2005c). *The Sydney Morning Herald*, 13 September 2005, announced 'suddenly, China seems to be holding the levers of the world economy'.

Figures poured out at the start of the twenty-first century, supplementing China's already astounding population figure with economic counterparts. In 2004 it overtook Japan to become the world's biggest importer of iron ore. Spring 2004 witnessed the great manhole mystery, 'when slowly at first but with mounting velocity, manhole covers started to disappear from roads and pavements all over the world' (Kynge 2005: 6). This had been sparked by the Chinese demand for scrap metal, and with it soaring prices, 'soon the gravitational pull of a resurgent "Middle Kingdom" was reaching the furthest sides of the world'. Scottish headlines of a 'great drain robbery' was but one example as was 'wherever the sun set, pilferers worked to satisfy China's hunger' (6) for industrial sources. China's iron and steel statistics were dramatic in 2006, where 'production has increased at a prodigious rate' (ISSB 2006). China imported 275 million tonnes of iron ore, the world's biggest, in 2005 and 161 million tonnes in the first half of 2006, up 23 per cent year-on-year and more than in all of 2003. In turn, China's rising iron ore imports were enabling massive expansion of its steel capacity. In terms of crude steel production in the first half of 2006 China produced 199 million tonnes, up 19 per cent on the first half of 2005. This accounted for 33 per cent of global production, compared to 12 per cent in 1995. Thus, China produced over 35 per cent of world steel in June 2006, having increased from approximately 12 million tonnes/month in 2001 to 37 million tonnes in June 2006. Not only was this fuelling China's own domestic industrialisation, but it was also helping her balance of trade, where China's steel exports jumped 22 per cent from June 2005–6, overtaking Japan, the EU and Russia to become the world's largest exporter.

According to Chinese figures, its merchandise trade surplus rose from $25.3 billion in 2003, to $32.6 billion in 2004, tripling to $102 billion in 2005. Its July 2006 surplus of $14.5 billion was the biggest ever recorded by any country in the world, a 'record . . . eclipsing' (Barboza 2006) Japan's famous trade surpluses of earlier decades. China's foreign exchange reserves, mostly gold and US dollars, similarly soared in the first decade of the century, reaching over $711 billion by 2005, and still 'mushrooming' (*Asia Times* 2006) to overtake Japan in February 2006 as the world's largest holder of foreign exchange reserves, and crossing the $1 trillion threshold by autumn 2006. In Europe, 2005 saw China's mass textiles production producing the 'Bra Wars' furore in the EU during the summer, and the Shanghai Automotive company buying up Rover. In the USA, the Chinese Lenovo computer giant took over IBM's PC division (Ling and Avery 2006).

As so often, profound uncertainties surrounded perceptions of the PRC, as with Ramgopal Agarwala's *The Rise of China: Threat or Opportunity* (2002) written around China's 'stellar' (113; also *Economist* 2000: 3) economic growth. Hu Jintao's visit to London in 2005 brought mention of China's economic 'miracle' as also being a 'threat' (Watts 2005). Admittedly some commentators argue otherwise, as in 'Undue fears of China Inc?' (Mooney 2005). Shaun Breslin argues that it was not so much the PRC as a national entity that should be looked at, but rather the supranational and transnational flow of commodity driven networks which had done much to generate Chinese economic growth, within which China was operating in a global division of labour at the low cost manufacturing cycle. China's economy is indeed growing but this was not exactly national economic power in a straightforward sense, that is, in thinking of 'power and production' there is a need for 'rethinking China's global economic role' (Breslin: 2005). One can, though, note that it is not just a question of 'power and production' but of 'power, production and perception'. Meanwhile, others point out the scale and strategic underpinning by the Chinese government, in a way not evident in earlier Japan-related economic fears of the 1980s, evident in the setting up of its Special Economic Zones like Shenzhen, and most visually in recent years with Shanghai's meteoric rise. However the very pace of China's economic growth led analysts to wonder if the central apparatus was still in charge of China, some analysts wondering if the 'largest command economy, isn't responding to commands' (Benjamin and Tweed 2006) from the centre to rein back growth. Quite simply, China continues to dramatically grow. The second quarter of 2006 saw China's ongoing cumulative growth rate of 10 per cent reaching further heights of 11.3 per cent. June 2006 saw China's industrial output surging at a record 19.5 per cent.

Access to primary industrial resources has become an issue, where China has already overtaken the United States as the largest player in the global commodities market, posing ever greater demands for resources like copper, aluminium, and cement and suchlike. For some commentators this represents 'the next Chinese threat', as 'China is going to be even hungrier for resource deals than it was before' (Mallaby 2005). Not only does China's search for industrial resources have implications for Chinese assertion in oil rich disputed territory on China's frontiers, like the South China Sea and Central Asia, but also further afield. For Hale, 'China's growing appetites' for resources is 'likely to be as transforming an event in geopolitics as America's arrival as a world power during the early decades of the twentieth century' with 'profound implications for the foreign policies of the United States, China's Asian neighbours, and the countries in the Third World that will soon emerge as China's primary suppliers' (2004: 137).

Such massive scale of industrialisation poses the question of China's environmental impact, where given the 'threat of China's rapacious appetite' for resources 'China is telescoping history . . . the past 25 years of economic growth have devastated China's environment; another 25 could do the same world wide' (Watts 2005). As this book, *China Stands Up*, was being readied for the publishers, news came of air monitoring stations in California picking up Chinese industrial emissions from across the Pacific, with it being reckoned that on some days already one-quarter of the particulate matters in the air above Los Angeles come from the polluted skies of China (Chea 2006). Yet again, though, Chinese officials were keen to defend China's international image, admitting it was affecting their own domestic environment but not those of other countries, Li Xinmin from the PRC's State Environmental Protection Administration said 'those reports saying 25% of pollution in Los Angles comes from China are not objective and are irresponsible and the conclusion is also doubtful' (BBC 2006).

China is the biggest producer and consumer of coal. In 2003 it overtook Japan to become the second biggest petroleum consumer, having accounted for around 40 per cent of the world oil demand growth during 2001–5. A China Century could become a dirty polluting century, perhaps the biggest long-term threat that China poses to the international system, 'China's staggering economic growth is an environmental time bomb that, unless defused, threatens to convulse the entire planet' (Chea 2006). Western commentators point out the dangers in China's industrialisation and consumption patterns following earlier Western patterns, but Chinese commentators can see that as double standards and of the West trying to pull up the drawbridge and retain initial advantages. Perceptions abound in this area. The Kyoto Protocol of 1998 was not signed by the USA, but was signed by China and most other countries. However, as US President George W. Bush noted with disquiet, 'the world's second largest emitter of greenhouse gases is China. Yet, China was entirely exempted from the requirements' (2001) in the initial protocols. From China's point of view, it was up to the United States, the largest polluter, to reduce emissions rather than blaming a lesser polluting China.

Access to energy resources is a rising priority for the PRC as the twenty-first century unfolds; 'energy security and its international relations' (Zha Daojing 2005) is becoming crucial in the PRC's 'global hunt for energy' (Zweig and Bi 2005). China's industrialisation continues to soar, and China has become an energy importer rather than exporter. China's 'thirst for resources' (Small 2005: vi) brings with it 'the politics of energy' (19–22) and diplomatic forays across the globe to secure such modern vital resources. The PRC is now 'driving world demand for energy' (Thomas 2004). Its 'dependency' (Umbach 2003) upon energy from the Middle East and Central Asia is worrying for China; in order 'to slake its thirst for oil, China scours backwaters of the world' (Mellor and Lim 2006). Indeed, China's 'oil obsession [and] energy appetite fuels Beijing's plans to protect vital sea lines' (Blumenthal and Lin 2006), and construct secure land routes. However, such PRC attempts to remedy the situation through securer access brings rising concern from other international actors. Robert B. Zoellick, US Deputy Secretary of State, despite his positive supportive comments on China as a 'stakeholder' in the international system, simultaneously warns that 'China's economic growth is driving its thirst for energy. In response, China is acting as if it can somehow "lock up" energy supplies around the world. This is not a sensible path' (2005).

In that setting, the summer of 2000 had already seen a 'milestone in the PRC's development as a global power' (Kane 2002: 129), as around 4,000 Chinese troops were sent by air and sea to help the Sudanese government maintain control of its vital oilfields against rebel attacks. The dispatch of troops to the Sudan was not just part of China's push for resources; it was also part of China's political, diplomatic, and military outreach, 'its psychological readiness to expand its influence beyond its national borders' (Thompson and Zhu Feng 2004: 4).

China's presence continued to make itself felt outside its East Asian neighbourhood, where maritime expansion saw the 'undersea dragons' (Goldstein and Murray 2004) represented by, a 'Great Wall at sea' (Cole 2001). 'China's new "imperial" Navy' (Elleman 2002) has 'expanding maritime ambitions in the Western Pacific and the Indian Ocean' (Lee Jae-hyung 2002), a 'dragon in paradise' manifested in 'China's rising star in Oceania' (Reilly 2003, also Shie 2006), and literally underpinned by 'underwater dragons: China's maturing submarine force' (Murray 2004) and China's general drive for 'command of the sea' (Holmes and Yoshihara 2005b). Chinese figures push for a stronger navy able to project power and gain access facilities, in 'China's "Caribbean"' (Holmes and Yoshihara 2006a) the South China Sea, and beyond. As such, China's challenge had become an issue for American naval strategists (Jensen 2000), disconcerted by a Chinese task force flotilla passing from the Indian Ocean into the Atlantic in August 2000, following its goodwill trips to Malaysia, Tanzania and South Africa.

Alfred Mahan, the leading naval advocate of sea-power and geopolitical thinker of a century ago, has gained increasing attraction for Chinese strategic thinking (Holmes and Yoshihara 2005a, 2006b). In Ni Lexiong's view 'we cannot give up our efforts to build up a strong navy simply because of hegemonic countries' suspicions of us. We should not be afraid of drawing hostile attention to us' for 'to live and survive in a world such as ours, we must develop a strong and powerful sea power' (2005: 7–8). Soft power maritime diplomacy (Holmes 2006) is supplementing the PRC's hard power increases. Diplomacy and naval strategy have been intertwined. Kane judges, 'China's maritime ideas are grand . . . awe-inspiring' (2002: 68, 132), and 'the PRC has laid the diplomatic foundations to become a force to be reckoned with at sea . . . Beijing's maritime expansion is central to a larger [strategic] policy aimed at putting China among the foremost global powers' (133, 139).

Still further afield, geopolitics has transformed EU–China economic links into an official 'strategic partnership' in 2003 (Scott 2007a, 2007b; also Shambaugh 2004). Chinese influence has been rising in Central Asia through the vehicle of the Shanghai Cooperation Organization. China's appearance, often oil-related, in Africa became widely noticed. A growing Chinese presence is discernible in Latin America, much to the evident discomfort of American strategists, with talk of China's strategy to constrain the United States within its own hemisphere (Mrozinski *et al.* 2002: 202) through economic penetration in Panama, setting up tracking stations in Cuba and announcing a 'strategic partnership' with Brazil in 2004. October 2003 saw China's first manned space flight, making China the third Space Power after the USA and Russia.

Chinese perspectives on the twenty-first century

Perceptions and feelings are noticeable, inside and outside China, on this undoubted rise and growing presence, which for many would seem to be 'leading China into the promised land of the long "lost" greatness, respect, prosperity, power' (Wang Fei-ling 2005: 676) of its Middle Kingdom days of glory. Yan Xuetong sees history at play since 'the rise of China is granted by nature . . . this history of superpower status makes the Chinese people very proud of their country on the one hand, and on the other hand very sad about China's current international status', for 'they believe China's decline is a historical mistake which they should correct . . . the rise of China is a long-term historical process' (2001: 33, 34) that is inevitable for the twenty-first century. This is no hypothetical chimera, as Zheng Yongnian puts it, 'China rises. This is today more fact than anticipation. The question is no more whether China will rise, but *how* it will rise and its impact on the world' (Zheng and Tok 2005: 5). PRC scholars like Shi Yinhong are clear on China's importance, where 'a rising China is certainly one of the most fundamental and profound facts in world politics today and tomorrow . . . critical reality in shaping the world power structure' (2002: 1). Indeed, 'befitting a power of its stature', China will 'assume a greater role of leadership, and developing the norms, rules and institutions that will define the international order of the 21st century' (Pang Zhongying 2006: 10). What seems clear is China's growing awareness of its growing presence, 'China is preoccupied, and almost fascinated, with the trajectory of its own ascent' (Brzezinski and Mearsheimer 2005).

Yet, amidst undoubted awareness of power advances, ambiguities remain. Yan Xuetong argues that 'the Chinese regard their rise as regaining China's lost international status rather than as obtaining something new. This psychological feeling results in the Chinese being continuously dissatisfied with their economic achievements until China resumes its superpower status' (2001: 34). Moreover, there are assumptions and frames of mind where 'the Chinese people take the rise of their nation for granted. They never concern themselves with the question of why China should be more advanced than other nations', but 'rather frequently ask themselves the question of why China is not the number one nation in the world' (34). A number one position is though something that other countries, especially any displaced by China, may well find disturbing. Conversely, there is also the way in which 'China's political and military leaders see threats everywhere. The full extent of the siege mentality of China's leaders is not always appreciated. This siege mentality results in elites viewing the foreign . . . environments as treacherous landscapes filled with threats and conspiracies' (Scobell 2002: 12), the stuff that misperceptions and IR security dilemma spirals flourish in.

A more reassuring strand of Chinese thought is expressed by Ni Feng, where, 'to use the popular Chinese catch phrases, China is seeking to *rongru shijie*, or integrate with the world' (2004: 146; also Jia Qingguo 2005a: 502). Xia Liping talks of 'China's efforts as a responsible power' (2003). As such, Ni Feng reckons 'China is repositioning itself from a revolutionary country that rejected the existing international regime to a responsible power within the system', that 'China has switched to a different strategic paradigm, one that sees the world in cooperative rather than confrontational terms . . . the main thrust of Chinese diplomacy today is not to create a new international order, but to join the existing order' (2004: 146–7).

At one level, the PRC frequently talks of the twenty-first century as providing opportunity and fortune. Zeng Peiyan, Minister at the State Development Planning Commission, asserts with some pride, that 'at this point in time as the human race enters the 21st century, China is increasingly becoming the focus of world attention . . . people can see with increasing clarity China's bright prospects in the new century' (2001: 11). However, China's previous humiliation continued to figure in China's 'security/insecurity discourse' (Callahan 2006: 187), the PRC's National People's Congress agreeing in April 2001 to re-establish a 'National Humiliation Day', officially called National Defense Education Day. 'Never forget' has become a mantra, typically shown in the *People's Daily* stories on 18 September 2004, 'Never forget History' and 'Never forget national humiliation'. Remembering China's national humiliation may have been a way to deflect external criticism of China, but it was also a way to mobilise internal support for the state and for military modernisation. This was why the 2004 National Humiliation Day posters, replete with marching troops, warships, planes and space rockets, had the caption 'Never forget national humiliation, strengthen our national defence' (Callahan 2006: 180 fig. 1).

As in the 1990s, China Threat arguments continue to be a prime concern for PRC rebuttal, concerned as it is with its reputation and security dilemma dynamics (Deng Yong 2006). This is well illustrated by the plethora of articles appearing in the *People's Daily*, online as well for maximum circulation, during June–July 2002. On 6 June it wrote that 'the "theory of the China threat" has been spreading like pestilence . . . in fact, [the] real threat comes from the creator of the 'theory of threat' (*People's Daily* 2002a), a theme pursued over the next few weeks (Liu Xiaobiao 2002; *People's Daily* 2002b; 2002d; Ren Yujun 2002). Another random point in time, summer 2006, had the *People's Daily* continuing to produce varied rebuttals; on 28 May 'China promotes its culture overseas to dissolve China threat' (2006a), 29 May, ' "China threat" fear countered by culture' (2006b), 1 June 'China not a threat to world energy security' (2006c), 5 July 'Stronger China poses no threat to other nations' (2006d), 8 July 'Who believes the new China threat theory?' (2006e), and 2 August 'Why is China always haunted by the China threat?' (2006f).

Apart from rebutting negative *China Threat* concerns of others, the PRC is also keen to offer more positive images of what it wanted to achieve in the world, a world in which words matter; with a 'long series of concepts used to define China's place in world politics' (Laliberté 2005: 5) and which reflect 'Chinese thinking on China's appropriate role in the world' (Suettinger 2004: 9). 'Multipolarity', the frequently used term in the 1990s, was joined by the phrase *heping jueqi* (peaceful rise) (Lin Shaowen 2004, Zheng Bijian 2005) in 2003, and in turn by the still more reassuring term *heping fazhan* (peaceful development) (PRC 2005). Other couplings are evident – multipolarity with the 'democratization of international relations', multipolarity with globalisation, globalisation with multilateralism.

China's embrace of globalisation has been partly for economic reasons, but also for strategic reasons (Moore 2005). First, 'mainstream Chinese strategic thinkers now believe that globalization, as manifested in transnational forces, international institutions, and greater need for multilateralism, can be used to "democratize" the U.S. hegemonic order to minimize unilateralist power politics' (Deng and Moore 2004: 118) on the part of America. Second, 'globalization as a way of making China rich and strong and simultaneously reducing international fears of fast-growing Chinese material power . . . a more cooperative form of interstate competition that increases prospects for China's peaceful rise' (Deng and Moore 2004: 118). As such the PRC reckons that a combination of multipolarisation multilateralism and economic globalisation may 'overcome the security dilemma fuelled by great-power transition' (134).

China's Great Power drive is in part a question of confidence of China's sense of herself as a great nation. Nationalism, a clearly emerging phenomenon in China in the 1990s, continues to increase in scope during the first decade of the twenty-first century, becoming 'one of the key focuses in the study of China's foreign policy' (Chen Zhimin 2005: 35; also Zhang Jian 2004). Lei Guang rightly discerns a 'realpolitik nationalism' generated from universalist IR realism entwined with an 'emotive nationalism' generated from particularist Chinese culture and history (2005: 508) at play in the PRC. For Wang Fei-ling, 'an increasing strong sense of nationalist aspiration and even ambition is clearly growing in China' but where 'a persisting sense of frustration, insecurity, and even victimization still seems to color people's feelings about themselves and about China's relations with western powers' (2005: 686). Yet China's growing strength also feeds in. Jia Qingguo argues that nationalism has got weaker in some ways in China, as in a greater readiness to adopt 'foreign' technologies and greater acceptance of marriages with non-Chinese (Jia 2005c: 15). However, nationalism has also got stronger in other ways, Jia seeing the Chinese as 'more nationalistic in their reactions to foreign criticisms and condemnations of China ... more nationalistic in that they take greater pride in China's achievements than before ... they begin to feel the rise in China's status in world affairs' (2005c: 15). He also saw them as becoming more nationalistic 'in the ways that they approach international affairs ... they have discovered the [IR] Realism language ... one hears more and more people using such terms as national interests' (16). For him, perceptions underpin this trend, since it was the external insulting disrespect of China by the world that was triggering the 'distrust' of the world by China. A mutually exacerbating perceptual spiral?

In the wake of continuing anti-Japanese frictions in 2005, Zhao Suisheng recognised that 'anxiety is growing in Asia and the West that a virulent nationalism has emerged out of China's "century of shame and humiliation"', and 'the question remains, can Beijing keep this nationalism reined in, or will it begin to accelerate out of control' (2005–6: 132). Chinese public opinion is influencing PRC foreign policy (Fewsmith and Rosen 2001). As such China's 'pragmatic nationalism' (Zhao Suisheng 2004; also 2005: 250–65) represents a continuing attempt by the PRC's leadership to control and channel such popular forces, 'state-led nationalism' (Zhao Suisheng 1998a). The PRC government treads a fine line (Seckington 2005), responding to, and to some extent providing outlets for heated nationalist furore, mainly directed against Japan and the USA. Yet it also seeks to control this 'bottom up' force, 'controlled expression of anti-American nationalism' (Zhao Suisheng 2005: 265), its 'state down' projection remaining generally more cooperative than confrontational.

Some nationalist writers feel that Deng Xiaoping's low profile cooperative foreign policy is no longer desirable in the face of American power projection and of China's own growth. For Yue Jianyong, 'our national spirit are all facing unprecedented challenges' from the United States through its attempts 'to maintain and increase the U.S. military and geo-political strategic advantage; to control China's economy and politics from within through the process of globalization; and to weaken China's nationalism culturally and destroy China's national spirit' (2003). In his mind, 'to use one single sentence to sum it up, the U.S.'s goal is to colonize China from within by using military threats' and 'as such, America's strategic objective is to completely and forever obliterate any possibility of China, a country with vast territory, challenging the United States so that the U.S. can maintain its status as the world's hegemon' (2003). In order to achieve 'economic self-strengthening' and to 'strengthen our military power', he thinks the PRC 'must use our national will of steel to facilitate the rise of strategic industries . . . a mission related to our vital national interests that will determine our national security and the survival of our nation' (2003). Zhang Binsen is particularly blunt in arguing that 'China should abandon the foreign policy of "taoguang yanghui"' (2003), that is, abandon the axiom of 'Hide our capacities and bide our time' since the time had come to reveal, and perhaps use, China's growing capacity.

For Zhang Binsen, geoculture and imagery is an issue, whereby 'stimulated by such a confrontation-based mentality, "demonization of the other" has become an effective cultural strategy' (2003) pursued in America and the West. Yet, faced with this American unilateralist onslaught, China is now in a different position from Deng's Xiaoping's days, 'our comprehensive national power has reached the level of a quasi-big power, and we are developing rapidly. This is an inevitable reality . . . as a rapidly rising big power' faced with 'menacing American "cultural unilateralism"' that 'we have to confront' (2003).

Both writers envisage a China not necessarily bound by the existing international system. For Yue Jianyong 'to accomplish this goal, if necessary, we must not be bound by international treaties' (2003). For Zhang Binsen, 'we should focus more on building and pursuing new international institutions and mechanisms, and not be entangled with preserving the old international order. The existing international principles can not effectively rein in the United States' (2003). Thus, 'since the existing international mechanisms can not be justly implemented, it is in our interest to destroy them completely, which can at least give us equal opportunity . . . , this is our pursuit' (2003).

Both writers are explicitly nationalist. For Yue Jianyong, 'China's nationalism gains its vigor from vastly numerous people and their genuine awareness of a national self-esteem, which has become the precious spiritual source of our unshakable national will, of our efforts to revive China and our Chinese nation' (Yue Jianyong 2003). For Zhang Binsen 'we must stress the realistic characteristics of the clash of civilizations . . . stress the clash between Chinese civilization, Islamic civilization, and Indian civilization on one hand, and the Western civilization on the other . . . we should promote nationalism' (2003). For once, Huntington receives some support outside the West for his controversial Clash of Civilizations thesis!

Nevertheless, China's policy of 'peaceful rise/development' has become the well established official message from the PRC. Yet there are ambiguities for China and for the outside world. As Wang Jisi argues in terms of debate over China's Peaceful Rise, 'what is obviously missing in the current discourse is any discussion of China's domestic political agenda', for 'both the advocates and the critics of Peaceful Rise avoid touching on the sensitivities of political reform at home as if it bore no importance to China's path of development ahead' (2006: 6). Peaceful rise and the democratisation of international relations have unstated linkages with calls for peaceful internal transformation and the democratisation of China's internal relations. Wang Jisi is optimistic that 'concerns about China's future will be dispersed as more observers will be caring about how the country is governed internally . . . in this sense the Peaceful Rise/Peaceful Development theory may be gradually eclipsed by upcoming events and new discourses may likely emerge' (2006: 8). However, others are less optimistic over the inevitability of political reform under PRC leadership.

Uncertainties, long cycles and Grand Strategy for a new century

These preceding considerations point to the undoubted clear significance, yet noticeable uncertainties surrounding China's likely place in the international system for this century. How far China's undoubted increase in power will destabilise the international system depends on uncertainties, both within and outside China.

Externally, the PRC's increasing participation in international organisations may be softening its views of the world, 'a participant not just in the international system, but in international society' (Harris 2002: 24). Internally, domestic politics remain problematic. Since 1989, China's leadership has had a 'siege mentality' (Wang Fei-ling 2005: 678) generated by Tiananmen Square and the collapse of communist rule in the Soviet Union, 'a chronic but realistic sense of being under siege' (678), where the internal pressures for democratisation and external pressures on Human Rights do threaten its hold on power. American politicians continue to argue that 'closed politics cannot be a permanent feature of Chinese society. It is simply not sustainable . . . we can cooperate with the emerging China of today, even as we work for the democratic China of tomorrow' (Zoellick 2005).

Wang Fei-ling pinpoints future uncertainties. The IR democracy = peace axiom may not be applicable since 'democratization may turn out to be a factor that will completely alter the nature of Chinese foreign policy and make it less conservative and more demanding' (Wang Fei-ling 2005: 682). Rising nationalism, rather than liberal democracy may mean that 'the internal constraints on Chinese power that must provide the assurance' (Wang

Fei-ling 2006) for the international community are not present. After all, in the immediate sense, 'unfortunately, some early signals from the rising Chinese power have been rather unsettling . . . a whole generation of angry youth has emerged' with 'one-sided views of the world that are often laughably ignorant and frighteningly arrogant' (2006). Similar cautions had been expressed for the future by Bao Tong, the former adviser to Zhao Ziyang in the late 1980s. In 1998 he wondered '[China] has already gone mad in the last 40 years. You have to ask yourself a question. What will it do on the international scene? Is it a source of stability or a potential source of instability' (Mufson and Pomfret 1998)? Different time scales were to be considered 'when it doesn't have enough power, its attitude will be restrained. But once it develops and becomes strong, what kind of a role is it going to play without a complete structural change?' (Mufson and Pomfret 1998), though with the proviso that China's internal world view of the outside world is not necessarily a reassuring one.

Meanwhile, China's rural masses are faced with unprecedented, and for many uncertainly disturbing changes in their lives. China needs to run hard, just to keep standing up. In 2006, it is clear that China's economic surge is creating marked and growing urban/rural, coastal/interior socio-economic divisions in its wake. Glittering Shanghai can be juxtaposed with Shanwei, the centre of rioting and crackdowns in December 2005. Indeed according to government figures some 74,000 demonstrations took place in 2004. All in all, talk of China 'soft' and 'hard' landing is uncertain with regard to both economic and political change. Such pressures were the underpinning for Gordon Chang's *The Coming Collapse of China* (2002; cf. Lin Liangqi 2002, Xiao Ding 2002), and feature in Steve Chan's caution over how far there was really a 'power transition' going on between the US and China (2005).

The question still remains how far will China's increasing integration within a global world economy also soften and smooth potential international frictions. Already as the twenty-first century beckoned Rosita Dellios considered 'that China cannot readily be demonized as the Communist "other" is evident in the unwavering support it receives from American business' (1999: 4). Indeed, George Gilboy argues that there is something of a 'phantom menace' at play in the way in which 'China's sudden rise as a global trading power has been greeted with a curious mix of admiration and fear', given that 'China now has a stake in the liberal, rules-based global economic system that the United States worked to establish over the past half century', and where 'Chinese firms continue to rely heavily on imported technology and components – severely limiting the country's ability to wield technological or trading power for unilateral gains' (2004: 3). The bottom line is that 'China, in other words, has joined the global economy on terms that reinforce its dependence on foreign technology and investment and restrict its ability to become an industrial and technological threat to advanced industrialized democracies' (3–4). However there may be different time scales at play here, 'is short term [economic] dependence seen as a necessary price to pay to improve China's long-term international position' (Saunders 2000a: 56) by creating mutual interdependence with the USA and strengthening China's own economic base? Will regional frameworks like the Pacific APEC community integrate China with the West, or did the first meeting of the East Asian Summit in December 2005, without an American presence, prove to be a harbinger for re-emerging Middle Kingdom pre-eminence by China?

Such issues raise questions of long-term cycles and long-term 'Grand' strategy at play, where 'the world's next superpower [China] is playing a very long game, one of the longest history has ever known, subordinating temptation and instinct not to alienate the US in the course of its breathless economic transformation' (Jacques 2003). Such horizons are used by Avery Goldstein, where 'China's contemporary grand strategy is designed to engineer the country's rise to the status of a true great power that shapes, rather than simply responds to the international system' (2001: 836). In the immediate short term, consolidation by China and reassurance of the international system remains a 'grand strategy [which] makes sense for a rising, but not dominant power surrounded by potential adversaries who are nervous about its intentions' (2003: 58). The China Threat analogies drawn from history by containment proponents of the 1990s seemed overdone, their 'historical analogies seem inappropriate'. Like post-1870 Germany, China still needs the breathing space and security, in her case to enable the Modernisation programme, first launched by Deng Xiaoping back in 1978, to come to fruition. The PRC's advocacy of multilateralism, its establishment of various 'strategic partnerships' with other states and actors, and reassuring language is indeed a very deliberate 'calculative strategy' (Swaine and Tellis 2000: xi) to get it through the immediate short-term period of danger at the start of the twenty-first century. Within that, the greatest challenge is with the United States, the existing hegemon alongside which China is rising, and perhaps overtaking.

Structural and perceptual uncertainties surround China for the coming century. For Avery Goldstein the approach taken by China since the late 1990s 'finesses questions about the longer term' (2003: 60). However, as Goldstein has noted this approach, 'a strategy of transition' (2005: 38) operating since the late 1990s and still set to run for another 30–50 years, avoids the longer-term issue of what happens once China has risen, once it has achieved its target of achieving similar standards of wealth and strength, with a much bigger base. For him 'the strategy is tailored to fit the requirements of an emerging China, to chart the course for its rise during a period of [American] unipolarity; it is not designed to guide China once it has risen and circumstances are fundamentally different' (38). Kissinger once said that China thinks in centuries. Certainly the Chinese leadership has seen the process as taking around fifty to seventy years to complete her long march (i.e. catching up sometime between 2030–50). China will have the greater capability by the second half of the twenty-first century, but how will it then choose to use it; what will its intents be for the international system? As Ashley Tellis notes in his paper 'A grand chessboard', China's peaceful rise will lead to a future where 'it becomes a true rival of the United States. At that point, China will face another strategic crossroads' (2005) vis-à-vis the United States, and indeed the world.

Uncertainties are still apparent. Paul Wolfowitz admits, 'I think one of the challenges about our relationship with China over the coming years, and even decades, is that you can't categorize it, you can't put it in a box. China's future is still very much to be shaped' (2002). His conclusion leaves open the future, 'it seems almost certain that China is going to be more powerful, certainly on the trajectory that it's on. The question is to what end is that applied' (2002)? There is an inherent unknowability for the future, 'both Beijing and Washington have questions about one another whose answers simply cannot be known in advance', that is, 'time and experience will enable Beijing, for example, to assess American assurances that it is not determined to "hold China down" but instead welcomes its growing role on the world stage (as the architects of peaceful rise hope)' (Goldstein 2005: 218–19). In turn, only 'time and experience will also enable Washington to assess Chinese assurances that it is not the sort of dangerous challenger the United States needs to confront (as American advocates of containment warn)' but 'instead the sort of state whose interests and ambitions the United States can safely accommodate and with whom it can peacefully co-exist (as advocates of engagement assert)' (219).

This uncertainty is compounded by the constraints of theory. Mearsheimer argues that China's rise would not be peaceful, precisely and specifically on the grounds of IR power transition theory. Yet a look at theory reveals several theories. Friedberg's consideration of the simple yet crucial question 'is conflict inevitable' (2005) between China and America, makes the point that there are different positions able to be taken from different IR theories. IR liberalism optimists pinpoint economic interdependence, international institutions, democratisation; but IR liberalism pessimists bring out China as an authoritarian regime in transition, the United States as a crusading liberal democracy, and mutually damaging interactive effects. IR realism pessimists pinpoint China's power rise, China's expanding aims, and an intense security dilemma; but realism optimists focus on China's power as limited and likely to remain so, on China's aims as limited, the security dilemma as muted. IR constructivist optimists consider identities, strategic cultures, and norms as flexible and softening via institutional contact; but IR constructivist pessimists consider such perspectives as rigid and hardening via shocks and crises. Consequently, given such theoretical variation, 'the future character of the U.S.–China relationship is also profoundly uncertain' (225: 8) even if profoundly important.

'Grand Strategy' is evoked quite clearly by Wang Yiwei's analysis in the *Beijing Review*. Different time scales are involved for Wang, as 'right now China is keeping a low profile but preparing to do what it wants to do' (2004b: 23). This is because 'after the Cold War, especially after 9/11, the international structure stepped into a period of great adjustment' (25) of American pre-eminence where 'the United States is today's only superpower' (23). In the longer term, though, a further adjustment or structural change is working its way through the International System in which 'China is a rising power' (23). Thus a crucial part of Chinese policy is to get through the current transition period, of post-Cold War American pre-eminence, where 'this buildup period is expected to last for twenty years. According to a widely accepted estimation, by 2020 China will become the second largest economic entity after the United States' (25). This current transition period 'will be used by China to serve its grand strategy of peaceful rise ... to grasp the 20 year period of opportunity, winning time at the cost of ... a degree of [short-term] concession' (25), a transition strategy which 'is compatible with China's [longer-term] grand strategy and should have more potential in the future' (25) – a future where 'China will be tomorrow's world power' (23).

Chinese analysis confirms this approach. Consequently, a 'new official doctrine' as approved at the 16th Communist Party Congress in November 2002 is to focus on a '20-year period of strategic opportunities' (Wang Jisi 2004: 6) through concentrating on domestic priorities and, crucially, avoiding strategic confrontation between China and the United States. Whilst cultivating other bilateral and multilateral ties in the region, the Asia–Pacific and Central Asia, 'this strategic situation will give China enough breathing space to enhance its stature and influence' (17) within a world where American power was pre-eminent in the immediate context. Meanwhile, in effect, from a stronger domestic base China can then re-emerge in the longer term at some point.

In IR realism terms, there is 'a global power shift in the making' within which 'today, China is the most obvious power on the rise' (Hoge 2004: 2), 'long cycles' (Kennedy and Modelski 1987, Dark 1998) and change are at play for the international system. Talk of the twenty-first century being 'China's Century' reflects this possibility, based on power, perception and position – an opportunity for some, a threat to others, above all a challenge. China's rise will in all likelihood prove to be the story of the twenty-first century for the international system, to which we can turn.

9 The international system and China in the twenty-first century

It was a fitting coincidence that as this manuscript was being completed in September 2006, opinions polls carried out by Pew Research Center showed 'China's neighbors worry far more about the country's military resurgence than about its massive economic surge, international polling suggests' (PGAP 2006). China's presence is such in this 'power shift ... China's neighbours are increasingly looking to Beijing' (Shambaugh 2005: 23). As such, China's march to Great Power status, and perhaps pre-eminence, can now be followed through considering China's relations with its immediate neighbours, Russia, Japan and India, as well as its relationship with the leading state in the international system – the USA.

Sino–Russian relations for the twenty-first century

Two strands continue to be involved in China's relations with Russia in the first years of the twenty-first century, the 'local' imperatives of two adjacent states, as well as the 'central' imperatives of balancing against the United States. The year 2001 saw China and Russia sign a Treaty of Good Neighbourly Friendship and Cooperation, which somewhat glossed over their relationship by recording that it was 'based on the historical tradition of good neighbourly friendship between their two peoples'. Further border agreements in 2004 and 2005 finally established the 4,300-kilometer border, albeit in a twenty-year treaty framework.

From China's point of view three features dominate her local relations with Russia. First, geographical access for its Manchurian provinces to the Pacific through the Tumen river project, second, access to the Russian market in the Far Eastern centres, and third, access to Russian oil and gas reserves in the Siberian tundra. In all of these settings Russia presented economic opportunities and openings for the PRC. From Russia's point of view, her power vis-à-vis the PRC continues to weaken at the local level as her population further declined in the first decade of the century, as did the quantity and quality of her military forces.

Demographics continues to make its presence felt. One scenario, a 'reverse Manchuria', is where 'the Russian Far East remains a titular part of Russia but is increasingly integrated into Beijing's sphere of influence. That is precisely what the conspiracy among geography, demography, power and time may create in Russia's Far East' (Menon 2003: 102). The simultaneous decrease of the Russian Far East and the adjacent continuing growth of the already much greater Chinese population in Northeast China continues to gather pace, a 6.1 per cent decrease in the Russian population, 7.2 million down to 6.7 million was forecast against an 11.4 per cent increase in the Chinese population, 105.2 million up to 120 million between the start of 2000 and end of 2010 (Motrich 2001: Table 1), in which from a Russian perspective 'the atrophy of human capital is pervasive' (Thornton and Ziegler 2002: 99). At the national level, the situation was also stark. By 2003, China's population of 1,319 million had increased by 1.2 per cent over the previous year whereas Russia's population of 141 million had suffered a 1 per cent drop from the previous year.

Population issues and perceptions continue to be wrapped in the long enduring spectre of demographic 'invasion' (Radyuhin 2003), peaceful but an invasion none the less. In *Pravda*, a classic Yellow Perilist profile appeared from Valery Davydov, that Chinese emigrants were about 'to conquer Siberia', that in the Russian Far East Chinese already numbered 480,000 people in which 'the Russian population is gradually becoming the minority,' and where such a Chinese challenge 'does not concern only the military policy, it can be said about the demographic and migration policies too . . . it is obvious, the problem has already become serious' (2004). Outside observers commented on the economic penetration as well as growing demographic profile of the Chinese (Lintner 2006, Wall 2006).

Victor Larin's polling of attitudes in the summer of 2003 showed China 'had impressed itself deeply on the mindset of Russians facing that country' (2004: 22). Chinese migration remained a high profile issue for 'politicians, journalists and academics to rave about' (22), in which 'the subject is clothed in myth and charged with politics' (32) and 'engrained fears of "yellow peril" going deeper' (40). Amidst 'distorted conception' (35) of actual immigration figures, 'the perception entrenched firmly in the residents' minds of an ongoing Chinese expansion . . . which is deliberately planned and orchestrated from Beijing' (35), with 76 per cent of Khabarovsk residents and 58 per cent of Vladivostok seeing such Chinese expansion as a threat to Russia's territorial integrity. The most recent poll, in 2006, on the question of 'China's growing military power' found that whereas 95 per cent of Chinese thought it was a 'good thing', 76 per cent of Russians thought it a 'bad thing' (PGAP 2006: 2).

Territorial agreements between China and Russia were not necessarily seen as permanent. This was encapsulated in the local comment that 'no treaties will protect you from the Yellow Peril. You can have a treaty but in ten or twenty years the Far East and Siberia will be flooded with Chinese and we should prepare ourselves to say good-bye to Russian culture and civilization in those areas' (Lomanov 2001: 2). In Moscow, Vilya Gelbras's study of Chinese migration fused geopolitical and geocultural fears in the strongest terms. As to the territorial boundary dispute, theoretically solved in the 2001 Treaty between Russia and China, Gelbras was sceptical, arguing that the treaty wasn't necessarily a permanent long-term resolution since 'the fact is that the treaty is in force only for twenty years' (2002: 137), and asserting that 'ordinary Chinese who arrive in Russia have their own understanding of who is the real owner of the land they want to settle. Often they directly note that the territory will be returned to China' (137). Such geocultural trends were dramatic and telling. Economics becomes demography and in turn politics since 'Beijing states that it needs to conquer approximately 10 per cent of the international market . . . then all more or less developed countries of the world, including Russia, will face a new major challenge, a rapid growth of Chinese migration' (137).

In terms of geo-economics, the economic gap continues to widen in the PRC's favour. Continuing Russian decline and Chinese expansion gave China roughly four times the size of Russia's GDP by 2002, thereby giving the Chinese leadership 'access to considerably greater resources than its Russian counterpart, with correspondingly greater choices in the deliberation of foreign policy goals' (Wilson 2004: 196). Indeed, for Donaldson 'in the economic arena, Russia and China have experienced one of the most stunning reversals of economic position in recent years' (2003: 721 fn. 21), or indeed more accurately a reversion to China's Middle Kingdom glories of advancement over Russia and other periphery barbarian states!

Such geocultural and geoeconomic concerns are muffled to some extent by the high-level strategic alignment carried out between Beijing and Moscow, with their 1996 'strategic partnership' further consolidated. The last territorial disputes were finally resolved in 2004. Military arms sales continued to expand amidst talk of economic opportunities. At the diplomatic level Sino–Russian convergence was seen in their common positions over the Iraq war at the UN. The unprecedented joint military manoeuvres in Shandong in September 2005, the first of its kind, was widely noticed and understood in that context.

An unstated but evident enough attempt to rein in America's unipolar hegemony was apparent, 'this is where the "strategic partnership" comes into play on many matters, the two take similar stances . . . both countries favour democratization in international relations, a multi-polar world' (Pang Zhongying 2005). IR realism and balance of power undertones are apparent. In fact, earlier Pang had been even more explicit, that 'the two countries basically share the same views on principles governing international relations, which are opposite [to] that of the United States. That means that China and Russia are standing together against the United States in this regard' (Pang 2002). As such, 'China and Russia are jointly engaged in maintaining [the] global strategic balance . . . they encounter common pressure from the United States in many fields . . . their closer relations and cooperation will indeed help ease U.S. pressure' (Pang 2002).

Concerns, however, are discernible in Russian circles over China's geo-political presence and potential challenge to Russian interests. One sort of comment picked up about China by Alexander Lomanov was how 'they are arming and can become a military threat', with the Chinese military budget surpassing the Russian one in 2001 by some $4–5 billion as a sign of the 'growing militarization of China' (2001: 2). Some military analysts (e.g. Tsygichko and Pionkovskiy) have warned in recent years of China's military superiority and potential threat to Russia being muffled by considerations of diplomatic correctness, in which demographic pressures could push the PRC into threats against Russia. Admittedly other Russian military analysts (Klimenko and Lutovinov) disagree, instead stressing the advantages of political and strategic cooperation, in effect against the USA. However Russian military, and economic strength, as well as demographic presence, continues to weaken in the East. In such a vein, Yevgeny Bendersky sees Russia being elbowed out of the East by China and left with a 'secondary role in Eurasian affairs in the near future' (2004). Whilst their current strategic partnership does serve to partly counterbalance American strength, it also accentuates China's own growth vis-à-vis Russia where the 'Russia–China relationship favors Beijing' (2004). A stark picture of power imbalance had already emerged, where 'at present, the Chinese military is well equipped, better motivated, and well trained vis-à-vis its Russian counterpart' (2004). Indeed, 'a major open question is the extent to which Russia is currently willing to underwrite China's successful emergence as one of the world's foremost states', for 'as the Russian Federation sells high-tech military items south of its border, it is contributing to China's emergence as a powerful military force in Eurasia – a force that some day will have a chance to overshadow Russia's' (2004).

Uncertainties are present with the Sino–Russian relationship. As to its future, Bendersky is uncertain, 'how Russia will adapt to a possible second-ary role in Eurasian affairs in the near future is still an unanswered question, especially given . . . these two states may yet find themselves at odds over issues highly sensitive to both' (2004). Harsh Pant raises uncertainties over the Sino–Russian partnership, 'Russia has reasons to worry about China's rising profile in east and Northeast Asia and about Chinese immigrants overrunning the Russian Far East . . . it would take an enormous effort to avoid geo-political confrontation', and 'given the divergence between their geo-political and strategic national interests, it is anyone's guess as to how far Russia and China would be able to maintain the current positive trend in their relationship' (2005: 34–35).

Some Chinese sources are well aware of this longer-term ambiguity. Follow-ing Putin's trip to China in October 2004, the language of Wang Yiwei's article in the *Beijing Review* was revealing, namely that 'Putin got what Putin wanted from China, approval of a powerful state [China] for Russia's accession to the WTO' (Wang Yiwei 2004b: 23). Moreover, 'Russia and China also resolved their long-standing dispute over their 4,300-km-long border, somewhat in Russia's favour' (23). Interestingly, perceptions could raise their head here to as 'more generally, people in China have all kinds of misunderstandings and questions regarding Sino–Russian relations and are unwilling to agree with Putin that Sino–Russian relations are enjoying the best period in their history . . . naturally there is distrust between the two' (23). Here Wang Yiwei's analysis is to 'link the outcome to the fact that China is a rising power, while Russia is a declining empire' (23). As Jonathan Pollack puts it, the difference was that 'whereas Russia has a keen strategic awareness of what it has lost; China has a keen strategic awareness of what it has begun to acquire' (2002a: 56) as a Power on the rise. Returning to Wang Yiwei's analysis in the *Beijing Review*, he considers that 'the decline of Russia is not yet over' (2004b: 23). Looking to the future, 'Sino–Russian relations will reach a turning point. This build-up period is expected to last for twenty years . . . then asymmetric Sino–Russian relations will have to become a strategic partnership (which recognizes China's dominance) or it has to change' (25). His words 'China's dominance' are particularly striking. All this paints a picture of long-term strategic vision, where 'in terms of strategic position, China has the upper hand. The Sino–Russian partnership should be and will be used by China to serve its grand strategy of peaceful rise'; in which 'to grasp the 20 year period of opportunity, winning time at the cost of territory is the basic choice for China . . . a degree of [short-term] concession in Sino–Russian relations is compatible with China's [longer-term] grand strategy' (25) of rising past Russia. As Weede noted, with China and Russia one is indeed faced with the 'rise and fall of two nations' (2003) within a bilateral relationship, to the advantage of China and detriment of Russia. Ferguson's summation at the end of the 2006 G-8 summit is that 'Russia's only remaining card in Asia seems to be China, and we can only surmise just who is playing who in that bilateral tango' (2006: 1) (i.e. the PRC). At the time of writing, China is in the driving seat of their bilateral relationship, reversing almost 200 years of previous Russian-centred dynamics.

Sino–Japanese relations for the twenty-first century

Historical images and sensitivities still remain high, with the writing and re-writing of history, and matters of 'apologies' from the past remaining highly emotive issues between Japan and China, and indeed for Korea and others in the region (Yang Daqing 2002). Some PRC scholars recognised the 'psychological estrangements' and 'antagonism between the Chinese and Japanese nations' as the century started (Shi Yinhong 2002: 7).

Heated issues spill over the cultural-political divides, for example, the Zhao Wei clothes issue of 2001, the 'New Thinking' debate of 2003–4, the 'snub diplomacy' surrounding Chikage Ogi's trip to China in 2003, the student riots of 2003 and the rioting that broke out following Japan's victory over China in the Asia World Cup in 2004, and Zhang Ziyi's role in the film *Geisha* in 2006. The discovery of a Chinese nuclear submarine in Japanese waters in 2004, explained as a 'mistake' by China, further raised Japanese concerns. Meanwhile, Junichiro Koizumi's election as Prime Minister in April 2001 brought immediate visits to the Yasakuni war shrine that summer, visits that continued to spark demonstrations and vehement denunciations in China, and which saw an ongoing halt in summit meetings. Koizumi's explanation of his trip as a private individual matter of no concern to others was not accepted by China, especially as he kept making them each subsequent year 2002–6 during his tenure as Prime Minister. Already by 2002 Chinese analysts like Jiang Wenran were recognising that 'the bilateral strategic relationship is at its lowest point since the early 1970s', in which 'a dangerous dynamic of a bilateral threat perception is developing: both sides increasingly view the other as a potential national security threat' (2002: 153).

Understated but real signs of Japanese uncertainties over China, witting and unwitting testimony therein, are apparent in Koizumi's speech *The Future of Asia* that he delivered at the symposium on *Emerging China and the Changing Regional Framework* in 2002. There, in carefully crafted language, Koizumi asserts that 'as China has gained economic strength rapidly and acceded to the WTO there are people who regard China as a threat', so 'for China to play a role commensurate with its size in this region, it is essential that China respects universal values and the rules of the international community. At times we experience difficulties with China'. Japan's foreign minister, Taro Ase, was heard to describe China more bluntly as 'it's a neighboring country with nuclear bombs, and its military expenditure has been on the rise for 12 years. It's beginning to pose a considerable threat' (Associated Press 22 December 2005), an undiplomatic statement which drew immediate protests from Beijing.

Other political figures also emphasise the dangers from China. A former ambassador, Hisahiko Okazaki, apart from noting a military 'buildup driven by humiliation' sees it as meaning a 'China threat only a matter of time . . . it is only a matter of time before the issue of China's emerging military strength will have to be confronted head-on' (2005). Shintaro Ishihara, the popular author and Mayor of Tokyo, drew attention to China's challenge to Japan and the region with his 'questions about the rising giant' (2005), where 'Asia is facing a crisis of greater severity than that seen during the cold war due to China's insistence on hegemony' (2005), and where 'the government is inciting a dangerous kind of nationalism in order to divert public frustration' (2005). The ironical thing was that Beijing uses virtually identical language about Japan! Koizumi's replacement in September 2006 as Prime Minister, Shinzo Abe had an even more hawkish confrontational background; with Abe's newly appointed Defence Chief, Fumio Kyuma causing a small furore by immediately labelling China's military growth as a 'threat' (AFP 2006) to Japan on his first day in office. All this is in addition to territorial disputes over isles and waters, economic friction, and continuing power rivalry between two powers 'rising simultaneously' and with 'uncertainty over one another's strategy' (Yang Bojiang 2006).

All in all, Gries sees a 'new chapter . . . second wave' (2005b: 848) overriding the earlier 1990s anti-Americanism, widely disseminated through a virulent web-based 'Internet nationalism' *wangluo minzuzhuyi*, whereby 'Chinese hatred of Japan still runs deep, and given that Japanese nationalism is also emerging, things don't bode well for 21st century Sino–Japanese relations' (832). Psychological factors remain a 'root cause' (Hu Jintao 2006) for their poor relationship. In short, 'today, at the onset of the 21st century, Chinese animosity towards Japan is unquestionably out of control' (Gries 2005b: 849; also Gries 2005c). Whereas over half of the Japanese polled in 2002 viewed China positively, by 2006 it had virtually halved to 28 per cent, the Chinese figure being an even lower 21 per cent. Opinion polls in 2006 found that 'negative characteristics' and 'antipathy' still predominated, 'in particular both countries consider each other competitive, greedy and arrogant' (PGAP 2006: 3).

Their respective nationalisms have become a two way process, emerging from behind the shadow of China's post-war Communist ideology and Japan's post-war effacing pacifism. Instead 'not only do the growing nationalistic sentiments in Japan and China mirror each other, but they are also fuelling each other, with identical political consequences: leaders in both countries are trying to ride on the tides of nationalism' (Huang 2005: 5; also Chellaney 2006). In effect 'this has enabled nationalistic sentiments to hijack both leaderships' (Huang 2005: 5), as Japanese leaders use nationalism to increase popularity and PRC leadership uses it to maintain domestic political legitimacy. Something of a security dilemma is in play, as each nationalism becomes more affronted by the other, indeed with the other state portrayed and perceived as the antagonistic 'Other'.

The moves towards Japanese re-armament, already discernible in the 1990s were quickened in the following decade, where 'Japan may talk a lot about the dangers of North Korea, but the real objective of its rearmament is China' (Johnson 2005). Japan's defence links with the United States were also further strengthened in 2002 and 2005 with their *Common Strategic Objectives* and *Transformation and Realignment for the Future* (Japan–USA 2005) agreements. Given the rise of China, it was no surprise to also see classic IR balancing tactics at play in Japan's convergence with India, from China's point of view an increasing encirclement of her. As the Japanese Foreign Minister put it, when visiting India in 2003, 'ever-closer cooperation on the security and defence front is crucial for both Japan and India . . . both countries share common interests and concerns regarding these issues' (Kawaguchi 2003). The Indian commentator, with reason, considered that 'while Ms. Kawaguchi did not spell out what the rest of the shared agenda was, it is not difficult to figure out – China', where 'India and Japan, as wary neighbours of a rising China, have great interest in exchanging thoughts on where Beijing's military modernisation and security philosophy are headed' (Mohan 2003).

Sino–Indian relations for the twenty-first century

If the twenty-first century is seeing the rise of China, it is also seeing the rise of India. For many, India is becoming a credible rival to China and for some a credible partner. In part it is a matter of size as a neighbour, where India's 2003 population of 1,067 million enables it to match that of China's 1,319 million; unlike Russia's 141 million, Japan's 141 million and Australia's 20 million. Moreover, India's population growth is higher than China's, and likely to overtake China's population in the next few decades.

'Power and population' (Eberstadt 2004) are in play with such demographic projections. Power and perceptions are also intermixed, in which 'the dominant *Gestalt* dominant among both Chinese and Chinese analysts is an image of competition and rivalry' (Garver 2002: 264). Both countries are on the rise; indeed Ching Ch'ien-peng argues that 'even if the territorial dispute were resolved, India and China would still retain a competitive relationship in the Asia–Pacific region, being as they are, two Asiatic giants aspiring to Great Power status' (2004: 117). Similarly Gu Xuewu argues that 'this simultaneous quest for power . . . on the same continent, at the same time . . . makes competition for political, diplomatic, military and economic resources on an international scale inevitable' (2003: 173). Meanwhile at the popular level, despite some glossing official rhetoric, there are still 'particularly dangerous . . . psychological estrangements' (Shi Yinhong 2002: 7) and antagonism at play between the Chinese and Indian nations. Three complicating features remain. One is their territorial dispute, the cause of war in 1962, and far from resolved in 2006. Second is their status as rising powers with geopolitical interests that often clash. Third is their mutual encirclement strategies, which cause classic IR security dilemma escalation. A nuclear arms race also adds a competitive spiral element to their relationship, following India's 1998 nuclear explosions.

The PRC's response to India has been twin-tracked in the twenty-first century. On the one hand, there have been continuing attempts to reach accommodation with India. China's own Great Power concerns and regional reassurance diplomacy have seen her stressing win-win economic cooperation with India. Atal Vajpayee's visit of 2003 was reciprocated by Wen Jiabao's return visit of 2005. Both Chinese and Indian sources in the political and media spheres are ready to forecast the twenty-first century as an 'Asian Century' based on the twin driving power of China's and India's economies. Both India and China extol the desirability of multipolarity. Indeed Wen Jiabao's trip to India in April 2005 saw official agreement between the two states to establish a China–India Strategic and Cooperative Partnership for Peace and Prosperity, a development noticed with enthusiasm in China (Zhao Huanxin 2005) but with an edge of concern in the United States (Lancaster 2005). A formal Sino–Indian 'strategic dialogue' mechanism was set up later on in the year. Such broad political engagement was mirrored with some military engagement, a *Memorandum of Understanding* being drawn up in 2006 over military confidence boosting measures.

However, balancing and containment has been, and remains, a feature of relations between India and the PRC. India's rise, and the issues at dispute between the PRC and India, meant in 2001 that 'China may feel highly vulnerable in its relationship with India' (Li Nan 2001: 41). Li's 'may' has become reality, overturning Susan Shirk's comment, that 'the Chinese really do not see India as any kind of strategic threat to China' (2002: 109). Shirk's dismissal of the India factor for China has become dated in view of India's continuing rise, India's closer alignments with Japan and the USA, India's encirclement strategies towards the PRC, and the PRC's own encirclement strategy towards India. Both sea and land avenues are present in 'China's strategy of containing India' (M. Malik 2006), as also in India's mirror strategy towards China (Batabyal 2006), amidst their developing 'Great Game' and IR security dilemma dynamics.

On land, China's 'unprecedented' (Mahapatra 2005) military build-up in Tibet poses a direct and immediate military threat for India. China's occupation of Tibet gives China strategic depth and a potential offensive platform against India from its Himalayan heights, able to be realised with her construction of highway and railway, 'China's strategic masterstroke' (Borah 2006) infrastructure and installation of various missile systems weapons. These missile systems are irrelevant to quelling domestic discontent inside Tibet, but do point towards the north Indian heartland, the capital Delhi and other major Indian cities like Calcutta. Indian analysts are acutely aware of these implications. Such 'power projection' makes 'India vulnerable to Chinese pressure' (Singh 2006: 21). For Mahapatra this is 'not only aimed at overwhelming India militarily, but to enable Chinese coercive diplomacy in respect of the border dispute . . . [and] triple the PLA's offensive power against India' (2005). Installation of medium range ballistic missiles lets the PRC immediately and easily threaten India, whereas the main centres of China, Beijing, Shanghai, Guangzhou remain far away from India. As Bhartendu Singh puts it, 'the strategic challenges must not be overlooked . . . Imagine a scenario where China penetrates a Maoist-led Nepal and makes deep inroads into the Indo-Gangetic plains' (2006: 20).

At sea, China's 'expanding maritime ambitions' in the western Pacific and the Indian Ocean (Lee Jae-hyung 2002), her 'oceanic offensive' (Smita 2005) brings her right around India's eastern, southern and western flanks. Since 1999 Chinese naval vessels have been making calls at Singapore, Malaysia, Pakistan and South Africa, all part of what Vijay Sakhuja calls 'Chinese creeping assertiveness in the Indian Ocean' (2006: 33) to test its strategic reach. China's 'string of pearls' (Mohan 2005) policy saw links with Myanmar and Bangladesh strengthened, moves to establish a base in the Maldives, more blue water operations and links with Pakistan reaching new heights.

Partly, this was a question of further land links, with Pakistan envisaged as an energy corridor for China, enabling vital oil imports to flow from the

Middle East by-passing India, and solving China's 'Malacca [Straits] dilemma' (Storey 2006) of being choked and controlled by India and the US. Partly, it was a question of China pledging vital support and financial funding in 2001 for Pakistan's Gwadar deep-water port project. This was started in 2002, with its phase-1 set for completion in late 2006. Its strategic importance for Sino–Indian relations is that it can provide long range berths for Chinese naval units, serving as 'China's naval outpost on the Indian Ocean' (Niazi 2005), and a crucial 'pearl' (Ramachandran 2005; Chaturvedy 2006) in China's Grand Strategy of power projection. Such Chinese projection literally, and strategically, cuts across India's own 'Mahanian visions' for making the Indian Ocean India's Ocean.

From India's point of view, as this century opened, *The Hindu* newspaper (22 April 2001) judged that 'one of the major policy challenges for India in the 21st Century will be to respond to China as a growing economic and military super power'. Chinese sources do recognise India's doubts about China, 'by and large, in India, there is no doubt about the "rise of China", but there are doubts about the "*peaceful* rise of China" . . . the resolution of bilateral issues and the establishment of trust still have a long way to go' (Zhang Guihong 2005: 163, 159). India's perceptions cover a spectrum, appeasement, 'containment-cum-encirclement policy' and 'balanced engagement' (Zhang Guihong 2006: 93). Whilst economics has given appeasers, or co-operators the most room, security and military issues have generated these 'containment-cum-encirclement' strategies by India. In effect a hedging policy has been followed, engagement but also balancing against the PRC in various ways. After all the PRC remains 'India's principal long-time adversary in Asia, China' (Nayar and Paul, 2003: 209). In short, 'fears and misgivings' (Ganguly 2002) are evident for India concerning the rise of China in Asia. Consequently, and faced with encirclement from China, India also has been attempting some de facto encirclement of China of her own, and some balancing with others against China: 'India's response is a good example of how China's buildup is already eliciting counterbalancing responses around her periphery' (Waldron 2005: 723; also Batabyal 2006).

On land, India has jumped over China's strategic proxy Pakistan. The fall of the Taliban brought in a friendly pro-Indian government, whilst still further north on China's borders, an 'Indian military shadow over Central Asia' (Maitra 2002) was apparent as Tajikistan gave India airforce facilities at Farkhor and then Ayni, and India become a land base player in the Great Game opening up in Central Asia (Ramachandran 2006), alongside and if need be across China. Military links established between India and Mongolia in 2005, 'to counter China' (Chaube 2006), completes this picture.

At sea, Indian ships have been patrolling the Malacca Straits since 2002, highlighting Chinese concerns over secure access to oil supplies in times of trouble. Indian naval units have been deployed into the South China Sea in 2000, 2003, 2004 and 2005 for bilateral and unilateral operations. China's concerns have been evident at various points, 'world powers such as . . . India have increased their military infiltration in the South China Sea regions, pushing the issue towards a more complicated and internationalized level. The situation allows no room for optimism' over China's undisturbed hegemony in these waters (*Outlook East Weekly* 2004). An initial India–Vietnam defence agreement in 1994 was further strengthened by a joint protocol on defence cooperation in March 2000, which includes sharing of strategic threat perceptions and intelligence, 'convergence of interests' (Kapila 2001) with an 'encircle-and-contain-China thrust' (Srinivasan 2000). Naval exercises between India and Vietnam in 2000, not surprisingly, drew protests from China. Meanwhile discussions have taken place on naval berthing rights for Indian ships, possibly at Cam Ranh deep-water bay. In the 1980s this had been a Soviet base and the scene for Chinese fears of encirclement. Its possible use by the Indian Navy reawakens such fears for the PRC. Japan's naval operations with India in the Indian Ocean are matched by naval operations between India and Japan in East Asian waters facing China. The first ever joint Indian–Chinese naval operation off Shanghai in November 2003 does not negate the much larger naval rivalry at play, in which India's navy, including aircraft carriers, which the PRC did not have, is the stronger.

However, asymmetrical perceptions are at play, China seeing India as fairly unimportant in its calculations, whereas China looms much larger for Indian analysts. India can feel itself slighted or downgraded by Chinese commentators. Yan Xuetong's analysis of 'China's foreign policy towards Major Powers' discusses 'other major powers' in the shape of the USA, Russia, Europe and Japan, but ignores India (2002). On the one hand 'Indians tend to be deeply apprehensive regarding China. Chinese, on the other hand, tend not to perceive a serious threat and find it difficult to understand why Indians might find China and its actions threatening' (Garver 2003a: 109). In part, this has an element of deliberate Chinese propaganda and media projection and manipulation, downgrading of possible threat situations so as to legitimize its own gains in the meantime over Tibet and elsewhere, through maintaining a rosy tinted status quo. In part, though, this reflects the real situation of India being less of a threat to China than China is to India, both in terms of India's relatively inferior economic and military strength vis-à-vis China and in terms of India's sparser network of local allies in comparison to China. China's projection into South Asia has been more substantial than India's projection into China's backyards of Southeast Asia and Central Asia, though India was becoming more noticeable there in the first decade of the twenty-first century.

An important factor in the Sino–Indian relationship is India's relations with other powers, in which an IR balancing against China is discernible. Indian convergence towards Japan has already been noted. Similar convergence with the United States is also taking place, with shared concerns over China. Indeed Beijing is well aware of these balancing moves against it.

Even as some modest economic links were reopened between Tibet and northern India in July 2006, it was still noticed by the PRC sources how 'current China-India bilateral relations show some tension . . . The United States and Japan are big powers . . . both countries are trying to prop up and engage India, which has led to more complicated and delicate relations between China and India' (Zhang Lijun 2006b: 12). This is why, whereas China's concerns over India 'mainly refer to strategic constellations [India's balancing with other powers] and thereby to a relatively abstract level, Indian perceptions of threat seem to be much more concrete and precise' (Gu Xuewu 2003: 175), territorial and military issues.

Indian convergence with the United States, amidst common concerns over China, became apparent during 2005–6. Incoming US Secretary of State, Condoleezza Rice, had already pointed out common concerns with India over China as a threatening 'competitor' for both, 'India is an element in China's calculation and it should be in America's too. India is not a great power yet, but it has the potential to emerge as one', thus making India's co-option alongside America against China all the more useful (2000: 56). Whilst China denounced US plans to create its National Missile Defence system, dubbed 'son of Star Wars', India gave it enthusiastic support. Post-9/11, Indo–American military links were established. Following Fernandes's trip to Washington in 2002, joint US–Indian naval exercises took place in the Malacca Straits drawing unease from Chinese sources about India wanting to be 'the international maritime police' (Qian Feng 2002). Joint defence links and agreements were drawn up in summer 2005, followed by Bush's presidential trip in spring 2006, with India's place as a Great Power, and a democratic one unlike the PRC, openly and explicitly accepted by the USA.

Amidst this Indo–American security convergence, a 'China factor' (Cherian 2006, Zhang Lijun 2006a: 13) remains discernible for Indian and Chinese analysts. Chinese analysts see the 'dramatic . . . implications for China' (Zhang Guihong 2005: 277) of the US–India strategic partnership, with India 'used by the United States as a "card" for balancing China . . . a potential counterbalance to growing Chinese influence' (287, 290) in South Asia and the Asia-Pacific'. The *People's Daily* headlined developments as 'Washington draws India in against China' (7 July 2005). In Beijing, this is why Zhang Lijun thinks 'most importantly, India is the best bet to restrict a future strong China, as per U.S. regional strategy in Asia' (2006a: 14). The 'Great Game' (Scott n.d) between India and China, and their encirclement of each other, overlaps with the other Great, or perhaps even Greater Game between China and the United States. As Zhang Guihong notes the 'US–India strategic partnership in South Asia and the Indian Ocean, and US–Japan military alliance in east Asia and west Pacific Ocean are two major concerns for China in the new big power games in the Asia-Pacific region' (2005: 290). This takes us to the state of play in Sino–US relations.

Sino–American relations for the twenty-first century

Amongst various bilateral relationships that between the United States and China will probably turn out to be the single most important one, both for themselves (Saunders 2000b: 64, J. Roy 2005: 14) and indeed for the world (Roy 2003: 125, Mahbubani 2005: 49, Kissinger 2005). It is thus given more space here. Their relationship has grown beyond immediate regional matters, as China's leader notes 'China-US relations have gone far beyond the bilateral context and become increasingly global in nature' (Hu Jintao 2006; also Rice 2002).

Distrust of the US is apparent, 'many Chinese still view the United States as a major threat to their nation's security and domestic stability' (Deng Yong 2005: 39). However, the US remains too strong to directly take on in conflict (Ness 2002). Moreover, China's Dengist parameters are still valid, so that 'China, therefore, must maintain a close relationship with the United States if its modernization efforts are to succeed. Indeed, a cooperative partnership with Washington is of primary importance to Beijing, where economic prosperity and social stability are now top concerns' (Deng Yong 2005: 39), both for China's rise as a nation and for PRC regime survival. However, alongside a degree of bandwagoning cooperation, 'China continues to pursue more limited strategies to curb U.S. power' through 'bargaining, binding, and buffering' (Gries 2005d: 407). Power and perceptions give an ironical outcome as 'both Washington and Beijing, in other words, frequently treat each other as giant Gullivers to be tied down by tiny Lilliputians' (408).

Strategic uncertainties continue. As Kissinger puts it, 'the relationship between the United States and China is beset by ambiguity', in which 'attitudes are psychologically important' (2005). Conversely, 'if one were to name a single metric by which the Chinese government judges itself, it would be the United States. Of course Chinese fascination and rivalry with the United States are in part reciprocated by an irrational US romanticism about China' (Waldron 2005: 728). In terms of the 'identity and conflict in Sino–American relations' (Gries 2006), IR security dilemma and constructivism concerns are discernible, 'cooperative actions by one side have often been viewed as noncooperative behavior by the other' (Johnston 2003: 53). On the one hand 'there is scepticism among some Chinese analysts about even relatively benign U.S. overtures', but on the other hand 'American concerns about the potential malevolence of China's intentions in the region have translated into concrete military and political steps to hedge against Chinese power'; but then 'China picks up these hedging signals and interprets them in malign ways . . . as more sinister and less driven by uncertainty than its proponents in the United States claim' (53).

The PRC is reluctant, with the exception of Taiwan, to take the USA on directly (Wang Jisi 2005), though its charm diplomacy in Asia enables something of a 'Gulliver strategy' for restraining the US through various multilateral restrictions and constraints' (2, 3). A point continually made to reassure such neighbours was that America's actual quantitative strength and network of alliance bases and facilities was far greater than anything China yet had in the military field (*People's Daily* 2005b). However, it is precisely because the 'US military lead is so great' (Foot 2006: 89; also Sutter 2004: 1), and because of the PRC's focus on longer-term economic modernisation, that Foot considers China's strategy in a US hegemonic world order to be one of 'accommodating and hedging' with their being 'little substance' (89) to fears of China directly challenging US military power.

Yet, the US has its own concerns about a rising China (Pan 2004); typified in *China's Growing Military Power* (Scobell and Wortzel 2002), and Sutter's perception that 'China remains the sole large power today building an array of more modern military forces to attack Americans' (2003: 1; also Christensen 2001). China as 'the forgotten nuclear power' (Roberts and Manning 2000, cf. Wang Mei-ling 1998, Nathan and Tien 2003) is more noticeable as other Great Powers reduce their arsenals. Outer space is a field of competition (McCabe 2003; Murray and Antonellis 2003), with the Rumsfeld Commission report seeing 'a space Pearl Harbor' (USA 2001: viii–ix) threat posed by China's emerging presence in space (xiv), and in which 'the prevailing assessments in Beijing and Washington are notable for their unmistakable apprehension of each other' (Martel and Yoshihara 2003: 24). China's ASAT breakthrough in January 2007 exacerbates this. Economics also comes into the picture, as with the U.S.–China Security Review Commission's 2002 *The National Security Implications of the Economic Relationship between the United States and China* and its warning over trade and investment patterns. As Denny Roy notes 'China's rapid economic development raises the prospect of a serious PRC–U.S. rivalry, with global ramifications comparable to last century's Cold War' (D. Roy 2003: 125).

Behind the military and economic frictions lay structural dynamics between a rising Power, the PRC, and an established Power, the USA (Haass 2005; also Russ Munro 2000). IR theory can be troubling, Gilpin's *system governance thesis*, Organski and Kugler's *power transition thesis* (cf. Steve Chan 1999: 208–9), Waltz's *balance of power* framework, Jervis's *security dilemma* logic, Doyle's *democratic peace thesis*, neo-liberalist *functionalist* focus on the weak international institutions in the Asia–Pacific, all 'point in the same troubling direction' (A. Goldstein 2003: 59) of competition and potential conflict. China's rise can be causally juxtaposed with a consequent American fall, for Wang Yiwei 'the United States is today's only superpower and China will be tomorrow's world power' (2004b: 23). The stakes are rightly and starkly summed up by Garver, 'history is replete with confrontations between incumbent paramount powers and rising aspirant powers . . . one over-arching question we face as the twenty-first century unfolds before us is whether Sino–American relations will replay this bloody, costly drama of confrontation' (1999: xi). In structural terms American policy makers are very sensitive to the PRC, 'the most credible prospective rival to the United States in the decades to come' (Pollack 2002a: 53), with 'China's challenge to *Pax Americana*' (Feigenbaum 2001b; also 2001a). In geopolitical terms, Robert Ross had argued for geopolitical stability for the twenty-first century, whereby Chinese land hegemony in continental East Asia was balanced by an American maritime hegemony in the Pacific, with neither being able or wanting to penetrate to the other's core areas (1999). However, post-2001 saw US land forces appearing in continental Asia. In turn, China edges out in the Pacific 'the American lake', to try to establish its own 'command of the sea' (Holmes and Yoshihara 2005b).

The new George W. Bush administration 2001–8 came into office signalling a shift away from Clinton's attempts at 'constructive strategic partnership' and engagement. Condoleezza Rice came into her post as NSC advisor arguing 'China is a rising power . . . a strategic competitor, not the "strategic partner" the Clinton administration once called it' (Rice 2000: 55–6). Sino–American relations plummeted in the wake of the April 2001 spy plane incident, where American and Chinese fighter planes bumped into each other over the South China Sea coast off China, in disputed airspace. The Chinese pilot was killed as his plane crashed, with the American plane having to force land on Chinese soil, there to face detention of its crew, the dismantling of the American plane and tortuous negotiations over their return and over the form of words to use over the incident. Chinese opinion was furious, but it also gave the new administration and the American public grounds for 'seeing China as enemy' (Pfaff 2001). In this 'event full of symbolism' (Yu Zhang 2005: 77), Chinese nationalism was in the forefront with images of earlier humiliations coming to the surface, though American containment proponents like Kagan and Kristol saw the events as 'a national humiliation' (Kagan and Kristol 2001a, 2001b) for the USA. American readiness to use the word 'regret' rather than offer an 'apology' caused friction and was a veritable East–West 'culture clash' (Gries and Peng 2002) within the dynamics of this 'apology diplomacy' (174).

Ambiguities and uncertainties continued to surface under Bush's presidency, 'one administration, two voices' (Jia Qingguo 2005b), divided between the softer 'engagement' RED team approach typified by Powell, and the harder 'containment' BLUE team approach (Waller 2001) represented by Defence Secretary Donald Rumsfeld and Paul Wolfowitz. However, the destruction of New York's Twin Towers by al-Qaeda operatives in September 2001 (9/11), to some extent brought in a 'new era' (Lowell 2002) where 'the eerie normalcy of Sino–American relations in the aftermath of the 9/11 attacks constitutes one of the unanticipated consequences of those events' (Pollack 2003: 617). Jiang Lingfie, in the *Beijing Review*, noted with some relief that the new 'Islamic Threat' replaced the 'China Threat' in American eyes, so that the conflict between the US and China was 'no longer the most important confrontation in the world', it had 'altered U.S. judgement of where the threat comes from, and also changed [its] attitude regarding China as the real strategic opponent, thus easing the tension in Sino–U.S.

relations' (2002: 7–8). China's 9/11 support of America, it's 'about face' (Eckholm 2001), led it to seek consensus with the USA, in part through common concerns over Islamic fundamentalism (Pollack 2002b).

The visit of the new Chinese Premier, Wen Jiabao, to Washington in December 2003 saw Bush using the term 'partner in diplomacy' (Dobbs 2003, Sanger 2003) to describe a re-established Sino–American relationship. China could feel more secure as 'China Threat' perceptions of the 1990s receded. As Secretary of State Powell noted 'the September 11 attacks led us to shuffle priorities' (2004: 32). However, Malik sees such post-9/11 improvement in China's position as 'minor, and transitory in nature' (2002: 23). He argues that 'no other major power has been as much affected by the geopolitical shifts unleashed by the U.S. counter offensive [against 'international terrorism'] as China,' whereby 'if China was on a roll prior to 9/11, in a complete reversal of roles post 9/11, it is now the United States that is on a spectacular roll' (30). This brought 'lurking fears of American encirclement and containment of China – a hot topic among Chinese strategists and foreign policy analysts' (28; also Austin 2002). PRC voices argued 'the new US cold war approach towards China remains unchanged ... Sept.11 has not changed the nature of international relations in the East Asia region. The war on anti-terrorism has not changed the balance of power in East Asia', for 'as long as the rising trend of Chinese economic and military strength persists, the conflict between China and the new American imperialists could prove to be a long story' (Pang Zhongying 2002; also Zhai Kun 2002: 9, Gu Xuewu 2003: 177) in the twenty-first century. The profile by the veteran politician Qian Qichen 'U.S. strategy to be blamed' was clear, 'the United States has tightened its control of the Middle East, Central Asia, Southeast Asia and Northeast Asia' (2004), and was a threat to China. Immediately commented on in US State Department briefings (USA 2004), it was quickly taken off the Internet archives by an embarrassed PRC leadership (Stockwin 2004).

The *National Security Strategy of the United States* report, submitted to US Congress by President Bush on 27 September 2002, reflects the post-9/11 ambiguities between the US and China. On the one hand, it claims 'we welcome the emergence of a strong, peaceful and prosperous China' (Bush 2002: 27). On the other hand it warns 'in pursuing advanced military capabilities that can threaten its neighbors in the Asia-Pacific region, China is following an outdated path that, in the end, will hamper its own pursuit of national greatness' (27). As always, Chinese sources have been quick to respond. For Pang Zhongying 'China perceives this comment as a warning to itself' (2002a). American sources are ready to point to China's challenge to the USA. The Pentagon's *Military Power of the People's Republic of China* became mandatory annual reports after 2000, with China highlighted on a regular basis (e.g. USA 2002), and generating ongoing immediate PRC rebuttals (e.g. Ren Yujun 2002, Zhan Yan 2003a, 2003b). Deng Xiaoping's 1990s maxim for China to 'hide our capabilities and bide our time' was repeatedly invoked (USA 2002: 7; 2003: 12) as indicating deliberate 'strategic ambiguity, including strategic denial and deception . . . a mechanism to influence the policies of foreign governments and the opinions of the general public and elites in other countries' (USA 2002: 8) and 'a long-term strategy to build up China's CNP with a view to maximizing China's options in the future' (USA 2003: 12). In other words 'China may thus be planning for the day when it feels more able to contest American strategic predominance' (Pollack 2002a: 61). The *US–China Security Review Commission* report of summer 2002 was another public call. It was welcomed by commentators like Tom Donnelly, Senior Fellow at the influential *Project for the New American Century*, as 'China without illusions . . . Washington wakes up to Beijing's intentions' (2002); though one of its members, William Reinsch, a Clinton figure, lamented that the majority report 'adds to the paranoia about China' (Reinsch 2002).

Powell's replacement as Secretary of State, Condoleezza Rice, recognises, even if not necessarily welcoming, China's arrival, 'China is a very important – I used to say emerging power, but I'll say emerged power' (2005) that the US couldn't ignore. However as 9/11 recedes 'attention has returned to the military and economic rise of China and the challenges to American security' (Ross 2005: 81; also Menges 2005). In this climate, Shambaugh notes 'there has been a notable shift in Sino–American mutual imagery in recent years', a 'shift . . . towards the hardening of negative and demonized images in both countries . . . a predominantly disapproving and critical set of mutual perceptions' (2003: 236). In the public domain 'positive perceptions of the other are rarely articulated, and have been increasingly replaced by strong inventive and mutual demonization in the national media and specialist publications in each country' (236).

Such perceptions are perhaps discernible in the *Atlantic Monthly* cover backdrop of Chinese military on a warship, with a brooding menacing, indeed rather demonic-eyed, Chinese sailor in the foreground. Inside was Robert Kaplan's hard hitting, and widely reported blunt nine-page article, 'How we would fight China'. Kaplan argues 'the Middle East is just a blip. The American military contest with China in the Pacific will define the twenty-first century. And China will be a more formidable adversary than Russia ever was' (2005b: 49; also 2005a). Fundamental geo-politics are involved, 'in the coming decades China will play an asymmetric back-and-forth game with us in the Pacific' in which 'the result is likely to be the defining military conflict of the twenty-first century: if not a big war with China, then a series of Cold War-style standoffs that stretch out over years and decades' (49, 51). Kaplan was rubbished by Thomas Barnett as doing a 'strategic lap dance for the U.S. Navy and Pacific Command . . . amazed the magazine printed it, its that bad' (2005b). Alongside Kaplan, the *Atlantic Monthly* issue for June 2005 contained the two-page argument by Benjamin Schwarz, 'Managing China's rise'. He argues that 'the United States, however, has such a jump on Beijing in its command, control, communications, computer, and intelligence capabilities' that 'American strategic supremacy in East Asia will grow, not diminish, in the coming years' (2005: 28; cf. Corpus 2006 for threat of Chinese asymmetrical warfare strategies). Talk of China's naval threat is to 'exaggerate' (Schwarz 2005: 27). However, Kaplan's article got the larger treatment and probable impact.

Rumsfeld famously raised the question of China's intentions and secretiveness (2005a, 2005b), and initiated a radical shift during 2005–6 of military resources from the Atlantic and Europe into the Pacific to face China. The shift of military resources to Guam in 2005–6, and the VALIANT SHIELD and RIMPAC exercises off Guam and Hawaii in 2006 sent a clear warning message to China of American power projection for the region. This was acknowledged as a hedging insurance against a bellicose China, ironical given China's own hedging strategy against the USA (Small 2005: 37–46). During 2006, the US *Quadrennial Report* considered that 'of the major and emerging powers, China has the greatest potential to compete militarily with the United States' (USA 2006b: 29) with their annual *Military Power of the People's Republic of China* report immediately noting China's 'rapid rise' and echoing Rumsfeld's own words, asking 'why these continuing large and expanding arms purchases? Why these continuing robust deployments?' (USA 2006a: 1) by China. America's military links with Japan, Australia and India were all tightened up in 2005–6, a hedging and containment strategy that had China in mind. For Klare these events were a 'momentous shift', a 'revving up the China Threat' in which 'the pendulum has now swung toward the anti-Chinese, prepare for war position' (2005). By Summer 2006 alliance adjustments and force deployments were apparent, 'the grand strategy of the Bush administration . . . the containment of China', which Klare thought might trigger further attempts by China to catch up, further US justification for accelerating containment policies, and so on, 'a self-fulfilling loop of distrust, competition and crisis' (2006).

China's military spending hit the headlines in Spring 2006 as the PRC announced an increase of 14.7 per cent to 283.8 billion yuan or $35.3 billion. It was the percentage rate that caught the headlines in the USA. However China's response was one of reassurance, her ambassador at Washington stressing 'I want to emphasize the point that China's peaceful development poses and will pose no threat to any other country . . . China pursues a national defense policy of a defensive nature', for 'as our economy grew in recent years, there had been appropriate increase on the defense expenditure, most of which was used to increase pay and allowances for the troops', and 'only a small percentage was spent on additional equipments' (Zhou Wenzhong 2005). He also makes the comparative point that 'China's defense expenditure, per capita or total, is much lower than any of the other major country in the world. The total for 2004 was about 27.5 billion U.S. dollars, which is only 5.77% of that of the U.S.' (2005). The Pentagon reckoned that Chinese figures were only half to one-third of their real level, that is, c. $50– 80 billion, but even that was still much less than the American budget of

$450 billion dollars in 2006. Moreover American budget increases had generally risen higher than China's in percentage terms over recent years. Indeed the tactic of running the Soviet Union into the ground by ramping up defence spending, which the USSR was eventually unable to match, has been suggested in some American circles as part of a 'prepare to fight' strategy.

American commentators continue to disagree with each other over China's intents and America's future. Mearsheimer continues to argue that the PRC poses a military threat to the US, that conflict is virtually inevitable, and that the US should carry out containment policies (2001a, 2005; also Boot 2005, cf. Nye 2006). Yet, in *Foreign Policy*'s 'Clash of the titans' Zbigniew Brzezinski's advocacy of engagement was counterpoised with Mearsheimer's advocacy of containment, Marshier's sense that it was 'better to be Godzilla than Bambi', and his recognition that 'the United States does not tolerate peer competitors' (Brzezinski and Mearsheimer 2005; also Steve Chan 2004: 130). In such a vein Max Boot, senior fellow at the Council on Foreign Relations, argues not only for external containment but also for deliberate 'internal subversion . . . American technology should be used to crack open, not cement, the authority of the Communist party' (2005: 39), sentiments guaranteed to feed negative images of America in the PRC leadership. Hardliners in America are matched by hardliners in the PRC. American eyebrows were raised in 2005 as Major General Zhu Chenghu raised the prospect of China abandoning its no first use of nuclear weapons policy, threatening that 'if the Americans are determined to interfere [in Taiwan], then we will be determined to respond . . . the Americans will have to be prepared that hundreds of [US] cities will be destroyed by the Chinese' (Kahn 2005).

In parallel with military strategic considerations are economic considerations, a basic point underpinning Stephen King's 'How Big a Threat to West is Growth of China?' (2004). Chinese attempts to buy up the Californian oil company, Unocal, raised alarm bells in Washington (Mallaby 2005). China's trade surplus with the USA continues to increase, the largest bilateral imbalance in the world. About 70–80 per cent of China's ballooning foreign exchange reserves, currently valued at just over $1 trillion are held in $dollars, China in effect bankrolling the spiralling American budget deficit, giving the PRC a 'whip hand' (Gundzik 2006) over the USA. China's economic impact is paramount for Henry Paulson, US Treasury Secretary, shown as he prepared to set off to China in September 2006. Paulson recognises that 'the U.S. economy and the Chinese economy are highly interdependent' (2006). He considers that 'because of its size and its role in world markets, China is, by definition, already a global economic leader and deserves to be recognized as a leader' (2006). However, he is concerned that sentiments 'increasingly blaming China for economic dislocations in their nations . . . increasingly viewing China with apprehension' are reflected in 'the level of anti-trade and anti-China sentiment in the United States' (2006).

His caution is that 'both in China and in the United States, we must not allow ourselves to be captured by harmful political rhetoric or those who engage in demagoguery' (2006). The stakes are high, 'the tasks faced by Beijing are so daunting that the biggest risk we face is *not* that China will overtake the U.S., but that China *won't* move ahead with the reforms necessary to sustain its growth and to address the very serious problems facing the nation' (2006). Consequently 'I agree with former Deputy Secretary of State Bob Zoellick, China should be a responsible stakeholder. As a global economic leader, China should accept its responsibility as a steward of the international system'.

The stakeholder concept has already proved to be an important contribution by the then Under-Secretary of State Robert Zoellick, with the concept of China as a supportive 'stakeholder' (2005) in the international system. The PRC broadly welcomed it (*People's Daily* 2005c), though China's current leader, Hu Jintao reined in the phrase at the 2006 PRC–US summit, stressing that 'China and the United States are not only stakeholders, but they should also be constructive partners' (Hu Jintao 2006; also PRC 2006, Wang Jianwei 2006) (i.e. equal players). Chinese analysts point out, 'if "stakeholder" is only used to facilitate the U.S. demands upon China, it will not serve as a solid basis for a stable relationship . . . the U.S. should treat China in a more reciprocal fashion' (Wang Jianwei 2006: 1). Uncertainties over America's relationship with China are evident with Zoellick, 'I think everyone in the world wants to believe and wishes China the best for its peaceful development, but nobody is willing to bet their future on it' (2006). In such uncertain times 'it's not surprising that people will hedge their relationships', as countries 'need to have some reassurance that China will be a constructive player in the international system. And that's what the notion of a responsible stakeholder is about', although he also concedes 'the U.S. and others also need to be responsible stakeholders in the system' (Zoellick 2006) alongside China.

The stakes remain high for the Sino–American relationship, 'managing the rise of China constitutes one of the most important challenges facing the United States in the early 21st century' (Swaine and Tellis 2000: 1), as it does for the PRC, and indeed the international system. Yu Bin rightly highlighted the security significance of the Sino–American relationship, whereby 'for both countries, the twenty-first century will undoubtedly test, for the first time in modern history, whether the rise of a major power can be peaceful and relatively low-cost, for both China and the rest of the world' (1999: 202). He also wondered 'can the United States – which fought its way onto the world stage during the twentieth century – be able to tolerate, absorb, and manage the rise of a major, non-Western power without a last-ditch fight' (1999: 202). That remains a stark question. Geopolitical and geoeconomic issues are joined by basic geocultural nuances. For Martin Jacques 'the 21st century will be grim indeed . . . if China will be demonised for its political system and its profound cultural differences', since 'for the first time in modern history, a non-white, non-European-based society will be a global superpower . . . the US will need to learn to contain its primordial desire to have an enemy' (2005c). One ironical situation may well be simultaneous balancing against the USA by China, Russia and Europe coupled with parallel balancing against China by the USA, Japan and India.

Epilogue

Back to the future: 1949 revisited

If Mao returned and surveyed China's prospects in the twenty-first century against his 'Standing Up' speech of 1949, he would see that China was standing up tall and high within the international system. China's strength is the highest it has been for two hundred years, and it is still rising. The Chinese giant is still growing. Mao's roll call of China's humiliations from the nineteenth and early twentieth centuries would indeed seem increasingly remote from China's present settings. Mao, the romantic student of China's earlier 'Golden Age', could justifiably feel that China had become respected in a substantial way in the international system. In retrospect, the proclamation of the PRC, two months after Mao's iconic 'Standing Up' speech, proved to be a decisive moment for China's modern history, enabling a robust developing China to emerge, ready to take on the world on its own terms.

What of Mao's specific elements in his 1949 speech? Domestically did China stand up and establish its own domestic jurisdiction and territorial integrity? Her Qing-period territorial integrity has been mostly recovered, with the exception of the Russian Far East and Taiwan. Tibet and Sinkiang were regained by 1950, Hong Kong and Macao at the end of the century. Intervention in Korea against the United States in the 1950s and China's split from the Soviet bloc in the 1960s showed the PRC's readiness to stand up to the two superpowers.

Not only has China stood up to both superpowers in various ways, she has made her presence felt vis-à-vis other powerful regional neighbours, India, Vietnam and Japan for example. China also at times has stood up and claimed wider ideological significance for the world. In earlier decades this was seen with Mao's revolutionary model. At present it can be seen with its current anti-hegemonism and Third World economic development model, which has brought a Chinese presence back into Africa and Latin America. Meanwhile, China has stood up and shown herself ready to develop significant strategic relationships across the world with an evolving European Union, and to re-establish from a position of strength a partnership with Russia. It has become virtually impossible for the United States to ignore or marginalise China in her calculations. In economic, as well as strategic terms, China has become a factor of recognised importance in the International System. China is a global power for the first time in her history.

Finally, Mao's 1949 speech had looked back to China's Century of Humiliation, whose legacy the PRC has continued to react against, and looked forward to creating a new vibrant Chinese civilisation. It is important that Zhai Qiang stresses Mao's 'awareness of China's traditional images of itself and other countries' in which 'determined to end his country's humiliations at the hands of imperialism, Mao intended to transform it from a backward nation, to a modern state and re-establish its central position in the world' (2000: 221). Talk of China's Middle Kingdom can become a clumsy rhetorical tool for 'China bashing' but in reality there may be something of a return to that still older pattern of Chinese prestige and respect, in which 'there are already signs of the expansion of their soft-power resources' (Nye 2005: 88–9; also Lampton 2005: 317–19, Gill and Huang 2006). Of course, China's increasing soft power allure situations will co-exist with other power centres, and with it the issues of Western economic, political and social values modifying China's own civilisation. Huntington argued for a 'Clash of Civilisations' thesis but perhaps overlooked this interactive nature involved in any meetings of cultures and civilisations. It is at this level that the story of the twenty-first century may indeed revolve around the 'symphony of civilizations' (Gossett 2006) at play in China's place in the international system, in the biggest East–West encounter process.

Bibliography

Abadi, J. (1998) 'The Sino–Indian conflict of 1962', *Journal of Third World Studies*, 15: 11–29.

Acheson, D. (1949) 'Letter of Transmittal', 30 July 1949, in *The China White Paper*, Stanford: Stanford University Press, 1967, iii–xvii.

—— (1950a) 'Remarks by the Secretary of State Acheson before the National Press Club, Washington, January 12, 1950', in R. Dennett and R. Turner (eds), *Documents on American Foreign Relations. XII. January 1–December 31, 1950*, Princeton: Princeton University Press, 426–33.

—— (1950b) 'Address by the Secretary of State Acheson before the Commonwealth Club of California, San Francisco, March 15, 1950', in R. Dennett and R. Turner (eds), *Documents on American Foreign Relations. XII. January 1–December 31, 1950*, Princeton: Princeton University Press, 519–21.

—— (1967) *Present at the Creation. My Years in the State Department*, New York: W.W. Norton.

AFP. (2006) 'Japanese defense chief says military growth of China a threat', *Sino Daily*, 27 September 2006.

Agarwala, R. (2002) *The Rise of China*, New Delhi: Blackwell.

Albright, M. (1997) 'American principle and purpose in East Asia', 15 April, <http://usinfo.state.gov/regional/ea/easec/albright.htm> (accessed 1 July 2006).

Alexseev, M. (2002) 'Chinese migration in the Russian Far East', in J. Thornton and C. Ziegler (eds), *Russia's Far East*, Seattle: University of Washington Press, 319–47.

—— (2003) 'Economic valuations and interethnic fears: perceptions of Chinese migration in the Russian Far East, *Journal of Peace Research*, 40.1: 89–106.

Ali, S. (2005) *US–China Cold War Collaboration*, London: Routledge.

Allen, G. (1952) 'White Australia and the Asian population problem', *Eastern World*, 6.7: 17–18.

Amalrik, A. (1970) *Will the Soviet Union Survive Until 1984?*, New York: Harper & Row.

Anderson, C. (2003) 'An American dilemma: race and realpolitik in the American response to the Bandung Conference, 1955', in B. Plummer (ed.), *Window on Freedom. Race, Civil Rights, and Foreign Affairs, 1945–1988*, Chapel Hill: University of North Carolina Press, 115–40.

Anderson, W. (1999) 'Overcoming uncertainties: U.S.–China strategic relations in the 21st century', *Occasional Paper*, Institute for National Security Studies, 29, October, <http://www.usafa.af.mil/inss/OCP/ocp29.pdf> (accessed 1 July 2006).

Anonymous. (1995) 'The ballad of the bleeding heart liberal', <http://members. ozemail.com.au/~natinfo/poems01/the-ballad-of-the-bleeding-heart-liberal.html>
Arbatov, A. (1992) *The System: An Insider's Life in Soviet Politics*, New York: Times Books.
Armstrong, J. (1977) *Revolutionary Diplomacy. Chinese Foreign Policy and the United Front Doctrine*, Berkeley: University of California Press.
Asia Times. (2006) 'China's mushrooming forex reserve', 19 September.
Atlantic Monthly. (1889) 'The break-up of China and our interest in it', 84, August: 276–80.
Aubin, S. (1998) 'China: yes, worry about the future', *Strategic Review*, 26, Winter: 17–20.
Austin, G. (2002) 'The China periphery: the new US challenge and Beijing's response', *Briefing Paper*, European Institute for Asian Studies, 02/03.
Australia. (1965) 'Vietnam. Ministerial statement', *Commonwealth of Australia. Parliamentary Debates (Hansard). House of Representatives*, 29 April, Canberra: Commonwealth of Australia, 1060–1.
—— (1966) *Viet Nam February 1966 to October 1966*, Canberra: Department of External Affairs.
—— (1997) *In the National Interest. Australia's Foreign and Trade Policy White Paper* Canberra: Commonwealth of Australia.
Australian Financial Review. (1996) 'Security links with the U.S.', 29 July.
Baldwin, H. (1951) 'China as a military power', *Foreign Affairs*, 30.1: 51–62.
Banerjee, D. (1996) 'Myanmar and Indian security concerns', *Strategic Analysis*, 19, August: 691–705.
Baral, J., Mohapatra, J. and Mishra, S. (1989) 'Rajiv Gandhi's China diplomacy: dynamics and problems', *International Studies* 26.3: 257–70.
Barboza, D. (2006) 'China posts a surplus sure to stir U.S.', *New York Times*, 11 July.
Barnett, D. (1960) *Communist China and Asia*, New York: Harper & Brothers.
Barnett, T. (2005) 'Kaplan's strategic lap dances for the U.S. navy and Pacific Command', *Newsletter From Thomas P.M. Barnett*, 16 May, <www .thomaspmbarnett.com/journals/barnett_16may2005.doc> (accessed 1 July 2006).
Basu, B. (1998) 'Indo–Japan naval cooperation', *Strategic Analysis*, 22, May: 321–3.
Batabyal, A. (2006) 'Balancing China in Asia', *China Report*, 42.2: 179–97.
BBC. (2006) 'China hit by rising air pollution', *BBC News*, 3 August, <http://news .bbc.co.uk/2/hi/asia-pacific/5241844.stm>.
Bedeski, R. (1983) *The Fragile Entente: The 1978 Japan–China Peace Treaty in a Global Context*, Boulder: Westview Press.
Belden, J. (1950) *China Shakes the World*, London: Victor Gollanz.
Bendersky, Y. (2004) 'Russia–China relationship favors Beijing', *Asia Times*, 12 August.
Benjamin, M. and Tweed, D. (2006) 'Largest command economy, isn't responding to commands', *News*, Bloomberg.com, 31 July, http://www.bloomberg.com/apps/ news?pid=20601109&sid=abQaz5BqhoVU&refer=home (accessed 1 August 2006).
Bernier, J. (2003) 'China's strategic proxies', *Orbis*, 47.4: 629–43.
Bernstein, R. (1997) 'China basher bashes bashing', *New York Times*, 29 June.
Bernstein, R. and Munro, R. (1997a) 'China: the coming conflict with America', *Foreign Affairs*, 76.2: 18–32.

—— (1997b) *The Coming Conflict With China*, New York: Alfred A. Knopf.

Betts, R. and Christensen, T. (2000–01) 'China: getting the questions right', *National Interest*, 62, Winter: 17–29.

Bhushan, S. (1973) *China's Shadow on India and Bangladesh*, New Delhi: Institute for Socialist Education.

Bland, J. (1912) *Recent Events and Present Policies in China*, London: William Heinemann.

Blank, S. (1994) *The New Russia in the New Asia*, Carlisle Barracks: Strategic Studies Institute.

Bloom, W. (1990) *Personal Identity, National Identity and International Relations*, New York: Cambridge University Press.

Blumenthal, D. and Lin, Joseph. (2006) 'Oil obsession. Energy appetite fuels Beijing's plans to protect vital sea lines', *Armed Forces Journal*, June, http://www.armedforcesjournal.com/2006/06/1813592/ (accessed 1 September 2006).

Bo, Yibo. (1992) 'The making of the "Leaning to one side" decision', *Chinese Historian*, 5.1: 57–62.

Boot, M. (2005) 'Project for a new Chinese century', *Weekly Standard*, 11.4: 36–9.

Borah, R. (2006) 'Qinghai-Tibet railway: China's strategic masterstroke', *Peace & Conflict*, 9.8: 17–18.

Brahm, L. (1996) *China as No. 1*, Singapore: Butterworth–Heinemann.

—— (ed.) (2001) *China's Century*, New York: John Wiley.

Brawley, S. (1995) *The White Peril. Foreign Relations and Asian Immigration to Australasia and North America 1919–78*, Sydney: University of South Wales Press.

Breslin, S. (2005) 'Power and production: rethinking China's global economic role', *Review of International Studies*, 31: 735–53.

Broinowski, A. (1992) *The Yellow Lady: Australian Impressions of Asia*, Melbourne: Oxford University Press.

Broomfield, E. (2003) 'Perceptions of danger: the China Threat theory', *Journal of Contemporary China*, 12: 265–84.

Brown, A. (1904) *New Forces in Old China*, New York: F.H. Revell.

Brown, M., Owen, R., Lynn-Jones, S. and Miller, S. (eds) (2000). *The Rise of China. An International Security Reader*, Cambridge: MIT Press.

Brzezinski, Z. (2000) 'Living with China', *National Interest*, 59, Spring: 5–21.

Brzezinski, Z. and Mearsheimer, J. (2005) 'The clash of the titans', *Foreign Policy*, January–February 2005, http://www.carnegieendowments.org/publications/index.cfm?fa=print&id=16538.

Bundy, M. (1964) 'Progress and problems in East Asia', *Department of State Bulletin*, 19 October: 537.

Bundy, M. and Rusk, D. (1964) 'Rusk and Bundy interviewed on Red China's nuclear testing', *Department of State Bulletin*, 2 November, 614–17.

Burr, W. and Richelson, J. (2000–01) 'Whether to "strangle the baby in the cradle": the United States and the Chinese nuclear program, 1960–64', *International Security*, 25, Winter: 54–99.

Burstein, D. and Keijzer, A. de. (1998a) *Big Dragon: China's Future: What it Means for Business, the Economy, and the Global Order*, New York: Simon & Schuster.

—— (1998b) 'The "Chinese Threat" is overblown', *American Enterprise*, 9, July–August: 44–8.

Bush, W. (2001) 'President Bush discusses global climate change', 11 June, <www.whitehouse.gov/releases/2001/06/20010611-2.html> (accessed 1 July 2006).

—— (2002) *National Security Strategy of the United States*, September 2002, <http://www.globalsecurity.org/military/library/policy/national/nss-020920.pdf> (accessed 1 July 2006).

Buszynski, L. (2004) *Asia Pacific Security – Values and Identity*, London: Routledge.

Buzan, B. (2004) 'How and to whom does China matter?', in B. Buzan and R. Foot (eds), *Does China Matter? A Reassessment. Essays in Memory of Gerald Segal*, London: Routledge, 143–64.

Byman, D., Cliff, R. and Saunders, P. (1999) 'U.S. policy options toward an emerging China', *Pacific Review*, 4.12: 421–51.

Cable, V. and Ferdinand, P. (1996) 'China as an economic giant', *International Affairs*, 70.2: 55–69.

Callahan, W. (2004a) 'National insecurities: humiliation, salvation and Chinese nationalism', *Alternatives*, 29: 199–218.

—— (2004b) 'Historical legacies and non/traditional security: commemorating National Humiliation Day in China', Paper presented to *Traditional and Non/ traditional Security in Northeast Asia* conference, Beijing, April 2004, <http://www.dur.ac.uk/chinese.politics/papers%20conference%20Beijing/callahan.pdf> (accessed 1 July 2006).

—— (2005) 'How to understand China: the dangers and opportunities of being a rising power', *Review of International Studies*, 31: 701–14.

—— (2006) 'History, identity and security. producing and consuming nationalism in China', *Critical Asian Studies*, 38.2: 179–208.

Campbell, I. (2004) 'The Chinese century begins,' *Washington Times*, 1 May.

Candlin, A. (1966) 'The Chinese nuclear threat', *Army Quarterly*, April: 50–60.

Cantril, A. (1964) 'Perception of the Sino–Indian border clash', *Public Opinion Quarterly*, 28.2: 233–42.

Cao, Yong. (2005) 'From communism to nationalism: China's press in the transition of dominant ideology', *Global Media Journal*, 4.6, <http://lass.calumet.purdue.edu/ cca/gmj/sp05/graduatesp05/gmj-sp05gradinv-cao.htm>.

Carletti, F. (1965) *My Voyage Around the World*, London: Methuen.

Carpenter, T. and Dorn, J. (eds) (2000) *China's Future*, Washington: Cato Institute.

Carter, J. (1995) *Keeping Faith. Memoirs of a President*, Fayetteville: The University of Arkansas Press.

Casey, R. (1954) *Friends and Neighbours: Australia and the World*, Melbourne: F.W. Cheshire.

Chan, Gerald. (1999) *Chinese Perspectives on International Relations*, London: Macmillan.

Chan, Steve. (1999) 'Chinese perspectives on world order', in T. Paul and J. Hall (eds), *International Order and the Future of World Politics*, Cambridge: Cambridge University Press, 197–212.

—— (2004) 'Exploring puzzles in power transition theory: implications for Sino– American relations', *Security Studies*, 13.3: 103–41.

—— (2005) 'Is there a power transition between the U.S. and China', *Asian Survey*, 65.5, 687–701.

Chang, Felix. (1999) 'The unraveling of Russia's Far Eastern Power', *Orbis*, 43.2: 257–85.

Chang, Gordon. (1988) 'JFK, China and the Bomb', *Journal of American History*, 74.4: 1287–1310.

—— (2002) *The Coming Collapse of China*, New York: Random House.

—— (2003) 'Is this China's Century?', *China Brief*, 3.16, <http://www.jamestown.org/publications_details.php?volume_id=19&issue_id=2887&article_id=23435> (accessed 1 July 2006).

Chang, Maria Hsia. (2001) *Return of the Dragon. China's Wounded Nationalism*, Colorado: Westview Press.

Chaturvedy, R. (2006) 'Interpreting China's grand strategy at Gwadar', *Peace & Conflict*, 9.3: 4–6.

Chaube, K. (2006) 'India mulling Mongolian military base to counter China', *India Daily*, 5 May.

Chea, T. (2006) 'China's growing pollution reaches U.S.', *Associated Press*, 28 July.

Chellaney, B. (2006) 'Japan–China: Nationalism on the rise', *International Herald Tribune*, 15 August.

Chen, Jian. (1994) *China's Road to the Korea War*, New York: Columbia University Press.

—— (2001) *Mao's China and the Cold War*, Chapel Hill: University of North Carolina Press.

Chen, Jian and Wilson, D. (1998) 'New evidence on Sino-Soviet rapprochement', *Cold War International Project Bulletin*, 11, Winter: 155–75.

Chen, Yi. (1969) 'Further thoughts by Marshal Chen Yi on Sino-American relations', *Cold War International Project Bulletin*, 11, Winter: 170–1.

Chen, Yi, Ye Jianging, Xu Xiangqian and Nie Rongzhen. (1969) 'Our views about the current situation', 17 September, *Cold War International Project Bulletin*, 11, Winter 1998: 170.

Chen, Zhimin. (2005). 'Nationalism, internationalism and Chinese foreign policy', *Journal of Contemporary China*, 14, February: 35–53.

Cheow, Eric. (2004a) 'Paying tribute to Beijing: an ancient model for China's new power', *International Herald Tribune*, 21 January.

—— (2004b) 'Asian security and the re-emergence of China's tributary system', *China Brief*, 4.18: 7–9.

Cherian, J. (2006) 'The China Factor', *Frontline*, 25 February–10 March, 14–16.

Chervonenko, S. (1998) 'The short version of the negotiations between CPSU and CCP delegations September 1960', Minutes, *Cold War International History Project. Bulletin*, 10, March: 172–3.

Chi, Haotian. (1996) 'U.S.–China military ties', in M. Pillsbury (ed.), *Chinese Views of Future Warfare*, Honolulu: University Press of the Pacific, 2002, 61–7.

Chiang, Kai-shek. (1947) *China's Destiny*, New York: Roy Publishers.

Ching, Ch'ien-peng. (2004) *Domestic Politics, International Bargaining and China's Territorial Disputes*, London: RoutledgeCurzon.

Christensen, T. (1997) 'Chinese realpolitik', *Foreign Affairs*, 75.5: 37–52.

—— (1998) 'Parsimony is no simple matter: International Relations theory, Area Studies, and the rise of China', Paper presented to *Program on International Politics, Economics, and Security*, Chicago, 28 February, unpublished.

—— (1999a) 'China, the U.S.–Japan Alliance, and the security dilemma in East Asia', *International Security*, 23.4: 49–80.

—— (1999b) 'Pride, pressure, and politics: the roots of China's world view', in Deng Yong and Wang Fei-ling (eds), *In the Eyes of the Dragon. China Views the World*, Lanham: Rowman & Littlefield, 239–56.

—— (2001) 'Posing problems without catching up. China's rise and challenges for U.S. security policy', *International Security*, 25.4: 5–40.

Clark, G. (1967) *Is Asian Communism a Threat to Australia?*, Australian Institute of Political Science, <http://www.gregoryclark.net/auscomps.html> (accessed 1 July 2006).
—— (1968) *In Fear of China*, London: The Cresset Press.
—— (2002) 'Remembering a war – the 1962 India–China Conflict', 24 October, <www.gregoryclark.net/redif.html> (accessed 1 July 2006).
Clark, M. (1954) *From the Danube to the Yalu*, New York: Harper.
Clinton, W. (1997) 'Remarks by President Clinton and President Jiang Zemin at arrival ceremony', The White House, Office of the Press Secretary, 29 October, <http://www.nti.org/db/china/engdocs/clji1097.htm> (accessed 1 July 2006).
—— (1999) 'President Clinton outlines China policy', 7 April, <http://www.nti.org/db/china/engdocs/pres0499.htm> (accessed 1 July 2006).
Cohen, P. (2002) 'Remembering and forgetting national humiliation in twentieth-century China', *Twentieth-century China*, 27.2: 1–39.
Cohen, W. (1997) 'China's strategic culture', *Atlantic Monthly*, 279.3: 103–5.
—— (2000) *America's Response to China*, 4th edn, New York: Columbia University Press.
Cole, B. (2001) *Great Wall at Sea: China's Navy Enters the 21st Century*, Annapolis: Naval Institute Press.
Committee of 100. (2001a) 'American attitudes toward Chinese Americans and Asian American', Survey, April, <http://www.committee100.org/Published/surveyfaqs.html> (accessed 1 July 2006).
—— (2001b) 'Conversations with Americans about Chinese Americans and Asian Americans', May, <http://www.committee100.org/Published/C100survey.pdf> (accessed 1 July 2006).
Confino, A. (1997) 'Collective memory and cultural history, *American Historical Review*, 10.2: 1386–1403.
Cordingley, P. and Hsieh, D. (1997) 'China's answer is still No', *Asiaweek*, 17 January.
Corpus, V. (2006) 'If it comes to a shooting war', *Asia Times*, 20 April.
Cossa, R. (2004) 'Non-military challenges in Pacific Asia', 7th Waldbrol Group Meeting on the European and Euro-Atlantic coordination on security policies vis-à-vis the Asia–Pacific', 12–13 December, <http://swp-berlin.org/common/get_document.php?id=1165&PHPSESSID=f40e015f3b2065db816954ee6aab6b10> (accessed 1 July 2006).
Cox, M. (1998) 'New China: new Cold War?', in I. Booth (ed.), *Statecraft and Security. Cold War and Beyond*, Cambridge: Cambridge University Press, 224–46.
Crankshaw, E. (1965) *The New Cold War. Moscow v. Pekin*, Harmondsworth: Pelican.
Cranmer-Byng, J. (1973) 'The Chinese view of their place in the world', *China Quarterly*, 53.1: 67–79.
Croft, M. (1959) *Red Carpet to China*, New York: St Martin's Press.
Cronin, R. (1997) 'Japan–U.S. security cooperation', *Congressional Research Service Report for Congress*, Washington, 30 October.
Cruz, C. (2000) 'Identity and persuasion: how nations remember their pasts and make their future', *World Politics*, 52.3: 275–312.
Cumings, B. (1997) 'Boundary displacement: Area Studies and International Studies during and after the Cold War', *Bulletin of Concerned Asian Scholars*, 29.1: 6–26.

Da, Jun. (1996) 'True threat comes from those trumpeting "China Threat"', *Beijing Review*, 11–17 November: 7–8.

DAFR. (1950) *Documents on American Foreign Relations. XII. January 1–December 31, 1950*, R. Dennett and R. Turner (eds), Princeton: Princeton University Press.

—— (1964) *Documents on American Foreign Relation 1963*, R. Stebbins (ed.), New York: Harper & Row.

Dai, Xiaohua. (1997) 'Why and how the US media work to demonize China', *Beijing Review*, 4–10 August: 8–11.

Dark, K. (1998) *The Waves of Time. Long Term Change and International Relations*, London: Pinter.

David, P. (1967) 'The coming Chinese communist nuclear threat and U.S. sea-based A.B.M options', *Orbis*, 11.1: 45–79.

Davydov, V. (2004) 'Chinese emigrants to conquer Siberia', *Pravda*, 16 July.

DBPO. (1987) 'The Anglo–American relations and Cold War strategy January–June 1950', *Documents on British Policy Overseas. Series II. Vol. II*, R. Bullen (ed.), London: HMSO.

—— (1991) 'Korea 1950–1951', *Documents on British Policy Overseas. Series II. Vol. IV*, H. Yasamee and K. Hamilton (eds), London: HMSO.

—— (2002) 'Britain and China, 1945–1950', *Documents on British Policy Overseas. Series I. Vol. VIII.*, S. Ashton (ed.), London: Frank Cass.

Degraffenreid, K. (1999) 'Editor's introduction', in K. Degraffenreid (ed.), *The Cox Report – China and National Security, The Report of the Select Committee on U.S. National Security and Military/Commercial Concerns with China*, Washington: Regnery.

Dellios, R. (1999) 'China–United States relation', *Culture Mandala*, 3.2, August: 1–20.

Deng, Xiaoping. (1974) 'Chairman of Chinese delegation Teng Hsiao-ping's speech', *Peking Review*, 19 April: 6–11.

—— (1984–94) *Selected Works of Deng Xiaoping*, 3 vols., Beijing: Foreign Languages Press.

—— (1991) 'Deng puts forward new 12-character guiding principle for internal and foreign policies', *Ching Pao* (Hong Kong), 172, 5 November: 84–6, FBIS HK0611100091.

Deng, Yong. (1988) 'Managing China's hegemonic ascension', *Journal of Strategic Studies*, 21: 21–43.

—— (1997) 'Chinese relations with Japan', *Pacific Affairs*, 70.3: 373–91.

—— (1999) 'Conception of national interests', in Deng Yong and Wang Fei-ling (eds), *In the Eyes of the Dragon. China Views the World*, Lanham: Rowman & Littlefield, 47–72.

—— (2000) 'Escaping the periphery: China's national identity in world politics', in Hu Weixing, Chan Gerald and Zha Daojiong (eds), *China's International Relations in the 21st Century*, Lanham: University Press of America, 41–70.

—— (2001) 'Hegemon on the offensive: Chinese perspectives on US global strategy', *Political Science Quarterly*, 116.3: 343–65.

—— (2005) 'Better than power: "international status" in Chinese foreign policy', in Deng Yong and Wang Fei-ling (eds), *China Rising*, Lanham: Bowman & Littlefield, 51–72.

—— (2006) 'Reputation and the security dilemma: China reacts to the China Threat theory', in A. Johnston and R. Ross (eds), *New Directions in the Study of China's Foreign Policy*, Stanford: Stanford University Press, 186–216.

Deng, Yong and Moore, T. (2004) 'China views globalization. Toward a new Great-Power politics?', *Washington Quarterly*, 27.3: 117–36.

Deng, Yong and Wang, Fei-ling. (1999) 'Introduction: toward an understanding of China's world view', in Deng Yong and Wang Fei-ling (eds), *In the Eyes of the Dragon. China Views the World*, Lanham: Rowman & Littlefield, 1–19.

Der Speigel. (1964) 'Kampf den Mongolen' ['The fight against the Mongols'], 5 August, 17–20.

Dewey, T. (1952) *Journey to the Far Pacific*, London: Oldham's Press.

Dikotter, F. (1992) *The Discourse of Race in Modern China*, Stanford: Stanford University Press.

Dittmer, L. (1981) 'The strategic triangle: an elementary game theoretical analysis', *World Politics*, 33.4: 485–515.

Dittmer, L. and Kim, S. (eds) (1993) *China's Quest for National Identity*, New York: Cornell University Press.

Dobbs, L. (2003) 'Our new diplomatic partner', *U.S. News & World Report*, 22 December.

Dockrill, M. (1989) 'The Foreign Office, Anglo–American relations and the Korean truce negotiations July 1951–July 1953', in J. Cotton and I. Neary (eds), *The Korean War in History*, Manchester: Manchester University Press, 100–19.

Donaldson, R. (2003) 'The arms trade in Russian–Chinese relations: identity, domestic politics, and geopolitical positioning', *International Studies Quarterly*, 47.3: 709–32.

Donnelly, T. (2002) 'China without illusions', *Weekly Standard*, 29 July: 19–20.

Downen, R. (1984) *The Tattered China Card: Reality or Illusion in United States strategy?*, Washington: The Council for Social and Economic Studies.

Downs, E. and Saunders, P. (1998–99) 'Legitimacy and the limits of nationalism. China and the Diaoyu Islands', *International Security*, 23.3: 114–46.

Dunlop, W. (1889) 'The march of the Mongol', *Asiatic Quarterly Review*, 7: 19–45.

Dutta, S. (1998) 'China's emerging power and military role', in J. Pollack and R. Yang (eds), *In China's Shadow: Regional Perspectives on Chinese Foreign Policy and Military Development*, Santa Monica: RAND, 91–114.

Eberstadt, N. (2004) 'Power and population in Asia', *Policy Review*, Hoover Institution, 123, February–March, 3–27.

Eckholm, E. (2001) 'China's about-face. Support for U.S. on terror', *New York Times*, 30 September.

Economist. (1996) 'China looming', 17 August, 13–14.

—— (2000) 'A Survey of China. Now comes the hard part', supplement, 8 April.

—— (2004) 'Peaceful rise. Even when China is trying hard to be conciliatory, it scares its neighbours', 26 June, 67–8.

Edwardes, M. (1962) *Asia in the Balance*, Harmondsworth: Penguin.

Eisenhower, D. (1954) 'Press Club news conference', 7 April, in H. Jones (ed.), *Safeguarding the Republic. Essays and Documents in American Foreign Relations 1890–1991*, New Jersey: Mcgraw-Hill College, 201.

—— (1981) *The Eisenhower Diaries*, R. Ferrell (ed.), New York: Norton.

Elegant, R. (1963) *The Centre of the World. Communism and the Mind of China*, London: Methuen.

—— (1967) 'China's next phase', *Foreign Affairs*, 46.1: 137–50.

—— (1996) 'Foreign illusions about influencing China lead to kowtows', *International Herald Tribune*, 18 July.

Elleman, B. (2002) 'China's new "imperial" navy', *Naval War College Review*, 55, Summer: 143–54.

Elman, C. and Elman, M. (1997) 'Diplomatic history and international relations theory', *International Security*, 22.1: 5–21.

Elman, C. and Elman, M. (eds) (2001) *Bridges and Boundaries. Historians, Political Scientists and the Study of International Relations*, Cambridge: MIT Press.

Erlanger, S. (1997) 'Searching for an enemy and finding China', *New York Times*, 6 April.

Escobar, P. (2005) 'Never mind the party, let's party!', *Asia Times*, 2 February.

Fairbank, J. (1969) 'China's foreign policy in historical perspective', *Foreign Affairs*, 47.3: 448–63.

—— (ed.) (1968) *The Chinese World Order*, Cambridge: Harvard University Press.

Feigenbaum, E. (2001a) 'Violence and major power coordination in Asia', in D. Lampton (ed.), *Major Power Relations in Northeast Asia*, Tokyo: Japan Center for International Exchange, 113–30.

—— (2001b) 'China's challenge to *Pax Americana*', *Washington Quarterly*, 24.3: 31–43.

Ferguson, J. (2006) 'The Group of Eight wrap up', *PacNet*, 36, 20 July.

Fernandes, G. (1998) 'China bigger threat to India than Pakistan', Interview, *Agence France–Presse*, 3 May.

Fewsmith, J. and Rosen, S. (2001) 'The domestic context of Chinese foreign policy', in D. Lampton (ed.), *The Making of Chinese Foreign and Security Policy, in the Era of Reform: 1978–2000*, Stanford: Stanford University Press, 151–87.

Financial Times. (1998) 'China "Greatest threat to India"', 5 May.

Fishman, T. (2004) 'Will the 21st century become the Chinese Century?', *New York Times Magazine*, 4 July.

—— (2005) *China, Inc.*, New York: Scribners.

Fitzgerald, J. (1997) 'Chinese, dogs and the state that stands on two legs', *Bulletin of Concerned Asian Scholars*, 29.4: 54–61.

—— (1999) 'China and the quest for dignity', *National Interest*, 55, Spring: 47–59.

Fix, J. (1966) 'China – the nuclear threat', *Air University Quarterly Review*, March–April: 38–9.

Fokkema, D. (1971) *Report from Peking*, London: C. Hurst.

Foot, R. (1990) 'The search for a modus vivendi: Anglo–American and China policy in the Eisenhower era', in W. Cohen and A. Iriye (eds), *The Great Powers in East Asia 1953–1960*, New York: Columbia University Press, 143–63.

—— (2001) 'Chinese power and the idea of a responsible state', *China Journal*, 45, January: 1–19.

—— (2006) 'Chinese strategies in a US hegemonic global order', *International Affairs*, 82.1: 77–94.

Freeman, C. (1998) 'An interest-based China policy', in H. Binnendijk and R. Montaperto (eds), *Strategic Trends in China*, Washington: National Defense University Press, 123–4.

Friedman, E. (1997) 'The challenge of a rising China: another Germany', in R. Lieber (ed.), *Eagle Adrift: American Foreign Policy at the End of the Century*, New York: Longman, 215–45.

Friedberg, A. (2005) 'The Future of US-China relations: Is conflict inevitable?', *International Security*, 30.2: 7–45.

FRUS. (1976) 'Korea', *Foreign Relations of the United States 1950. Vol. VII.*, E. Gleason (ed.), Washington: United States Government Printing Office.

—— (1986) 'China', *Foreign Relations of the United States 1955–1957. Vol. III.*, J. Glennon (ed.), Washington: United States Government Printing Office.

—— (1996a) 'National security policy', *Foreign Relations of the United States. 1961–63. Vol. VIII*, D. Mabon (ed.), Washington: United States Government Printing Office.

—— (1996b) 'Northeast Asia', *Foreign Relations of the United States 1961–1963. Vol. XXII*, E. Keefer et al. (eds), Washington: United States Government Printing Office.

—— (1998) 'China', *Foreign Relations of the United States 1964–1968. Vol. XXX*, H. Schwar (ed.), Washington: United States Government Printing Office.

—— (2003) 'Foundations of Foreign Policy, 1969–1972', *Foreign Relations of the United States 1969–1976. Vol. I*, L. Smith and D. Herschler (eds), Washington: United States Government Printing Office.

Fu, Lo-shu. (ed.) (1966) *A Documentary Chronicle of Sino–Western Relations (1644–1820)*, Tuscon: University of Arizona Press.

Funabashi, Yoichi. (2003) 'China's "Peaceful ascendancy"', *YaleGlobal*, 19 December.

Gaddis, J. (1996) 'History, science, and international relations', in N. Woods (ed.), *Explaining International Relations Since 1945*, Oxford: Oxford University Press, 32–48.

—— (1997) *We Now Know: Rethinking Cold War History*, Oxford: Clarendon Press.

Ganguly, S. (2002) 'Assessing India's response to the rise of China', in C. Pumphrey (ed.), *The Rise of China in Asia*, Carlisle: Strategic Studies Institute, 95–104.

Garnett, S. (1996) 'The Russian Far East as a factor in Russian–Chinese relations', *SAIS Review*, 16.2, 1–19.

Garrett, B. (1979) 'China policy and the strategic triangle', in R. Lieber, K. Oye and D. Rothchild (eds), *Eagle Entangled: U.S. Foreign Policy in a Complex World*, New York: Longman, 228–63.

—— (1983) 'China policy and the constraints of triangular logic', in R. Lieber, K. Oye and D. Rothchild (eds), *Eagle Defiant. United States Foreign Policy in the 1980s*, Boston: Little, Brown, 237–71.

Garrett, B. and Glaser, B. (1997) 'Chinese apprehensions about revitalization of the U.S.-Japan alliance', *Asian Survey*, 37, April: 383–402.

Garver, J. (1982) *China's Decision for Rapprochement with the United States 1968–1971*, Boulder: Westview Press.

—— (1992) 'The Chinese threat in the Vietnam War', *Parameters*, 22.1: 73–84.

—— (1996) *Will China be Another Germany?*, Carlisle Barracks: U.S. Army War College.

—— (1998) 'China as Number One', *China Journal*, 39, January: 61–6.

—— (1999) 'Foreword', in Deng Yong and Wang Fei-ling (eds), *In the Eyes of the Dragon. China Views the World*, Lanham: Rowman & Littlefield, vii–xi.

—— (2001a) *Protracted Contest: Sino–Indian Rivalry in the Twentieth Century*, Washington: University of Washington Press.

—— (2001b) 'More from the "Say No club"', *China Journal*, 45, January: 151–8.

—— (2002) 'The *Gestalt* of Sino-Indian relations', in C. Pumphrey (ed.), *The Rise of China in Asia: Security Implications*, Carlisle: Strategic Studies Institute, 263–86.

—— (2003a) 'Asymmetrical Indian and Chinese threat perceptions', in S. Ganguly (ed.), *India as an Emerging Power*, London: Frank Cass, 109–34.

—— (2003b) 'The (former) coming war with America, *Journal of Contemporary China*, 12, August: 575–85.

Ge, Yang. (1995) 'China's rise: threat or not?', *Beijing Review*, 30 January–5 February: 23–5.

Gelbras, V. (1997) *China in Russia's Eastern Policy*, Washington: National Council for Eurasian and East European Research.

—— (2002) 'Chinese migration to the Russian Far East', <http://gsti.miis.edu/CEAS–PUB/200208Gelbras.pdf> (accessed 1 July 2006).

Gershman, J. (2001) 'We have seen the enemy, and it is China', *Foreign Policy in Focus*, 20 July.

Gertz, B. (2000) *The China Threat*, Washington: Regnery.

Gilbert, M. (1960) *Winston S. Churchill, Volume 3, 'Never Despair', 1945–1965*, Boston: Houghton Mifflin.

Gilboy, G. (2004) 'The myth behind China's miracle', *Foreign Affairs*, 83.4: 33–48.

Gill, B. (1996) *China and the Revolution in Military Affairs*, Carlisle Barracks: Strategic Studies Institute.

Gill, B. and Huang Yanzhong. (2006) 'Sources and limits of China's "soft power"', *Survival*, 48.2: 17–36.

Gilley, B. and Crispin, S. (1999) 'Limited engagement', *Far Eastern Economic Review*, 22 April.

Gittings, J. (1968) *Survey of the Sino–Soviet Dispute*, Oxford: Oxford University Press.

—— (1984) 'China: half a superpower', in N. Chomsky, J. Steele and G. Gittings (eds), *Super Powers in Collision*, 2nd edn, Harmondsworth: Penguin, 87–120.

Godwin, P. (1996) 'From continent to periphery: PLA doctrine, strategy and capabilities towards 2000', *China Quarterly*, 146, June: 464–87.

Goh, E. (2005) 'Nixon, Kissinger, and the "Soviet card" in the US opening to China', *Diplomatic History*, 29.3: 475–502.

Goldstein, A. (1997–98) 'Great expectations: interpreting China's arrival', *International Security*, 22.3: 36–73.

—— (2001) 'The diplomatic face of China's grand strategy', *China Quarterly*, 168, December: 835–64.

—— (2003) 'An emerging China's emerging grand strategy', in J. Ikenberry and M. Mastanduno (eds), *International Relations Theory and the Asia–Pacific*, New York: Columbia University Press, 57–106.

—— (2005) *Rising to the Challenge: China's Grand Strategy and International Security*, Stanford: Stanford University Press.

Goldstein, L. (2003) 'When China was a "rogue state"', *Journal of Contemporary China*, 12, November: 739–64.

Goldstein, L. and Murray, W. (2004) 'Undersea dragons: China's maturing submarine Force', *International Security*, 28.4: 161–96.

Goldstein, S. (2001) 'Dialogue of the deaf?: the Sino–American ambassadorial-level talks, 1955–1970', in R. Ross and Jiang Changbin (eds), *Re-examining the Cold War. U.S. Diplomacy, 1954–1973*, Cambridge: Harvard University Press, 200–37.

Goncharov, S., Lewis, J. and Litai, L. (1993) *Uncertain Partners. Stalin, Mao and the Korean War*, Stanford: Stanford University Press.

Gong, Gerrit. (2001) 'The beginning of History: remembering and forgetting as strategic issues', *Washington Quarterly*, 24.2: 45–57.

Goodman, D. and Segal, G. (1997) 'Thinking strategically about China', in Goodman and Segal (eds), *China Rising*, New York: Routledge, 1–5.

Gordon, P. (1997) 'Uncertainty, insecurity and China's military power', *Current History*, 96, 252–7.

Gossett, D. (2006) 'A symphony of civilizations', *Asia Times*, 12 August.

Green, M. (1997) 'Interview, Ambassador Marshall Green', 15 January, <http://www.gwu.edu/~nsarchiv/coldwar/interviews/episode–15/green3.html> (accessed 1 July 2006).

—— (2001) 'The Defense Guidelines and China', in D. Lampton (ed.), *Major Power Relations in Northeast Asia*, Tokyo: Japan Center for International Exchange, 73–86.

Greenfield, K. (1992) 'Return of the Yellow Peril', *The Nation*, 11 May.

Gries, P. (1999) 'A "China threat"? Power and passion in Chinese "face nationalism"', *World Affairs*, 162.2: 63–75.

—— (2001) 'Tears of rage: Chinese nationalism and the Belgrade bombing', *China Journal*, 45, July: 25–43.

—— (2004) *China's New Nationalism: Pride, Politics and Diplomacy*, Berkeley: The University of California Press.

—— (2005a) 'Social psychology and the identity-conflict debate: is a "China Threat" inevitable?', *European Journal of International Relations*, 10.2: 235–65.

—— (2005b) 'China's "New thinking" on Japan', *China Quarterly*, 184, December: 831–50.

—— (2005c) 'Nationalism, indignation, and China's Japan policy', *SAIS Review*, 25.2: 105–14.

—— (2005d) 'China eyes the hegemon', *Orbis*, 49.3: 401–12.

—— (2006) 'Identity and conflict in Sino–American relations', in A. Johnston and R. Ross (eds), *New Directions in the Study of China's Foreign Policy*, Stanford: Stanford University Press, 309–39.

Gries, P. and Peng, Kaiping. (2002) 'Culture clash? Apologies East and West', *Journal of Contemporary China*, 11.30: 173–8.

Griffith, S. (1968) *The Chinese People's Liberation Army*, London: Weidenfeld and Nicolson.

Gu, George. (2004) 'How should we understand a Chinese Century?', *Sinomania*, <http://www.sinomania.com/CHINANEWS/Chinese_Century.html> (accessed 1 July 2006).

Gu, Ping. (1999) 'What is Segal up to by belittling China?', *People's Daily*, 16 September.

Gu, Xuewu. (2003) 'China and the great powers: mutual perceptions at the dawn of the 21st century', in E. Reiter and P. Hazdra (eds), *The Impact of Asian Powers on Global Developments*, Heidelberg: Physica-Verlag, 165–77.

Gundzik, J. (2006) 'Beijing holds whip hand over slowing US', *Asia Times*, 4 October.

Gurtov, M. (2002) 'Rising China', in Gurtov, *Pacific Asia*, Lanham: Rowman & Littlefield, 91–140.

Guzzini, S. (2000) 'A reconstruction of constructivism in international relations', *European Journal of International Relations*, 6.2: 147–82.

Haass, R. (2005) 'What to do about China', *US News & World Report*, 20 June 2005.

Halbwachs, M. (1992) *On Collective Memory*, Chicago: University of Chicago Press.

Hale, D. (2004) 'China's growing appetites', *National Interest*, 76, Summer: 137–47.

Hale, D. and Hale, L. (2003) 'China takes off', *Foreign Affairs*, 82.6: 36–53.

Hall, R. (1999) *National Collective Identity: Social Constructs and International Systems*, New York: Columbia University Press.

Halloran, R. (1998) 'China: restoring the Middle Kingdom', *Parameters*, 28.2: 56–68.

Halpern, A. (1962) 'Communist China's demands on the world', in M. Kaplan (ed.), *The Revolution in World Politics*, New York: John Wiley, 233–47.

Halperin, M. (1965) *China and the Bomb*, London: Pall Mall Press.

Han, Suyin. (1952) *A Many-splendoured Thing*, London: Jonathan Cape.

—— (1967) *China in the Year 2001*, London: C.A. Watts.

Harding, H. (1993) 'The concept of a "Greater China"', *China Quarterly*, 136, December: 660–86.

—— (1995) 'A Chinese colossus?', *Journal of Strategic Studies*, 18.3: 104–22.

Harper, N. (1955) 'Australia and Southeast Asia', *Pacific Affairs*, 28.3: 203–20.

Harries, O. (1999–2000) 'A year of debating China', *National Interest*, Winter: 141–7.

Harris, S. (2002) *Globalisation and China's Diplomacy*, Canberra: Australian National University.

—— (2003) 'Does China matter?', Canberra: Australian National University.

Harris, S. and Klintsworth, G. (eds) (1995) *China as a Great Power in the Asia–Pacific*, New York: St. Martins Press.

Hart, R. (1900) 'The Peking legations', *Cosmopolitan*, 30.2, December: 136.

Helms, J. (1992) 'Red China's military threat', 10 September, US Senate S13164-7, <http://www.fas.org/news/china/1992/920910-cr2.htm>.

Henley, L. (1996) *China's Capacity for Achieving a Revolution in Military Affairs*, Carlisle Barracks: Strategic Studies Institute.

Hensman, C. (1968) *Yellow Peril? Red Hope*, London: SCM Press.

Hevia, J. (2003) *English Lessons. The Pedagogy of Imperialism in Nineteenth Century China*, Durham: Duke University Press.

Hilsman, R. (1963a) 'The challenge to freedom in Asia', *Department of State Bulletin*, 8 July: 44.

—— (1963b) 'Redefinition of United States policy toward China', 13 December, in R. Stebbins (ed.), *Documents on American Foreign Relations 1963*, New York: Harper & Row, 1964, 301–11.

Hinton, H. (1966) *Communist China in World Politics*, London: Macmillan.

Hirschfeld, T. (1999) 'Assessing China's military potential', *East Asia*, 17.1: 95–107.

Hodder, R. (1999) 'China and the world', *Pacific Review* 12.4: 61–77.

Hoge, J. (2004) 'A global power shift in the making', *Foreign Affairs*, 83.4: 2–7.

Holmes, J. (2006) '"Soft Power" at sea: Zheng He and China's maritime diplomacy', *Southeast Review of Asian Studies*, 28, <http://www.uky.edu/Centers/Asia/SECAAS/Seras/2006/Holmes.doc21> (accessed 1 July 2006).

Holmes, J. and Yoshihara, T. (2005a) 'The influence of Mahan upon China's maritime strategy', *Comparative Strategy*, 24.1: 53–71.

—— (2005b) 'Command of the sea with Chinese characteristics', *Orbis*, 49.4: 677–94.

—— (2006a) 'China's "Caribbean" in the South China Sea', *SAIS Review*, 26.1: 79–92.

—— (2006b) 'Mao Zedong meets Alfred Thayer Mahan', *Australian Defence Force Journal*, 171, October: forthcoming.

Hooper, B. (1986) *China Stands Up. Ending the Western Presence 1948–1950*, Sydney: Allen & Unwin.

Hopf, T. (1998) 'The promise of constructivism in International Relations theory', *International Security*, 23.1: 171–200.

House Select Committee. (1999) *Report of the Select Committee on U.S. National Security and Military/Commercial Concerns with the People's Republic of China* [Cox Report], 3 January, <http://www.house.gov/coxreport/pdf>/overv.pdf> (accessed 1 July 2006).

—— (2006) *Hearing of the House International Relations Committee. Subject: China's Resurgence*, 10 May, <http://www.ait.org.tw/en/news/currentissues/060510-ChinaResurgence.asp> (accessed 1 July 2006).

Howe, H. (1996) 'China, Japan and economic interdependence in the Asia Pacific region', in H. Howe (ed.), *China and Japan*, Oxford: Clarendon Press, 98–126.

Hsuing, James. (1995) 'China's omni-directional diplomacy', *Asian Survey*, 35.6: 573–86.

Hu, Jintao. (2006) 'Remarks by President Hu Jintao of the People's Republic of China at welcoming luncheon at the White House hosted by President George W. Bush of the United States of America', 20 April, Ministry of Foreign Affairs of the People's Republic of China, <http://www.fmprc.gov.cn/eng/zxxx/t259220.htm> (accessed 1 July 2006).

Hu, Ping. (1994) 'China constitutes no military threat', *Beijing Review*, 21–27 November: 22.

Hu, Richard. (1999) 'India's nuclear bomb and future Sino–Indian relations', *East Asia*, 17, Spring: 40–68.

Hu, Yaobang. (1982) 'Create a new situation in all fields of socialist modernization', *Beijing Review*, 13 September: 11–40.

Huang, Jin. (2005) 'On Sino–Japanese tensions and the US approach', *Japan Economic Currents*, 58, October 2005, 4–8.

Huang, Xiaoming. (2000) 'Managing fluctuations in U.S.–China relations', *Asian Survey*, 40.2: 269–95.

Huang, Yasheng. (1999) 'A Chinese nightmare', *Newsweek*, 22 March.

Huck, A. (1984) 'Australian attitudes to China and the Chinese', *Australian Journal of Chinese Affairs*, 11, January, 157–68.

Hughes, C. (2006) *Chinese Nationalism in the Global Era*, London: Routledge.

Hunt, M. (1984) 'Chinese foreign relations in historical perspective', in H. Harding (ed.), *China's Foreign Relations in the 1980s*, New Haven: Yale University Press, 1–42.

—— (1996) *The Genesis of Chinese Communist Foreign Policy*, New York: Columbia University Press.

Huntington, S. (1993) 'The clash of civilizations', *Foreign Affairs*, 72.3: 22–49.

—— (1997) *The Clash of Civilizations and the Remaking of World Order*, New York: Simon & Schuster.

Inglis, D. (1965) 'The Chinese bombshell', *Bulletin of the Atomic Scientists*, May: 19–21.

Iriye, Akira. (1979) 'Culture and power: international relations as intercultural relations', *Diplomatic History*, 3.2: 115–28.

—— (1988) 'Images and diplomacy in Sino–American relations', in M. Hunt *et al.* (eds), *Mutual Images in U.S.–China Relations*, Washington: Wilson Center, 37–42.

—— (1990) 'Culture', *Journal of American History*, June: 99–107.

Iriye, Akira. (ed.) (1975) *Mutual Images. Essays in American–Japanese Relations*, Cambridge: Harvard University Press.

Isaacs, H. (1958) *Scratches on our Mind: American Views of China and India*, New York: John Day.

—— (1961) *The Tragedy of the Chinese Revolution*, 2nd edn, Stanford: Stanford University Press.

—— (1969) 'Color in world politics', *Foreign Affairs*, 47.1: 235–50.

—— (1972) *Images of Asia*, New York: Harper & Row.

Ishihara, Shintaro. (2005) 'Questions about a rising giant', *International Herald Tribune*, 23 April.

ISSB. (2006) 'China – the world's top exporter', Iron and Steel Statistics Bureau, July. http://www.issb.co.uk/.

Jacques, M. (2003) 'A year of thwarted ambition', *Guardian*, 27 December.

—— (2005a) 'The Middle Kingdom mentality', *Guardian*, 16 April.

—— (2005b) 'Cold War, take two', *Guardian*, 18 June.

—— (2005c) 'China is well on its way to being the other superpower', *Guardian*, 8 December.

Jain, P. (1997) 'Japan's relations with South Asia', *Asian Survey*, 37, April: 340–52.

Japan–USA. (1961) 'Joint statement of Japanese Prime Minister Ikeda and U.S. President Kennedy', 22 June, *Department of State Bulletin*, 45, 10 July: 57–8.

—— (1965) 'Joint statement of Japanese Prime Minister and U.S. President Johnson', 13 January; *Public Papers of the Presidents: Lyndon B. Johnson. 1965. Book 1: January 1 to May 31, 1965*, Washington: U.S Government Printing Office, 40–2.

—— (1967) 'Joint statement of Japanese Prime Minister Sato and U.S. President Johnson', 15 November, in *Public Papers of the Presidents of the United States: Lyndon B. Johnson. 1967. Book 2: July 1 to December 31, 1967*, Washington: U.S Government Printing Office, 1033–7.

—— (1996) 'Japan–U.S. joint declaration on security – alliance for the 21st century', 17 April, Ministry of Foreign Affairs of Japan, <http://www.mofa.go.jp/region/n-america/us/security/security.html> (accessed 1 July 2006).

—— (1997) 'The guidelines for Japan–U.S defense cooperation', September, Ministry of Foreign Affairs of Japan, <http://www.mofa.go.jp/region/n-america/us/security/guideline2.html> (accessed 1 July 2006).

—— (2005) 'U.S.–Japan Alliance: transformation and realignment for the future', 29 October, <http://www.mofa.go.jp/region/n-america/us/security/scc/doc0510.html> (accessed 1 July 2006).

Jencks, H. (1992) 'Chinese evaluations of "Desert Storm"', *Journal of East Asian Affairs*, 6.2: 447–77.

Jensen, P. (2000) 'Chinese sea-power and American strategy', *Strategic Review*, 28.3: 18–26.

Jervis, R. (1970) *The Logic of Images in International Relations*, Princeton: Princeton University Press.

—— (1976) *Perception and Misperception in International Politics*, Princeton: Princeton University Press.

Ji, You. (1997) 'A blue water navy', in D. Goodman and R. Segal (eds), *China Rising*, London: Routledge, 71–89.

Jia, Qingguo. (2005a) 'Peaceful development', *Australian Journal of International Affairs*, 59.4: 493–507.

—— (2005b) 'One administration, two voices: US China policy during Bush's first term', *International Relations of the Asia Pacific*, 6.1: 23–36.

—— (2005c) 'Disrespect and distrust: the external origins of contemporary Chinese nationalism', *Journal of Contemporary China*, 14.2: 11–21.

Jiang, Lingfie. (2002) 'Sino–U.S. relations and world politics since 9.11', *Beijing Review*, 3 January: 7–8.

Jiang, Wenran. (2002) 'The Japanese assessment of the "China Threat"', in H. Yee and I. Storey (eds), *The China Threat*, London: RoutledgeCurzon, 150–65.

Jiang, Zemin. (1995) 'Continue to promote the reunification of the motherland', 30 January, <http://www.fmprc.gov.cn/eng/ljzg/3568/t17784.htm> (accessed 1 July 2006).

—— (1997a) 'Jiang: peace and stability ensure a just, better world', *Beijing Review*, 12–18 May: 9–11.

—— (1997b) 'Speech by President Jiang Zemin at the public gathering to celebrate Hong Kong's return', *Beijing Review*, 14–20 July: 27–30.

—— (1997c) 'Enhance mutual understanding and build stronger ties of friendship and cooperation', *Beijing Review*, 24–30 November: 7–11.

—— (1999) 'Develop China–Europe cooperation and promote the establishment of a New International Order', *Beijing Review*, 12–18 April: 6–8.

—— (2000) 'Together to build a China–U.S. relationship oriented towards the new century', 8 September, <http://www.cfr.org/publication.html>?id=3803> (accessed 1 July 2006).

Johnson, C. (2005) 'No longer the "lone" superpower: coming to terms with China', *JPRI Working Paper*, 105, March, <www.jpri.org/publications/workingpapers/wp105.html> (accessed 1 July 2006).

Johnson, H. (1953) *China's New Creative Age*, London: Lawrence & Wishart.

Johnson, L. (1965) 'Pattern for peace in Southeast Asia', *Department of State Bulletin*, 26 April: 607.

Johnston, A. (1995) *Cultural Realism: Strategic Culture and Grand Strategy in Chinese History*, Princeton: Princeton University Press.

—— (1996) 'Cultural realism and strategy in Maoist China', in P. Katzenstein (ed.), *The Culture of National Security. Norms and Identity in World Politics*, New York: Columbia University Press, 216–68.

—— (1999) *The Cox Committee Report: An Assessment*, Stanford: Center for International Security and Cooperation.

—— (2003) 'Is China a status quo power', *International Security*, 27.4: 5–56.

—— (2004a) 'China's militarized interstate dispute behaviour 1949–1992', in G. Liu (ed.), *Chinese Foreign Policy in Transition*, New York: Aldine de Gruyter, 259–93.

—— (2004b) 'Chinese middle class attitudes towards international affairs: nascent liberalization?', *China Quarterly*, 179, September: 603–28.

Johnston, A. and Ross, R. (eds) (1999) *Engaging China. Managing a Rising Power*, London: Routledge.

Kagan, R. (1997a) 'What China knows that we don't: the case for a new strategy of containment', *Weekly Standard*, 20 January.

—— (1997b) 'China: the end of engagement', *Weekly Standard*, 10 November 1997.

—— (1999a) 'The price of "engaging" China', *New York Times*, 15 January.

—— (1999b) 'China's no. 1 enemy', *New York Times*, 11 May.

Kagan, R. and Kristol, W. (2001a) 'We lost', *Washington Post*, 13 April.

—— (2001b) 'A national humiliation', *Weekly Standard*, 16–23 April: 11–16.

Kahn, J. (2005) 'Chinese general sees U.S. as nuclear target', *New York Times*, 16 July.

Kaiser, R. (2000) '2025 vision: a China bent on Asian dominance', *Washington Post*, 17 March.

Kaiser, R. and Mufson, S. (2000) '"Blue Team" draw a hard line on Beijing', *Washington Post*, 22 February.

Kane, T. (2002) *Chinese Grand Strategy and Maritime Power*, Portland: Frank Cass.

—— (2004) 'China's foundations. Guiding principles of Chinese foreign policy', in G. Liu (ed.), *Chinese Foreign Policy in Transition*, New York: Aldine de Gruyter, 101–15.

Kang, D. (2001) 'Hierarchy and stability in Asian international relations', *American Asian Review*, 19.2: 121–60.

Kanwal, G. (1999) 'China's long march to world power status: strategic challenge for India', *Strategic Analysis*, 22, February: 1713–28.

Kapila, S. (2001) 'India-Vietnam strategic partnership', *SAAG Papers*, 177, January.

Kaplan, R. (1999) 'China: a world power again', *Atlantic Monthly*, 284.2: 16–18.

—— (2005a) 'The illusion of "managing" China', *Washington Post*, 15 May.

—— (2005b) 'How we would fight China', *Atlantic Monthly*, 295.5: 49–64.

Karasin, G. (1996) 'Russia and China: winging toward twenty-first century partnership', *Rossiiskiye Vesti*, 26 December, <http://www.fas.org/news/china/1996/msg00003i.htm> (accessed 1 July 2006).

Karmel, S. (2000) *China and the People's Liberation Army: Great Power or Struggling Developing State?*, New York: St Martin's Press.

Katzenstein, P. (1996) 'Introduction: alternative perspectives on national security', in Katzenstein (ed.), *The Culture of National Security. Norms and Identity in World Politics*, New York: Columbia University Press, 1–32.

Kaufman, V. (2001) *Confronting Communism. U.S. and British Policies Toward China*, Columbia: University of Missouri Press.

Kawaguchi, Yoriko. (2003) 'Towards a brighter future: advancing our global partnership', 8 January, <http://www.mofa.go.jp/region/asia–paci/fmv0301/india.html> (accessed 1 July 2006).

Keating, P. (2000) *Engagement. Australia Faces the Asia–Pacific*, Sydney: Macmillan.

Kennedy, D. and Krasner, S. (1997) 'Brothers under the skin: diplomatic history and internationals relations', *International Security*, 22.1, 34–43.

Kennedy, P. (1988) *The Rise and Fall of the Great Powers*, London: Hyman.

Kennedy, P. and Modelski, G. (1987) *Long Cycles in World Politics*, London: Macmillan Press.

Khalilzad, Z. (ed.) (1999) *The United States and a Rising China*, Santa Monica: RAND.

Khanna, R. (1999) 'Impact of China's ambitions to be a regional naval superpower', *Asian Defence Journal*, 8, August: 6–9.

Khong, Y. (1996) 'The United States and East Asia', in N. Woods (ed.), *Explaining International Relations Since 1945*, Oxford: Oxford University Press, 179–96.

Khrushchev, N. (1971) *Khrushchev Remembers*, London: Andre Deutsch.

Kim, S. (1996) *China's Quest for Security in the Post-Cold War World*, Carlisle Barracks: Strategic Studies Institute.

Kim, T. (1998) 'A reality check: the "Rise of China" and its military capability toward 2010', *The Journal of East Asian Affairs*, 12.2: 321–63.

King, S. (2004) 'How big a threat to West is growth of China?', *Independent*, 7 July.

Kipling, R. (1900) *From Sea to Sea*, London: Macmillan, 1919, 2 vols.

Kirby, S. (1960) 'Russia's largest satellite', *China Quarterly*, 1, January–March: 12–14.

Kissinger, H. (1971) 'My talks with Chou En–Lai', 14 July, <www.gwu.edu/~nscarchiv/NSAEBB/NSAEBB66/ch–40.pdf> (accessed 1 July 2006).

—— (1979) *White House Years*, Boston: Little, Brown.

—— (1982) *Years of Upheaval*, London: Weidenfeld and Nicholson.

—— (1994) *Diplomacy*, New York: Simon & Schuster.

—— (1999) 'Storm clouds gathering', *Washington Post*, 7 September.

—— (2005) 'China: containment won't work', *Washington Post*, 13 June.

Kissinger–Zhou. (1971) 'Memorandum of conversation', 9 July, <www.gwu.edu/~nscarchiv/NSAEBB/NSAEBB66/ch-34.pdf> (accessed 1 July 2006).

Klare, M. (2005) 'Revving up the China threat', *The Nation*, 13 October.

—— (2006) 'Containing China', *Asia Times*, 20 April.

Klein, C. (2003) *Cold War Orientalism*, Berkeley: University of California Press.

Klintworth, G. (1992) 'Chinese perspectives on India as a great power', in R. Babbage and S. Gordon (eds), *India's Strategic Future*, Houndsmill: Macmillan, 94–106.

Koizumi, J. (2002) 'The future of Asia', 21 May, <http://www.mofa.go.jp/region/asia–paci/future/speech0205.html> (accessed 1 July 2006).

Kornberg, J. and Faust, J. (2005) *China in World Politics*, 2nd edn, London: Lynne Rienner.

Kratochwil, F. and Lapid, Y. (eds) (1996) *The Return of Culture and Identity in IR Theory*, Boulder: Lynne Rienner.

Krause, J. and Renwick, N. (eds) (1996) *Identities in International Relations*, New York: St Martins.

Krausse, A. (1898) *China in Decay*, London: Chapman & Hall.

Krauthammer, C. (1995) 'Why we must contain China', *Time*, 31 July.

Kreisberg, P. (1996) 'The China factor', in P. Kreisberg (ed.), *South Asia and the Indian Ocean: The Strategic Environment, 1995–2010*, Alexandria: CRM/Center for Naval Analyses, 22–6.

Kristof, N. (1993) 'The rise of China', *Foreign Affairs*, 72.5: 59–74.

—— (2002) 'The chip on China's shoulder', *New York Times*, 18 January.

Kuchins, A. (1999) 'Russia and Great–Power security in Asia', in G. Chufrin (ed.), *Russia and Asia–Pacific Security*, Stockholm: SIPRI, 27–36.

Kulischer, E. (1953) 'Teeming Asia and the West', *Political Science Quarterly*, 68, 481–91.

Kynge, J. (2005) *China Shakes the World*, London: Weidenfeld & Nicolson.

Laliberté, A. (2005) 'China's "Peaceful Emergence"', *Papers*, CANCAPS, 38, August.

Lall, A. (1965) 'The political effects of the Chinese bomb', *Bulletin of the Atomic Scientists*, February: 21–4.

Lampton, D. (2001) *Same Bed Different Dreams. Managing U.S.–China Relations 1989–2000*, Berkeley: University of California Press.

—— (2005) 'China's rise in Asia need not be at America's expense', in D. Shambaugh (ed.), *Power Shift. China and Asia's New Dynamics*, Berkeley: University of California Press, 306–26.

Lancaster, J. (2005) 'India, China hoping to "Reshape the world order" together', *Washington Post*, 12 April.

Landsberger, S. (2004) 'Propaganda posters in the reform era', *Asian Economic and Political Issues*, 10: 27–57.

Lantis, J. (2005) 'Strategic culture', *Strategic Insights*, 4.10, http://www.ccc.nps.navy.mil/si/2005/Oct/lantisOct05.asp.

Larin, V. (1995) '"Yellow Peril" again', in S. Kotkin and D. Wolff (eds), *Rediscovering Russia in Asia*, New York: M.E. Sharpe, 290–301.

—— (2004) 'China factor in the mindsets of Russians living in border areas', *Far Eastern Affairs*, 32.3: 22–44.

Lattimore, O. (1949) *The Situation in Asia*, Boston: Little, Brown.

Lauren, P. (2003) 'Race from power: U.S. foreign policy and the general crisis of White supremacy', in B. Plummer (ed.), *Window on Freedom. Race, Civil Rights, and Foreign Affairs, 1945–1988*, Chapel Hill: University of North Carolina Press, 45–66.

Lawrance, L. (ed.) (1975) *China's Foreign Relations Since 1949 [Documents]*, London: Boston & Kegan Paul.

Layne, C. (1993) 'The unipolar illusion: why new Great Powers will rise', *International Security*, 17.4: 5–51.

Lee, Jae-hyung. (2002) 'China's expanding maritime ambitions in the Western Pacific and the Indian Ocean', *Contemporary Southeast Asia*, 24, December: 549–68.

Lee, Wen Ho. (2002) *My Country Versus Me*, New York: Hyperion.

Lei, Guang. (2005) 'Realpolitik nationalism. International sources of Chinese nationalism', *Modern China*, 31.4: 487–514.

Leifer, M. (1997) 'China in Southeast Asia', in D. Goodman and G. Segal (eds), *China Rising*, London: Routledge, 156–71.

Levi, W. (1953) *Modern China's Foreign Policy*, Minneapolis: University of Minnesota Press.

Lewis, J. and Litai, X. (1994) *China's Strategic Seapower*, Stanford: Stanford University Press.

Li, Hongshan. (1997) 'China talks back', *Journal of Contemporary China*, 6.14: 153–60.

Li, Jijun. (1994) 'Notes on military theory and military strategy', 1994, in M. Pillsbury (ed.), *Chinese Views of Future Warfare*, Honolulu: University Press of the Pacific, 2002, 221–31.

—— (1997) 'Traditional military thinking and the defensive strategy of China', 29 August, *Letort Paper*, 1, Carlisle Barracks: Strategic Studies Institute.

Li, Nan. (2001) *From Revolutionary Internationalism to Conservative Nationalism The Chinese Military's Discourse on National Security and Identity in the Post-Mao Era*, Washington: United States Institute of Peace.

Li, Peng. (1996) 'The impact of China's development and the rise of Asia on the future of the world', *Beijing Review*, 30 September–6 October: 6–11.

—— (1997) 'Speech by Premier Li Peng at the reception in Beijing celebrating the return of Hong Kong to the motherland', *Beijing Review*, 14–20 July: 24–6.

Li, Rex. (2004) 'Security challenge of an ascendant China', in Zhao Suisheng (ed.), *Chinese Foreign Policy*, New York: M.E. Sharpe, 23–57.

Li, Xiguang. (1996) 'US media: behind the demonization of China', *Beijing Review*, 21–27 November: 12.

—— (1998–9) 'The inside story of the demonization of China', *Contemporary Chinese Thought*, Winter: 13–77.

Li, Yan. (2000) 'Li Zhaoxing refutes "China Threat" theory', *People's Daily*, 29 December.

Lii, Haibo. (2004) 'Whose century is it?', *Beijing Review*, 14 October: 32.

Lilley, C. and Hunt, M. (1987) 'On social history, the state, and foreign relations', *Diplomatic History*, 11.3, 243–50.

Lilley, J. (1997) 'The "Fu Manchu" problem', *Newsweek*, 24 February.

Lim, R. (1998) 'Australian security after the Cold War', *Orbis*, 42.1, 91–103.

Lin, Biao. (1965) 'Long live the victory of People's War', *Peking Review*, 3 September, 9–30.

Lin, Liangqi. (2002) 'To our readers', *Beijing Review*, 4 July: 2.

Lin, Shaowen. (2004) 'China's "peaceful rise"', *People's Daily*, 2 May 2004.

Ling, Zhijun and Avery, M. (2006) *The Lenovo Affair*, New York: Wiley.

Lintner, B. (2006) 'The Chinese are coming . . . to Russia', *Asia Times*, 27 May.

Liu, Huaqing. (1994) 'Defense modernization in historical perspective', in M. Pillsbury (ed.), *Chinese Views of Future Warfare*, Honolulu: University Press of the Pacific, 2002, 115–18.

Liu, Ji. (2004) 'Making the right choices in twenty-first century Sino–American relations', in Zhao Suisheng (ed.), *Chinese Foreign Policy*, New York: M.E. Sharpe, 243–55.

Liu, Shaoqi. (1949a) *Internationalism and Nationalism*, Peking: Foreign Language Press.

—— (1949b) 'The opening speech at the Asia and Australia Trade Union Delegates Meeting', 16 November, in *Collected Works of Liu Shao-Ch'i*, Hong Kong: Union Research Institute, 1969, vol. 2, 175–82.

—— (1953) 'An address on the third anniversary of the Sino–Soviet Treaty of Friendship and Alliance and Mutual Assistance', 13 February, in *Collected Works of Liu Shao-Ch'i*, Hong Kong: Union Research Institute, 1969, vol. 2, 259–67.

Liu, Toming. (2001) 'Uses and abuses of sentimental nationalism: mnemonic disquiet in *Heshang* and *Shuobu*', *Modern Chinese Literature and Culture*, 13.1: 169–209.

Liu, Xiaobiao. (2002) 'From concocting "theory of threat" to dishing up "theory of collapse"', *People's Daily*, 14 June.

Liu, Yawei. (1998) 'Mao Zedong and the United States: a story of misperceptions, 1960–1970', in Li Hongshan and Hong Zhaohui (eds), *Image, Perception and the Making of U.S.–China Relations*, Lanham: University Press of America, 189–232.

Lloyd, J. (2000) 'Will this be the Chinese century?', *New Statesman*, 129, 10 January: 15–16.

Lomanov, A. (2001) 'On the periphery of the "clash of civilisations": discourse and geopolitics in Russian–Chinese relations', 1 August, *Contemporary Chinese Nationalism and Transnationalism*, CEU, <http://ceu.hu/courses/CIO/modules/Module06Lomanov/Lomanov_index.html> (accessed 1 July 2006).

London, J. (1993) 'The unparalled invasion', in E. Labor *et al.* (eds), *The Complete Short Stories of Jack London*, Stanford: Stanford University Press, 2.12, 36–40.

Lowe, P. (1989) 'The frustrations of alliance: Britain, the United States and the Korean War, 1950–1951', in J. Cotton and I. Neary (eds), *The Korean War in History*, Manchester: Manchester University Press, 80–99.

Lowell, D. (2002) 'East Asia in the "new era" in world politics', *World Politics*, 55.1, 38–65.

Lubman, S. (2004) 'The dragon as demon: images of China on Capital Hill', *Journal of Contemporary China*, 13, August: 541–65.

Lukin, A. (1998) 'The image of China in Russian border regions', *Asian Survey*, 38.9: 821–35.

—— (1999) 'Russia's image of China and Russian–Chinese relations', *East Asia: An International Quarterly*, 17, Spring: 5–39.

—— (2002) 'Russian perception of the China threat', in H. Yee and I. Storey (eds), *The China Threat*, London: RoutledgeCurzon, 86–114.

—— (2003) *The Bear Watches the Dragon*, New York: M.E. Sharpe.

Luo, Ruiqing. (1965) 'The people defeated Japanese fascism and they can certainly defeat U.S. imperialism too', *Peking Review*, 3 September, 31–9.

Lyman, S. (2000) 'The "Yellow Peril" mystique: origins and vicissitudes of a racist discourse', *International Journal of Politics, Culture and Society*, 13, 683–747.

MacArthur, D. (1964) *Reminiscences*, New York: McGraw-Hill.

Mackintosh, M. (1965) 'Yellow Peril 1975', *Sunday Times*, 19 December.

Mahapatra, A. (2005) 'Highland terror. China's unprecedented military build up in Tibet threatens India', *News Insight*, 1 August.

Mahbubani, K. (2005) 'Understanding China', *Foreign Affairs*, 84.5: 49–60.

Maitra, R. (2002) 'Indian military shadow over Central Asia', *Asia Times*, 10 September.

Malik, J. (1995) 'China–India relations in the post-Soviet era: the continuing rivalry', *China Quarterly*, 142, June: 317–55.

Malik, M. (2002) *Dragon on Terrorism: Assessing China's Tactical Gains and Strategic Losses Post–September 11*, Carlisle Barracks: Strategic Studies Institute.

—— (2006) 'China's strategy of containing India', *PINR*, 6 February.

Mallaby, S. (2005) 'The next Chinese threat', *Washington Post*, 8 August.

Mansfield, M. (1974) 'China and the United States', in F. Wilcox (ed.), *China and the Great Powers*, New York: Praeger Publishers, 49–61.

Mao, Zedong. (1954) *Selected Works of Mao Tsetung*, London: Lawrence & Wishart, 4 vols.

—— (1967) 'China should become the arsenal for world revolution', 7 July, in *Classified Chinese Communist Documents: A Selection*, Taipei: Institute of International Relations, National Chengchi University, 1978, 454–6.

—— (1969) *The Political Thoughts of Mao Tse-tung*, trans. and ed. S. Schram, Harmondsworth: Penguin.

—— (1974) *Mao Tse-tung Unrehearsed. Talks and Letters, 1956–71*, trans. and ed. S. Schram, Harmondsworth: Penguin.

—— (1977) *Selected Works of Mao Tsetung. Volume V*, Peking: Foreign Languages Press.

Marcuse, J. (1967) *The Peking Papers*, London: Arthur Barker.

Marland, B. (1996) 'China isn't a militarist power', *International Herald Tribune*, 15 November.

Marshall, S. (1953) *The River and the Gauntlet. Defeat of the Eighth Army by the Chinese Communist forces, November, 1950, in the Battle of the Chongchon River, Korea*, New York: Morrow.

Martel, W. and Yoshihara, T. (2003) 'Averting a Sino–U.S. space race', *Washington Quarterly*, Autumn: 19–35.

Martin, E. (1986) *Divided Counsel: The Anglo–American Response to Communist Victory in China*, Lexington: University Press of Kentucky.

Masani, M. (1965) 'The challenge of the Chinese bomb – II', *India Quarterly*, 21.1: 15–28.

Mattoo, A. and Kanti, B. (eds) (2000) *The Peacock and the Dragon: India–China Relations in the 21st Century*, New Delhi: Har Anand Publishers.

Maxwell, N. (1970) *India's China War*, London: Jonathan Cape.

—— (1987) 'India–China: toward India's second China war?', *Mainstream*, 13 June: 27–30.

—— (2003) 'Forty years of folly. What caused the Sino–Indian border war and why the dispute is unresolved', *Critical Asian Studies*, 35.1: 99–112.

McAllister, I. and Ravenhill, R. (1998) 'Australian attitudes towards closer engagement with Asia', *Pacific Review*, 11: 119–41.

McCabe, T. (2003) 'The Chinese air force and air and space power', *Air & Space Power Journal*, 17, Fall: 73–83.

McCarthy, J. (1950) 'Joseph McCarthy's speech on communists in the State Department excerpt', 9 February, <http://www.cnn.com/SPECIALS/cold.war/episodes/06/documents/mccarthy/.> (accessed 1 July 2006).

McGuire, E. (2001) 'China, the fun house mirror: Soviet reactions to the Chinese Cultural Revolution, 1966–1969', *Berkeley Program in Soviet and Post–Soviet Studies*, Paper, 1 May, <http://repositories.cdlib.org/iseees/bps/2001_02-mcgu> (accessed 1 July 2006).

McMorris, S. (1967) 'World peace and the bombs of China', *Midwest Quarterly*, 9.1, October: 53–64.

McNamara, R. (1965) 'Buildup of U.S. forces in Vietnam', *Department of State Bulletin*, 30 August: 369.

—— (1967) 'Statement by the U.S. representative at the Geneva Conference', *Department of State Bulletin*, 30 October: 543–5.

Mearsheimer, J. (2001a) 'The future of the American pacifier', *Foreign Affairs*, 80.5: 46–61.

—— (2001b) *The Tragedy of Great Power Politics*, New York: Norton.

—— (2005) 'The rise of China will not be peaceful at all', *The Australian*, 18 November.

Medvedev, R. (1986) *China and the Superpowers*, London: Basil Blackwell.

Meisner, M. (1967) *Li Ta-chao and the Origins of Chinese Marxism*, Cambridge: Harvard University Press.

—— (1999) 'A habit of distrust. Mutual racism and arrogance undermine ties', *Los Angeles Times*, 30 May.

Mekay, E. (2005) 'The dawn of the Chinese Century?, *Inter-Press Service* IPS, 16 February, <http://www.ipsnews.org/print.asp?idnews=27484> (accessed 1 July 2006).

Mellor, W. and Lim Le-Min Lim. (2006) 'To slake its thirst for oil, China scours backwaters of the world', *International Herald Tribune*, 26 September.

Men, Jing. (2003) 'The search for an official ideology and its impact on Chinese foreign policy', *Regional Governance: Greater China in the 21st Century*, Durham, 24–5 October.

Mende, T. (1961) *China and Her Shadows*, London: Thames and Hudson.

Menges, C. (2005) *China: The Gathering Threat*, Thomas Nelson.

Mendl, W. (1979) 'China's challenge to Japan', *World Today*, July: 276–86.

Menon, R. (2003) 'The sick man of Asia: Russia's Far East', *National Interest*, 73, Fall: 93–106.

Menon, R. and Ziegler, C. (2002) 'Balance of power and U.S. foreign policy interest in the Russian Far East', in J. Thornton and C. Ziegler (eds), *Russia's Far East*, Seattle: University of Washington Press, 35–56.

Middleton, D. (1968) *America's Stake in Asia*, Philadelphia: J. B. Lippincott.

Millennium (1993) *Special Issue: Culture in International Relations*, 22.3.

Miller, J. (1900) *China. The Yellow Peril: at War with the World*, Chicago: American Publishing House.

Minakir, P. (1996) 'Chinese immigration into the Russian Far East', in J. Azrael and E. Pain (eds), *Cooperation and Conflict in the Former Soviet Union*, Santa Monica: RAND, 85–97.

Mitra, K. (1996) 'China in the 21st century: implications for India', *USI Journal*, 126, April–June: 202–9.

Mohan, C. (2003) 'After China, Fernandes warms up to Japan', *The Hindu*, 30 April.

—— (2005) 'There's a new game in Asia. India, Indian Ocean and China's "string of pearls"', *Indian Express*, 31 May.

Moller, K. (2006) 'The Beijing bluff', *Survival*, 48.2: 137–46.

Monk, W. (1953) 'New Zealand faces north', *Pacific Affairs*, 26.3: 220–9.

Mooney, P. (2005) 'Undue fears of China Inc?', *YaleGlobal*, 29 September.

Moore, P. (1999) 'How China plays the ethnic card', *Los Angeles Times*, 24 June.

Moore, T. (2005) 'Chinese foreign policy in an age of globalization', in Deng Yong and Wang Fei-ling (eds), *China Rising*, Lanham: Bowman & Littlefield, 121–58.

Mosher, S. (2000) *Hegemon. China's Plan to Dominate Asia and the World*, San Francisco: Encounter Books.

Motrich, E. (2001) 'Reaction of the population of the Russian Far East to the presence of Chinese people', May, <http://gsti.miis.edu/CEAS-PUB/200105Motrich.pdf> (accessed 1 July 2006).

Mrozinski, L., Williams, T., Kent, R. and Tyner, R. (2002) 'Countering China's threat to the Western hemisphere', *International Journal of Intelligence and Counter Intelligence*, 15, 195–210.

Mufson, S. and Pomfret, J. (1998) 'Chinese ex-official challenges party', *Washington Post*, 3 June.

Munro, R. (2000) 'China: the challenge of a rising power', in R. Kagan (ed.), *Present Dangers: Crisis and Opportunity in American Foreign and Defense Policy*, San Francisco: Encounter Books, 47–74.

Murphey, R. (1966) 'China and the dominoes', *Asian Survey*, 6.9: 510–515.

Murray, W. (2004) 'Undersea dragons: China's maturing submarine force', *International Security*, 28.4: 161–96.

Murray, W. and Antonellis, R. (2003) 'China's space program', *Orbis*, 47.4: 645–52.

Nair, V. (2001) 'The Chinese threat: an Indian perspective', *China Brief*, 1.9, 2001, <www.jamestown.org/publications_details.php?volume_id=17&issue_id=637&article_id=4586> (accessed 1 July 2006).

Nanda, P. (2002) 'Strategic significance of the Andamans', *Bharat Rakshak Monitor*, 5.3, November–December, <http://www.bharat–rakshak.com/MONITOR/ISSUE5-3/nanda.html> (accessed 1 July 2006).

Nathan, A. and Ross, R. (1997) *Great Wall and the Empty Fortress: China's Search for Security*, New York: W.W. Norton.

Nathan, J. and Tien, C. (2003) 'The "China threat"', *National Missile Defense*, 19, March, 35–54.

Nathan, K. (1999) 'China, India, and the Asian balance of power in the 21st century', *Asian Defence Journal*, 4, April: 6–9.

Nayar, B. and Paul, T. (2003) *India in the World Order*, Cambridge: Cambridge University Press.

Nehru, R. (1965) 'The challenge of the Chinese bomb – I', *India Quarterly*, 21.1: 3–14.

Nelson, L.-E. (1999) 'Washington: The Yellow Peril', *New York Review of Books*, 66.12, 15 July: 6–10.

Ness, P. van. (2002) 'Hegemony, not anarchy: why China and Japan are not balancing US unipolar power', *International Relations of the Asia–Pacific*, 2: 131–50.

New York Times (1998) 'India's new defence chief sees Chinese military threat', 5 May.

—— (2006) 'China eyes stronger military against threats', Reuters, 26 July.

Newman, B. (1962) *The Blue Ants: The First Authentic Account of the Russian–Chinese War of 1970*, London: Robert Hale.

Newman, R. (1961) *Recognition of Communist China?*, New York: Macmillan.

—— (2005) 'China's turn', *US News & Report*, 20 June.

New Zealand. (1881) *Parliamentary Debates. Volume 38*, Wellington: G. Didsbury, Government Printer.

Ng, Franklin. (1998) 'Chinese Americans: still the Yellow Peril?', in G. Campbell (ed.), *Many Americas: Critical Perspectives on Race, Racism and Ethnicity*, Dubuque: Kendall/Hunt, 186–9.

Ni, Feng. (1997) 'Enhanced US-Japanese security alliance: cause for concern', *Beijing Review*, 16–22 June: 7–8.

—— (2004) 'The shaping of China's foreign policy', in Kokubun Ryosei and Wang Jisi (eds), *The Rise of China and a Changing East Asian Order*, Tokyo: Japan Center for International Exchange, 139–51.

Ni, Lexiong. (2005) 'Sea power and China's development', *Liberation Daily*, 17 April 2005, <www.uscc.gov/researchpapers/translated_articles/2005/05_07_18_Sea_Power_and_Chinas_Development.pdf> (accessed 1 July 2006).

Niazi, T. (2005) 'Gwadar: China's naval outpost on the Indian Ocean', *China Brief*, 5.4: 6–8.

NIC (2000) *Global Trends 2015*, National Intelligence Council, NIC 2000-02, December, <http://www.cia.gov/cia/reports/globaltrends2015/> (accessed 1 July 2006).

Nixon, R. (1967) 'Asia after Viet Nam', *Foreign Affairs*, 46.1: 111–25.

—— (1978) *The Memoirs of Richard Nixon*, New York: Grosset & Dunlap.

Nolan, P. (1995) *China's Rise, Russia's Fall*, Basingstoke: Macmillan.

Norbu, D. (1997) 'Tibet in Sino–Indian relations', *Asian Survey*, 37, November: 1078–95.

North, R. (1960) 'The Sino–Soviet alliance', *China Quarterly*, 1, January–March: 51–60.

—— (1962) 'Peking's drive for Empire', in E. Pentony (ed.), *China, the Emerging Red Giant*, San Francisco: Chandler Publishing, 53–69.

Nye, J. (1995) 'The case for deep engagement', *Foreign Affairs*, 74.4: 90–102.

—— (1998) 'As China rises, must others bow?', *Economist*, 27 June: 21–24.

—— (2005) *Soft Power*, New York: Public Affairs.

—— (2006) 'Fear of Chinese guns', *San Francisco Chronicle*, 9 April.

Observer (1964) 'US policy towards China is in a blind alley', *People's Daily*, 19 February.

OECD. (1996) *China in the 21st Century*, Paris: OECD.

Okazaki, Hisahiko. (2005) 'China's growing strength a future threat', *Yomiuri Shimbun*, 20 November.

Oksenberg, M. (1987) 'China's confident nationalism', *Foreign Affairs*, 65.3: 501–23.

Ollapally, D. (1998) 'Foreign policy and identity politics', *International Studies*, 35.3: 253–68.

Ong, R. (2002) *China's Security Interests in the Post-Cold War Era*, Richmond: Curzon, 2002.

O'Sullivan, J. (2000) 'A Yellow peril? No', *National Review*, 1 May: 28–30.

Outlook East Weekly. (2004) 'The worrisome situation of the South China Sea – China facing the stepped-up military infiltration by the U.S., Japan and India', *liaowangdongfang zhoukan*, 12 January 2004, trans. <http://www.uscc.gov/researchpapers/2004/southchinaseamilitary.htm> (accessed 1 July 2006).

Overholt, W. (1993) *China. The Next Economic Superpower*, London: Weidenfeld & Nicolson.

—— (1994) *The Rise of China*, New York: Norton.

Pablo-Baviera, A. (2002) 'Perceptions of a China threat: a Philippine perspective', in H. Yee and I. Storey (eds), *The China Threat*, London: RoutledgeCurzon, 248–64.

Paloczi–Horvath, G. (1963) *Mao Tse-tung. Emperor of the Blue Ants*, New York: Doubleday.

Palumbo-Liu, D. (1998) 'Out of place: transnationalism, race and the new Cold War', *Stanford Journal of International Relations*, 1.1, <http://Stanford.edu/group/sjir/1.1.02_palumboliu.html> (accessed 1 July 2006).

Pan, Chengxin (2004) 'The "China threat" in American self-imagination', *Alternatives*, 29.3: 305–31.

Pang, Zhongying (2002) 'The US role in Sino-Russian relations', *Beijing Review*, 23 May, 7.

—— (2005) 'Shared interests of China, Russia', *China Daily*, 6 July.

—— (2006) 'China, my China', *National Interest*, 83, Spring: 9–10.

Panikkar, K. (1955) *In Two Chinas*, London: Allen & Unwin.

Pant, H. (2005) 'The Moscow – Beijing-Delhi "strategic triangle". An idea whose time may never come', *Crossroads*, 5.2: 19–46.

Park, M. and Taeho, K. (1998) 'Anchoring a new pattern of interdependence and strategic rivalry: China–Japan relations toward the 21st century', *Korean Journal of Defense Analysis*, 10, Summer: 121–40.

Parker, G. (1985) *Western Geopolitical Thought in the Twentieth Century*, London: Croom Helm.

Pastor, R. (1999) 'Is China a threat or a partner? The logic of the downward spiral', *Brown Journal of World Affairs*, 6, Summer/Fall: 3–14.

Paulson, H. (2006) 'Remarks by Treasury Secretary Henry M. Paulson on the International Economy', 13 September, http://www.treas.gov/press/releases/hp95.htm

Payne, R. (1947) *China Awakes*, London: William Heinemann.

—— (1951) *Mao Tse-tung. Ruler of Red China*, London: Secker and Warburg.

Pearson, C. (1893) *National Life and Character. A Forecast*, London: Macmillan.

Peffer, N. (1931) *China. The Collapse of a Civilization*, London: Routledge.

—— (1956) 'China in reappraisal', *Political Science Quarterly*, 71.4: 481–515.

Peking Review. (1963) 'Statement by the spokesman of the Chinese government – a comment on the Soviet government's statement of August 21', 6 September 1963, 7–16.

—— (1964) 'China successfully explodes its first atom bomb. Chinese Government statement', 16 October, ii–iii.

—— (1966a) 'Heroic Chinese People's Air Force punishes intruding U.S. aircraft', 23 September, 25–7.

—— (1966b) 'Mao Tse-tung's thought is the common treasure of the world's revolutionary people', 30 September, 18–22.

—— (1966c) 'Colour documentary "The great victory of Mao Tse-tung's thought" being shown – hailing China's three successful nuclear tests', 7 October, 31–32.

—— (1966d) 'China successfully conducts guided missile-nuclear weapon test', 28 October, ii–iii.

—— (1967a) 'China's first hydrogen bomb successfully exploded', 23 June, 6–7.

—— (1967b) 'No adverse current can block the mainstream of history', 14 July, 37.

—— (1975) 'Soviet social-imperialists covet Southeast Asia', 15 August: 20–1.

—— (1976a) 'Soviet social-imperialism – most dangerous source of war', 30 January: 9–13.

—— (1976b) 'Soviet social imperialism. Maritime hegemonic features fully exposed', 30 April: 25–6.

—— (1976c) 'What does the situation show one year after the European Security Conference?', 9 August: 11–13.

—— (1977a) 'Soviet social imperialism – most dangerous source of world war', 15 July: 4–10.

—— (1977b) 'Chairman Mao's theory of the Differentiation of the Three Worlds is a major contribution to Marxism–Leninism', 4 November: 10–41.

People's Daily [Online]. (2000) 'Li Peng on international situation, China's domestic policies', 27 June.

—— (2002a) '"Theory of threat" is groundless, erroneous: analysis', 6 June.

—— (2002b) 'Will China and US follow the tracks of Soviet–US Cold War?', 28 June.

—— (2002c) 'US media kicking up terrific racket about "China threat"', 16 July,

—— (2002d) 'Chinese spokesman rebuts "China threat" theory', 23 July.

—— (2003) 'Chinese Premier, Indian PM hold talks', 23 June.

—— (2005b) 'How there comes "Chinese military threat" theory', 24 March.

—— (2005c) 'New vocabulary ushers China–US relations into global scenarios', 22 December.

—— (2006a) 'China promotes its culture overseas to dissolve China threat', 28 May.

—— (2006b) '"China threat" fear countered by culture', 29 May.

—— (2006c) 'China not a threat to world energy security', I June.

—— (2006d) 'Stronger China poses no threat to other nations', 5 July.

—— (2006e) 'Who believes the new China threat theory?' 8 July.

—— (2006f) 'Why is China always haunted by the China threat?', 2 August.

Perry, W. (1994) 'U.S.–China military relationship memorandum for the Secretaries of the Army, Navy, and Air Force', August, National Security Archive, George Washington University, <http://www.gwu.edu/~nsarchiv/NSAEBB/NSAEBB19/12-01.htm> (accessed 1 July 2006).

—— (1995) 'U.S. strategy: engage China, not contain it', 30 October, *Defense Issues*, 10.109, <http://www.fas.org/news/china/1995/di10109.htm> (accessed 1 July 2006).

—— (1998) 'Preventive diplomacy and U.S. diplomacy', *Stanford Journal of International Relations*, 1.1, Summer–Fall 1998, <http://www.stanford.edu/group/sjir/1.1.07_perry.html> (accessed 1 July 2006).

Pesek, W. (2005) 'Welcome to the Chinese century?', *International Herald Tribune*, 15 February.

Pfaff, W. (2001) 'What's the rationale for seeing China as enemy?', *International Herald Tribune*, 2 July.

PGAP. (2006) *China's Neighbors Worry About Its Growing Military Strength*, Washington: The Pew Global Attitudes Project, 21 September.

Pillsbury, M. (2001a) 'China's perception of the USA', *Research Papers*, U.S.–China Economic and Security Review Commission, 19 October.

—— (2001b) 'China's military strategy toward the U.S.', *Research Papers*, U.S.–China Economic and Security Review Commission, 2 November.

—— (2005) *China Debates the Future Security Environment*, Honolulu: University Press of the Pacific.

Pollack, J. (1984) 'China and the global strategic balance', in H. Harding (ed.), *China's Foreign Relations in the 1980s*, New Haven: Yale University Press, 146–76.

—— (1999) 'The Cox Report's "Dirty little secret"', *Arms Control Today*, 29.3: 26–35.

—— (2002a) 'American perceptions of Chinese military power', in H. Yee and I. Storey (eds), *The China Threat*, London: RoutledgeCurzon, 43–64.

—— (2002b) 'Chinese security in the post-11 September world', *Asia-Pacific Review*, 9.2: 12–30.

—— (2003) 'China and the United States post-9/11', *Orbis*, 47.4: 617–27.

Portiakov, V. (1996) 'Are the Chinese coming? Migration processes in Russia's Far East', *International Affairs*, 42.1: 132–47.

Posen, B. and Ross, A. (1996–7) 'Competing visions for U.S. grand strategy', *International Security*, 21: 5–53.

Powell, C. (2004) 'A strategy of partnerships', *Foreign Affairs*, 83.1: 22–34.

Powell, R. (1965) 'China's bomb', *Foreign Affairs*, 43.4: 615–25.

PRC. (1998) *China's National Defense* 27 July 1998, White Paper, <http://www.China.org.cn/e–white/5/index.htm> (accessed 1 July 2006).

—— (1999) *Facts Speak Louder than Words and Lies Will Collapse by Themselves* Information Office of the State Council, 15 July, <http://www.fas.rg/sgp/news/1999/chinacox/> (accessed 1 July 2006).

—— (2005) *China's Peaceful Development Road*, 22 December, <http://news.xinhuanet.com/english/2005-12/22/content_3955754.htm> (accessed 1 July 2006).

—— (2006) 'China, US more than stakeholders but constructive partners', Embassy of the People's Republic of China in the United States of America, <http://www.china-embassy.org/eng/zmgx/t248828.htm> (accessed 1 July 2006).

Puska, S. (1998) *New Century, Old Thinking: the Dangers of the Perceptual Gap in U.S.–China Relations*, Carlisle: Strategic Studies Institute.

Pye, L. (1996) 'China: not your typical superpower', *Problems of Post-Communism*, 43.4: 3–15.

Qian, Feng. (2002) 'India wants to be "the international maritime police" of the Malacca Straits', *Renmin Wang*, 20 April, FBIS CPP200020420000026.

Qian, Qichen. (1997) 'Toward a China–US Relationship for the 21st Century', *Beijing Review*, 19–25 May: 7–11.

—— (2004) 'U.S. strategy to be blamed', *China Daily*, 1 November. Text rep. as 'US strategy to be blamed: former senior Chinese official', Ningbo Municipal Development Reform Commission, <http://www.nbdpc.gov.cn/big5/main_view.php?id=1099357912&theme=202> (accessed 1 July 2006); and as 'The insecurity of the American empire', *Guardian*, 10 November 2004.

Qiao, Liang and Wang, Xiangsui. (2002) *Unrestricted Warfare: China's Master Plan to Destroy America*, Panama City: Pan American Publishing.

Radyuhin, V. (2003) 'A Chinese "Invasion"', *The Hindu*, 23 September.

Ramachandran, S. (2005) 'China's pearl in Pakistan's waters', *Asia Times*, 4 March.

—— (2006) 'India's foray into Central Asia', *Asia Times*, 12 August.

Ramo, J. (2004) *The Beijing Consensus*, London: Foreign Policy Centre.

Ranganathan, C. (1998) 'India–China relations', *World Affairs*, 2.2: 104–20.

—— (2002) 'The China threat: a view from India', in H. Yee and I. Storey (eds), *The China Threat*, London: RoutledgeCurzon, 288–301.

Rappai, M. (1999) 'India–China relations and the nuclear realpolitik', *Strategic Analysis*, 23, April: 15–26.

Rees-Mogg, W. (2005) 'This is the Chinese century', *Times*, 3 January.

Reilly, B. (2003) 'Dragon in paradise: China's rising star in Oceania', *National Interest*, 72, Summer: 94–105.

Reinsch, W. (2002) 'Dissenting views of Commissioner William Reinsch', <http://www.uscc.gov/researchpapers/2000_2003/reports/diss_02.htm> (accessed 1 July 2006).

Ren, Xin. (1996) '"China threat" theory untenable', *Beijing Review*, 5–11 February: 10–11.

Ren, Yujun. (2002) 'US right wing forces tend to fan up "China threat theory" again, *People's Daily*, 17 July 2002.

Renmin Ribao 'People's Daily' and *Hongqi* 'Red Flag'. (1965) 'Apologists of neo-colonialism. Fourth comment on the open letter of the Central Committee of the CPSU', 22 October 1963, rep. *The Polemic on the General Line of the International Communist Movement*, Peking: Foreign Language Press.

Rice, C. (2000) 'Promoting the national interest' *Foreign Affairs*, 79.1: 45–62.

—— (2002) 'Press briefing by National Security Advisor, Dr. Condoleezza Rice, on the President's trip to Asia', 14 February, <http://usinfo.state.gov/regional/ea/easec/condoleeza.htm> (accessed 1 July 2006).

—— (2005) Interview, *New York Times*, 17 August.

Richardson, E. (1969) 'The foreign policy of the Nixon administration', *Department of State Bulletin*, 22 September: 260.

Riggs, R. (1951) *Red China's Fighting Hordes*, Harrisburg: Military Service.

Roberts, B. and Manning, R. (2000) 'China: the forgotten nuclear power', *Foreign Affairs*, 79.4: 59–63.

Rohmer, S. (1913) *The Mystery of Dr. Fu Manchu*, London: Methuen.

—— (1938) 'The birth of Fu Manchu', *Empire News* (Manchester), 30 January.

Ross, R. (1997) 'Beijing as a conservative power', *Foreign Affairs*, 76.2: 33–44.

—— (1999) 'The geography of the peace: great power stability in twenty-first century East Asia', *International Security*, 23.4: 81–118.

—— (2005) 'Assessing the China threat', *National Interest*, 81, Fall: 81–8.

Rotter, A. (2000) 'Saidism without Said: Orientalism and U.S. diplomatic history', *American Historical Review*, 105.4: 1205–17.

Roy, D. (1994) 'Hegemon on the horizon? China's threat to East Asian security', *International Security*, 19.1: 149–68.

—— (1996) 'The "China threat" issue', *Asian Survey*, 36.8: 758–71.

—— (2003) 'Rising China and U.S. interests', *Orbis*, 47.1: 125–37.

Roy, J. (2005) 'Rise of China and the outlook for U.S.–China relations', *Notes. The National Committee on United States–China Relations*, 33.1: 14–17.

Rozman, G. (1987) *The Chinese Debate about Soviet Socialism, 1978–1985*, Princeton: Princeton University Press.

—— (1998) 'Sino–Soviet relations in the 1990s', *Post–Soviet Affairs*, 14.2: 93–113.

—— (1999) 'China's quest for great power identity', *Orbis*, 43.3: 383–404.

—— (2000) 'Turning fortresses into free trade zones', in S. Garnett (ed.), *Rapprochement or Rivalry? Russia–China Relation in a Changing Asia*, Washington DC: Carnegie Endowment for International Peace, 177–202.

—— (2003) 'Sino–Japanese Relations: mutual images and the balance between globalization and regionalism', *Special Report*, Woodrow Wilson International Center, Asia Program, 113, July: 8–13.

Rumsfeld, D. (2005a) 'Remarks as delivered by Secretary of Defense Donald H. Rumsfeld, Shangri-La Hotel, Singapore, Saturday, June 4, 2005', <http://www.defenselink.mil/speeches/2005/sp20050604–secdef1561.html> (accessed 1 July 2006).

—— (2005b) 'Remarks as prepared for delivery by Secretary of Defense Donald H. Rumsfeld, Beijing, China, Wednesday, October 19, 2005', <http:/ www.defenselink.mil/speeches/2005/sp20051019–secdef2042.html> (accessed 1 July 2006).

Rusk, D. (1965) 'A conversation with Dean Rusk', *Department of State Bulletin*, 18 January: 64.

—— (1966) 'United States policy toward Communist China', *Department of State Bulletin*, 2 May: 686–95.

Sakharov, A. (1968) 'Thoughts on progress, peaceful coexistence, and intellectual freedom', *New York Times*, 22 July.

Sakhuja, V. (2006) 'Strategic shift in Chinese naval strategy in Indian Ocean', *Peace & Conflict*, 9.1: 32–3.

Salisbury, H. (1967) *Orbit of China*, London: Secker & Warburg.

—— (1969) *The Coming War Between Russia and China*, London: Secker & Warburg.

—— (1973) *To Peking – and Beyond*, London: Arrow Books.

Sampson, M. (1987) 'Cultural influences on foreign policy', in C. Hermann *et al.* (eds), *New Directions in the Study of Foreign Policy*, Boston: Allen & Unwin, 384–405.

Sanger, D. (2003) 'Bush lauds China leader as "Partner" in diplomacy', *New York Times*, 10 December.

SAR. (1972) *Sino–American Relations 1949–1971*, documented and introduced by R. MacFarquhar, Newton Abbot: David & Charles.

Saunders, P. (2000a) 'Supping with a long spoon: dependence and interdependence in Sino–American relations', *China Journal*, 43, January: 55–81.

—— (2000b) 'China's America watchers', *China Quarterly*, 161, March: 41–65.

Sautman, B. (1997) 'Racial nationalism and China's external behaviour', *World Affairs*, 160.2: 78–95.

Scalapino, R. (1974) 'China and the balance of power', *Foreign Affairs*, 52.2: 349–85.

—— (1993) 'China's multiple identities in East Asia' in L. Dittmer and S. Kim (eds), *China's Quest for a National Identity*, Ithaca: Cornell University Press, 215–36.

Scheer, R. (2004) *In Search of an Enemy: Wen Ho Lee and the Revival of the Yellow Peril*, New York: New Press.

Schultz, J. (1998) 'China as a strategic threat', *Strategic Review*, 26.1: 5–16.

Schulzinger, R. (2001) 'The Johnson administration, China, and the Vietnam War', in R. Ross and Jiang Changbin (eds), *Re-examining the Cold War*, Cambridge: Harvard University Press, 238–61.

Schwarz, B. (2005) 'Managing China's rise', *Atlantic Monthly*, 295.5: 27–8.

Scobell, A. (2002) *China and Strategic Culture*, Carlisle: Strategic Studies Institute.

—— (2004) 'Soldiers, statesmen, strategic culture, and China's 1950 intervention in Korea', in Zhao Suisheng (ed.), *Chinese Foreign Policy*, New York: M.E. Sharpe, 107–27.

—— (2005) 'Strategic culture and China', *Strategic Insights*, 4.10, <http://www.ccc.nps.navy.mil/si/2005/Oct/scobellOct05.pdf> (accessed 1 July 2006).

Scobell, A. and Wortzel, L. (eds) (2002) *China's Growing Military Power*, Carlisle: Strategic Studies Institute.

Scott, D. (2007a) 'China and the EU: an axis for the 21st Century?', forthcoming in *International Relations*, 27.1: 23–45.

—— (2007b) 'The EU–China "strategic dialogue"', forthcoming in D. Kerr and F. Liu (eds), *The International Politics of EU–China Relations*, London: British Academy/Oxford University Press.

—— (forthcoming) *China and the International System: Power, Presence and Perceptions in a 'Century of Humiliation'*, New York: State University of New York Press.

—— (n.d) 'Kipling and the "Chinese Question": international race relations, geo-culture and geo-politics, then and now', forthcoming.

—— (n.d) 'The great power "Great Game" between China and India', *Geopolitics*, forthcoming.

Seckington, I. (2005) 'Nationalism, ideology, and China's "Fourth Generation" leadership', *Journal of Contemporary China*, 14, February: 23–33.

Segal, G. (1980) 'China and the great power triangle', *China Quarterly*, 83, September: 490–509.

—— (1980–81) 'China's strategic posture and the great power triangle', *Pacific Affairs*, 53.4: 682–97.

—— (ed.) (1982) *The China Factor*, London: Croom Helm.

—— (1988) 'As China grows strong', *International Affairs*, 64.2: 217–31.

—— (1996) 'East Asia and the "constrainment" of China', *International Security*, 20.4: 107–35.

—— (1997) 'Enlitening China', in D. Goodman and G. Segal (eds), *China Rising*, London: Routledge, 172–91.

—— (1999) 'Does China matter?', *Foreign Affairs*, 78.5: 24–36.

Selth, A. (1996) 'Burma and the strategic competition between China and India', *Journal of Strategic Studies*, June: 13–30.

Selvage, E. (2001) 'The Warsaw Pact and nuclear nonproliferation 1963–1965', *Working Paper*, 32, April. <http://wwics.si.edu/index.cfm?fuseaction=library.document&topic_id=1409&id=909> (accessed 1 July 2006).

Shambaugh, D. (1991) *Beautiful Imperialists: China Perceives America, 1972–1990*, Princeton: Princeton University Press.

—— (1994a) 'Growing strong: China's challenge to Asian security', *Survival*, 36.2: 43–59.

—— (1994b) 'Pacific security in the Pacific Century', *Current History*, December: 423–9.

—— (2005) *Greater China: The Next Superpower?*, Oxford: Oxford University Press.

—— (1996a) 'Containment or engagement of China?', *International Security*, 21.2: 180–209.

—— (1996b) 'China and Japan towards the twenty-first century', in C. Howe (ed.), *China and Japan: History, Trends, and Prospects*, New York: Oxford University Press, 83–97.

—— (1996c) 'China's military in transition', *China Quarterly*, 142, June: 265–98.

—— (1997a) 'The United States and China: Cooperation or confrontation', *Current History*, 96, September: 241–45.

—— (1997b) 'Chinese hegemony over East Asia by 2015?', *Korean Journal of Defense Analysis*, 9, 7–28.

—— (1999) 'The future of China's foreign relations and security postures, 2000–2005', 24 September 1999, <http://www.cia.gov/nic/confreports_china future.html> #link_future.

—— (1999–2000) 'China's military views the world. Ambivalent security', *International Security*, 24.3: 57–79.

—— (2000) 'Sino–American strategic relations', *Survival*, Spring: 97–115.

—— (2003) 'Imagining demons: the rise of negative imagery in US-China relations', *Journal of Contemporary China*, 12, May: 235–7.

—— (2004) 'China and Europe: the emerging axis', *Current History*, September: 243–8.

—— (2005) 'Return to the Middle Kingdom?', in Shambaugh (ed.), *Power Shift. China and Asia's New Dynamics*, Berkeley: University of California Press, 23–47.

—— (ed.) (1995) *Greater China: The Next Superpower?*, Oxford: Oxford University Press, 1995.

Shao, Kuo-kang (1996) *Zhou Enlai and the Foundations of Chinese Foreign Policy*, New York: St Martin's Press.

Shee, Poon. (1998) 'The South China Sea in China's strategic thinking', *Contemporary Southeast Asia*, 19, March: 369–87.

Shen, Kuiguan. (1994) 'Dialectics of defeating the superior with the inferior', in M. Pillsbury (ed.), *Chinese Views of Future Warfare*, Honolulu: University Press of the Pacific, 2002, 213–19.

Shenkar, O. (2005) *The Chinese Century*, Upper Saddle River: Wharton School Publishing.

Shi, Yinhong. (2002) 'The rising China', Sasakawa Peace Foundation USA, 12 February 2002, <http://www.spfusa.org/Program/av2001/feb1202.pdf> (accessed 1 July 2006).

Shi, Zhe (1993) 'With Mao and Stalin: the reminiscences of Mao's interpreter, Part II. Liu Shaoqi in Moscow', trans. Chen Jian, *Chinese Historians*, 6.1: 67–90.

Shie, T. (2006) 'China woos the South Pacific', *PacNet*, 10A, 17 March.

Shih, Chih-yu. (2005) 'Breeding a reluctant dragon: can China rise into partnership and away from antagonism?', *Review of International Studies*, 31: 755–74.

Shinn, J. (ed.) (1996) *Weaving The Net: Conditional Engagement with China*, New York: Council on Relations Press.

Shirk, S. (2002) 'Chinese perspectives of India', in C. Pumphrey (ed.), *The Rise of China in Asia*, Carlisle: Strategic Studies Institute, 105–10.

Shlapentokh, V. (1995) 'Russia, China and the Far East', *Communist and Post-Communist Studies*, 28.3: 307–17.

Short, A. (1990) 'British policy in Southeast Asia: the Eisenhower era', in W. Cohen and A. Iriye (eds), *The Great Powers in East Asia 1953–1960*, New York: Columbia University Press, 246–71.

Si, Chen. (1996) 'Chinese say "No" to the United States', *Beijing Review*, 21–7 October 1996: 13.

Simmonds, J. (1970) *China's World*, New York: Columbia University Press.

Singh, B. (2006) 'China comes closer', *Peace & Conflict*, 9.6: 20–1.

Singh, J. (1998) 'Against nuclear apartheid', *Foreign Affairs*, 72.5: 41–52.

Singh, S. (1997) 'Sinicisation of Myanmar and its implications for India', *Issues and Studies*, 33.1: 116–33.

Skidelsky, R. (2005) 'The Chinese shadow', *New York Review of Books*, 52.18, 17 November.

Small, A. (2005) *Preventing the Next Cold War: A View from Beijing*, London: Foreign Policy Centre.

Smita. (2005) 'China's "Oceanic offensive"', *Peace & Conflict*, 8.10: 1–2.

Smith, D. (1955) 'The Chinese enigma', *Political Quarterly*, 26.4: 360–70.

Smith, W. (1950) *Moscow Mission 1946–1949*, London: William Heinemann.

Snow, E. (1937) *Red Star Over China*, London: Victor Gollanz.

Solovev, V. (1900) *A Short Tale of the Anti-Christ*, <http://praiseofglory.com/taleantichrist.htm> (accessed 1 July 2006).

Solzhenitsyn, A. (1974) *Letter to the Soviet Leaders*, London: Collins.

Song, Xianlin and Sigley, G. (2000) 'Middle Kingdom mentalities', *Communal/Plural*, 8.1, 47–64.

Spence, J. (1990) 'Chinese fictions in the twentieth century', in R. Winks and J. Rush (eds), *Asia in Western Fiction*, Honolulu: University of Hawaii Press, 100–16.

—— (2005) 'The once and future China', *Foreign Policy*, January–February, <http://www.carnegieendowments.org/publications/index.cfm?fa=print&id=16538>.

Spender, P. (1969) *Exercises in Diplomacy. The Anzus Treaty and the Colombo Plan* Sydney: Sydney University Press.

Srinivasan, R. (2000) 'The good, the bad, and the ugly', *Rediff.com*, 9 May, <http://www.rediff.com/news/2000/may/09rajeev.htm> (accessed 1 July 2006).

Steel, R. (1967) The "Yellow Peril" revisited', *Commentary*, 43.6: 58–65.

Stephan, J. (1994) *The Russian Far East*, Stanford: Stanford University Press.

Stephanson, A. (1998) 'Diplomatic history in the expanded field', *Diplomatic History*, 22.4: 595–603.

Stevenson, W. (1959) *The Yellow Wind*, London: Cassell.

Stockwin, H. (2004) 'The Qian Qichen op-ed', *China Brief*, 4 December, <http://www.jamestown.org/email-to-friend.php?article_id=2368984> (accessed 1 July 2006).

Stoessinger, G. (1971) *Nations in Darkness: China, Russia and America*, New York: Random.

Storey, I. (1999–2000) 'Living with the colossus: how Southeast Asian countries cope with China', *Parameters*, 29, Winter: 111–25.

—— (2002) 'Singapore and the rise of China', in H. Yee and I. Storey (eds), *The China Threat*, London: RoutledgeCurzon, 205–26.

—— (2006) 'China's Malacca dilemma', *China Brief*, 6.8: 4–6.

Strahan, N. (1996) *Australia's China*, Cambridge: Cambridge University Press.

Studeman, M. (1998) *Dragon in the Shadows: Calculating China's Advances in the South China Sea*, Monterey: Naval Postgraduate School.

Studwell, J. (2002) *The China Dream*, London: Profile Books.

Suettinger, R. (2004) 'The rise and descent of "Peaceful rise"', *China Leadership Monitor*, 12, Fall: 1–10.

Sun, Fo. (1944) *China Looks Forward*, London: George Allen.

Sun, Yat-sen. (1929) *San Min Chi I. The Three Principles of the People*, Shanghai: The Commercial Press.

Sutter, R. (2003) 'China's rise in Asia – are US interests in jeopardy', *American Asian Review*, 21.2: 1–21.

—— (2003–4) 'Why does China matter?', *Washington Quarterly*, 27.1: 75–89.

—— (2004) 'China's peaceful rise and U.S. interests in Asia – status and outlook, *PacNet*, 27, 24 June, <pacnet@hawaiibiz.rr.com> (accessed 1 July 2006).

Swaine, M. (1997) 'Don't demonize China', *Washington Post*, 18 May.

Swaine, M. and Tellis, A. (2000) *Interpreting China's Grand Strategy*, Santa Monica: RAND.

Talbott, S. (1981) 'The strategic dimension of the Sino–American relationship', in R. Solomon (ed.), *The China Factor*, Englewood Cliffs: Prentice-Hall, 81–113.

Tamamoto, M. (2003) 'Ambiguous Japan', in J. Ikenberry and M. Mastanduno (eds), *International Relations Theory and the Asia-Pacific*, New York: Columbia University Press, 191–212.

Tang, Jiaxuan. (1999a) 'US Secretary of State Madeleine K. Albright and Chinese Foreign Minister Tang Jiaxuan. Joint Press availability', 1 March, <http://www .nti.org/db/china/engdocs/usch0399.htm> (accessed 1 July 2006).

—— (1999b) 'Tang on international situation and China's diplomatic work', *Beijing Review*, 22–28 March 1999: 6–11.

Taylor, G. (1921) 'The evolution and distribution of race, culture, and language', *Geographical Review*, 11.1: 54–119.

Taylor, R. (1996) *Greater China and Japan*, London: Routledge.

Tellis, A. (2005) 'A grand chessboard', *Foreign Policy*, January–February, <http:// www.carnegieendowments.org/publications/index.cfm?fa=print&id=16538> (accessed 1 July 2006).

Terrill, R. (1975) *800,000,000 The Real China*, Harmondsworth: Penguin.

Thayer, C. (2002) 'Vietnamese perspectives of the "China Threat"', in H. Yee and I. Storey (eds), *The China Threat*, London: RoutledgeCurzon, 265–87.

Thomas, A. (2004) 'The peaceful rise of China: what does it mean for Australia and the Region?', *AsiaLink*, 27 July, <http://www.asialink.unimelb.edu.au/cpp/ transcripts/pdf/Thomas.pdf> (accessed 1 July 2006).

Thomas, G. (2001) *Seeds of Fire: China and the Story Behind the Attack on America*, Tempe: Dandelion Books.

Thompson, D. and Zhu, Feng. (2004) 'New national strategy provides insight into China's rise', *China Brief*, 4.17: 3–5.

Thornton, J. and Ziegler, C. (2002) 'The Russian Far East in perspective', in Thornton and Ziegler (eds), *Russia's Far East*, Seattle: University of Washington Press, 3–34.

Time. (1979a) 'Teng Hsiao-ping', 1 January.

—— (1979b) 'Visionary of a New China', 1 January.

—— (1986) 'Deng Xiaoping', 6 January.

Timperlake, E. and Triplett, W. (1999) *Red Dragon Rising: Communist China's Military Threat to America*, Lanham: Regnery.

Trenin, D. (1999) *Russia's China Problem*, Moscow: Carnegie Moscow Centre.

Troyakova, T. (2000) 'A view from the Russian Far East', in S. Garnett (ed.), *Rapprochement or Rivalry? Russia–China Relation in a Changing Asia*, Washington DC: Carnegie Endowment for International Peace, 203–25.

Truman, H. (1947) 'Special message to the Congress on Greece and Turkey: the Truman Doctrine', 12 March, *Public Papers of the Presidents of the United States: Harry S. Truman, 1947*, Washington: Government Printing Office, 1963, 176–80.

—— (1951) 'President Truman's special message to Congress on Mutual Security Program', 24 May, *Public Papers of the Presidents: Harry S. Truman, 1951*, Washington: Government Printing Office, 1965, 309.

Tsang, Steve. (1999) 'Japan's role in the Asia Pacific: the views from Greater China', *Security Dialogue*, 30, December: 413–24.

Tsou, Tang. (1963) *America's Failure in China. 1941–50*, Chicago: University of Chicago Press.

Tucker, N. (1995–96) 'China as a factor in the collapse of the Soviet Empire', *Political Science Quarterly*, 110.4: 501–18.

Umbach, F. (2003) 'Future impacts of Chinese and Asian dependency upon energy from the Middle East and Central Asia', in E. Reiter and P. Hazdra (eds), *The Impact of Asian Powers on Global Developments*, Heidelberg: Physica-Verlag, 143–63.

USA (1949) 'The position of the United States with respect to Asia', NSC 48/1, 23 December, in T. Etzold and J. Gaddis (eds), *Containment: Documents on American Policy and Strategy, 1945–1950*, New York: Columbia University Press, 1978, 259.

—— (1952) 'United States objectives and courses of action with respect to Southeast Asia', NSC 124/2, 25 June, in D. Mabon (ed.), *Foreign Relations of the United States 1952–1954. Volume XII, East Asia and the Pacific. Part I*, Washington: Government Printing Office, 1984, 127–34.

—— (1954) 'United States objectives and courses of action with regard to Southeast Asia', NSC 5405, 16 January, in D. Mabon (ed.), *Foreign Relations of the United States 1952–1954. Volume XII, East Asia and the Pacific. Part I*, Washington: Government Printing Office, 1984, 367–76.

—— (1963) 'Communist China's advanced weapons program', 24 July, <http://www.gwu.edu/~nsarchiv/NSAEBB/NSAEBB19/01–14.htm> (accessed 1 July 2006).

—— (1984) 'The President's visit to the People's Republic of China', National Security Decision Directive 140, 21 April, <http://www.gwu.edu/~nsarchiv/NSAEBB/NSAEBB19/08–05.htm> (accessed 1 July 2006).

—— (1998) *The United States Security Strategy for the East Asia–Pacific Region 1998*, November, Department of Defense, *DefenseLINK*, <http://www.defenselink.mil/pubs/easr98/> (accessed 1 July 2006).

—— (2001) *Report of the Commission to Assess United States National Security Space Management and Organization*, 11 January, <www.space.gov/docs/fullreport.pdf> (accessed 1 July 2006).

—— (2002) *Military Power of the People's Republic of China*, Annual Report, Department of Defense, July, <http://www.defenselink.mil/news/Jul2002/d20020712china.pdf>. Accessed 1 July 2006.

—— (2003) *Military Power of the People's Republic of China*, Annual Report, Department of Defense, 28 July, <http://www.defenselink.mil/pubs/20030730Chinaex.pdf> (accessed 1 July 2006).

—— (2004) 'Transcript: State Department noon briefing, November 1', http://canberra.usembassy.gov/hyper/2004/1101/epf101.htm> (accessed 1 July 2006).

—— (2006a) *Military Power of the People's Republic of China*, Annual Report, Washington: Office of the Secretary of Defense.

—— (2006b) *Quadrennial Defence Report*, Washington: Office of the Secretary of Defense.

US–China Security Review Commission. (2002) *The National Security Implications of the Economic Relationship Between the United States and China*, Washington, DC: Government Printing Office.

Utley, F. (1951) *The China Story*, Chicago: Henry Regnery.

Vajpayee, A. (1998) 'Nuclear anxiety: India's letter to Clinton on the nuclear testing', *New York Times*, 13 May.

Vertzberger, Y. (1984) *Misperceptions in Foreign Policy Making: the Sino–Indian Conflict, 1959–1962*, Boulder: Westview.

Vitkovskaya, G., Zayonchkovskay, Z. and Newland, K. (2000) 'Chinese migration into Russia', in S. Garnett (ed.), *Rapprochement or Rivalry? Russia–China Relation in a Changing Asia*, Washington, DC: Carnegie Endowment for International Peace, 347–68.

Vogel, F. (ed.) (1997) *Living With China. US–China Relations in the Twenty First Century*, New York: Norton.

Voskressenski, A. (1997) 'The perceptions of China by Russia's foreign policy elite', *Issues & Studies*, 33.3: 1–20.

Waldron, A. (1995) 'Deterring China', *Commentary*, 100.4: 17–21.

—— (1998) 'The Chinese military threat', *American Enterprise*, July/August: 40–3.

—— (2005) 'The rise of China', *Review of International Studies*, 31: 715–33.

Walker, R. (1956) *China under Communism*, London: George Allen and Unwin.

Wall, D. (2006) 'Chinese reoccupying Russia?', *Japan Times*, 5 May.

Waller, J. (2001) 'Blue Team takes on Red China', *Insight on the News*, 4 June.

Waltz, K. (1979) *Theory of International Politics*, Reading: Addison-Wesley.

—— (1993) 'The emerging structure of international politics', *International Security*, 18, Fall: 44–79.

Wanandi, J. (2004) 'China and Asia Pacific regionalism', in Ryosei Kokubun and Wang Jisi (eds), *The Rise of China and a Changing East Asian Order*, Tokyo: Japan Center for International Exchange, 37–48.

Wang, Baocun and Li, Fei. (1995) 'Information warfare', in M. Pillsbury (ed.), *Chinese Views of Future Warfare*, Honolulu: University Press of the Pacific, 2002, 327–41.

Wang, Dong. (2003) 'The discourse of Unequal Treaties in modern China', *Pacific Affairs*, 76.3: 399–425.

Wang, Fei-Ling. (1997) 'Ignorance, arrogance and radical nationalism: a review of *China Can Say No*', *Journal of Contemporary China*, 6.14: 161–5.

—— (1999) 'Self-image and strategic intentions', in Deng Yong and Wang Fei-Ling (eds), *In the Eyes of the Dragon, China Views the World*, Lanham: Rowman & Littlefield, 21–45.

—— (2005) 'Preservation, prosperity and power: what motivates China's foreign policy?', *Journal of Contemporary China*, 14, November: 669–94.

—— (2006) 'Heading off fears of a resurgent China', *International Herald Tribune*, 11 April.

Wang, Gungwu. (1999) *China and Southeast Asia*, Singapore: Singapore University Press.

Wang, Jianwei. (1999) 'Managing conflict: Chinese perspectives on multilateral diplomacy and collective security', in Deng Yong and Wang Fei-Ling (eds), *In the Eyes of the Dragon, China Views the World*, Lanham: Rowman & Littlefield, 73–96.

—— (2000) *Limited Adversaries. Post-Cold War Sino–American Mutual Images*, Oxford: Oxford University Press.

—— (2006) 'Can "stakeholder" hold U.S.–China relations?', *PacNet*, 17A, May 11.

Wang, Jisi. (1994) 'Pragmatic nationalism: China seeks a new role in world affairs', *Oxford International Review*, 6.1: 28–30.

—— (1995) 'Conflit de civilisations: fondement théoriques et significations pratiques', *Cultures & Conflits*, 19–20: 107–40.

—— (1996) 'US China policy', *Beijing Review*, 21–7 October: 6–9.

—— (1998) 'International relations theory and the study of Chinese foreign policy', in T. Robinson and D. Shambaugh (eds), *Chinese Foreign Policy: Theory and Practice*, New York: Clarendon Press, 481–505.

—— (2001) 'Beauty – and beast', *Wilson Quarterly*, 25.2: 61–65.

—— (2004) 'China's changing role in Asia', in Kokubun Ryosei and Wang Jisi (eds), *The Rise of China and a Changing East Asian Order*, Tokyo: Japan Center for International Exchange, 3–22.

—— (2005) 'China's search for stability with America', *Foreign Affairs*, 84.5: 39–48.

—— (2006) '"Peaceful rise": a discourse in China', Public Lecture, LSE, 5 May, <http://www.lse.ac.uk/collections/CWSC/pdf>/wang_jisi_lecture_notes.doc> (accessed 1 July 2006).

Wang, Jisi and Zou, Sicheng. (1996) 'Civilizations: clash or fusion?', *Beijing Review*, 15–21 January: 8–12.

Wang, Jisi, Shi, Yinhong and Zhang, Baijia. (1997) 'Scholars refute book's views on U.S.–China relations', Interview, *Beijing Review*, 2–8 June: 10–12.

Wang, Ling-chi. (1999) 'China spy scandal taps reservoir of racism', *JINN Magazine* Pacific News Service, 5.6, 18 March, <www.pacificnews.org/jinn/stories/5.06/990318–china.html> (accessed 1 July 2006).

Wang, Mei-ling. (1998) 'Creating a virtual enemy: U.S.–China relations in print', in Li Hongshan and Long Zhaohui (eds), *Image, Perception and the Making of U.S.–China Relations*, Lanham: University Press of America, 73–97.

Wang, Naiming. (1997) 'Adhere to active defense and modern People's War', in M. Pillsbury (ed.), *Chinese Views of Future Warfare*, Honolulu: University Press of the Pacific, 2002, 37–44.

Wang, Qingxin. (1994) 'Toward political partnership: Japan's China policy', *Pacific Review*, 7.2: 171–82.

—— (2000) 'Cultural norms and the conduct of Chinese foreign policy', in Hu Weixing, Gerald Chan and Zha Daojiong (eds), *China's International Relations in the 21st Century*, Lanham: University Press of America, 143–69.

Wang, Yiwei (2004a) 'The dimensions of China's peaceful rise', *Asia Times*, 14 May.

—— (2004b) 'Beijing hands Moscow a long rope', *Beijing Review*, 11 November: 23–5.

Wang, Zhongchun. (2005) 'The Soviet factor in Sino–American normalization, 1969–1979', in W. Kirby, R. Ross and G. Li (eds), *Normalization of U.S.–China Relations*, Cambridge: Harvard University Press, 147–74.

Wang, Zhongren. (1997) ' "China threat" theory groundless', *Beijing Review*, 14–20 July: 7–8.

Warner, D. (1961) *Hurricane From China*, New York: Macmillan.

Watts, J. (2005) 'A miracle and a menace', *Guardian*, 9 November.

Watts, W. (1999) *Americans Look at Asia*, Henry Luce Foundation Project, October, <http://www.hluce.org/images/usasia_report_1099.pdf> (accessed 1 July 2006).

Weede, E. (2003) 'China and Russia: on the rise and decline of two nations', *International Interactions*, 29: 343–64.

Weinberger, C. (1999) 'Foreword' in K. Degraffenreid (ed.), *The Cox Report – China and National Security, The Report of the Select Committee on U.S. National Security and Military/Commercial Concerns with China*, Washington: Regnery.

Westad, O. (ed.) (1998) *Brothers in Arms. The Rise and Fall of the Sino–Soviet Alliance 1945–1963*, Washington: Stanford University Press.

White, H. (2005) 'The limits to optimism: Australia and the rise of China', *Australian Journal of International Affairs*, 59.4: 469–80.

White, T. and Jacoby. A. (1946) *Thunder Out of China*, New York: William Sloane.

Whiting, A. (1960) 'The logic of communist China's policy', *Yale Review*, 50.1: 3–17.

—— (1989) *China Eyes Japan*, Berkeley: University of California Press.

—— (1996) 'The PLA and China's threat perceptions', *China Quarterly*, 146, June: 596–615.

Whitney, J. (1880) *The Chinese and the Chinese Question*, New York: Thompson & Moreau.

Wilkinson, E. (1990) *Japan Versus the West. Image and Reality*, London: Penguin.

Wills, J. (1984) *Embassies and Illusions. Dutch and Portuguese Envoys to K'ang-hsi, 1666–1687*, Cambridge: Harvard University Press.

Wilson, J. (2004) *Strategic Partners. Russian–Chinese Relations in the Post-Soviet Era*, New York: M.E. Sharpe.

Wingrove, D. (1990) *Chung Kuo. The Middle Kingdom*, New York: Dell.

Wint, G. (1955) *Spotlight on Asia*, Harmondsworth: Penguin.

—— (1958) *Dragon and Sickle. How Communist Revolution Happened in China*, London: Pall Mall Press.

—— (1960) 'China and Asia', *China Quarterly*, 1, January–March: 61–71.

Wishnick, E. (1998) 'Prospects for the Sino–Russian partnership', *Journal of East Asian Affairs*, 12, Summer–Fall: 418–51.

—— (2001) *Mending Fences. The Evolution of Moscow's China Policy From Brezhnev to Yeltsin*, Seattle: University of Washington Press.

—— (2002) 'Chinese migration to the Russian Far East', Publications Centre for East Asian Studies, <http://gsti.miis.edu/CEAS–PUB/200209wishnick.pdf> (accessed 1 July 2006).

Wolfowitz, P. (1997) 'Bridging centuries: fin de siecle all over again – international relations', *National Interest*, 47, Spring: 3–8.

—— (2002) 'International Institute for Strategic Studies conference on East Asia security', 29 May, U.S. Department of State, http://fpc.state.gov/10566.htm.

Wortzel, L. (1994) 'China pursues traditional great-power status', *Orbis*, 38.2: 157–76.

—— (1996) *The ASEAN Regional Forum*, Carlisle Barracks: Strategic Studies Institute.

—— (ed.) (1999) *The Chinese Armed Forces in the 21st Century*, Carlisle Barracks: Strategic Studies Institute, Army War College.

Xia, Liping. (2003) 'China's efforts as a responsible power', in D. Lovell (ed.), *Asia–Pacific Security*, Canberra: Asia Pacific Press, 70–7.

Xiang, Lanxin. (1998) 'The China debate and the civilization debate', *Issues & Studies*, 34.10: 79–92.

—— (2006) 'Why Washington can't speak Chinese', *Washington Post*, 16 April.

Xiao, Ding. (2002) 'Is China about to collapse?', *Beijing Review*, 4 July: 15–7.

Xinhua. (1994) 'Li Peng denies "China Threat"', 2 January.

Xu, Guangqiu. (2001) 'Anti-Western nationalism in China, 1989–99', *World Affairs*, 163.4: 151–62.

Yahuda, M. (1978) *China's Role in World Affairs*, London: Croom Helm.

—— (1999a) 'China's search for a global role', *Current History*, 98, September: 266–70.

—— (1999b) 'China's foreign relations: the long march, future uncertain, *China Quarterly*, 159, September: 650–9.

Yan, Xuetong. (1997) 'Dangers of neo-McCarthyism', *Beijing Review*, 7–13 July: 7–8.

—— (2001) 'The rise of China in Chinese eyes', *Journal of Contemporary China*, 10.26: 33–9.

—— (2002) 'China's foreign policy towards major powers', Sasakawa Peace Foundation USA, 22 October 2002, <http://www.spfusa.org/Program/av2002/oct2202.pdf> (accessed 1 July 2006).

Yang, Bojiang. (1996) 'Why U.S. Japan joint declaration on Security Alliance', *Contemporary International Relations* 6.5: 1–12.

—— (2006) 'Redefining Sino-Japanese relations after Koizumi', *Washington Quarterly*, 129–37.

Yang, Daqing. (2002) 'Mirror for the future or the history card? Understanding the "history problem"', in M. Soderberg (ed.), *Chinese–Japanese Relations in the Twenty-first Century*, London: Routledge, 10–31.

Yang, Xiyue. (1999) 'Power relations in today's world', *Beijing Review*, 1–7 March: 6–7.

Yasutomo, D. (1977) 'Sato's China policy, 1964–1966', *Asian Survey*, 17.6: 530–44.

Yates, S. (1999) 'The impact of China's emerging global role on U.S. policy', *Brown Journal of World Affairs* 6, Summer/Fall: 35–41.

Yee, H. and Zhu, Feng. (2002) 'Chinese perspectives of the China threat', in H. Yee and I. Storey (eds), *The China Threat*, London: RoutledgeCurzon, 21–42.

Yeltsin, B. (1993) 'Yeltsin okays Russian foreign policy concept', *Current Digest of the Post-Soviet Press*, 45.17, 26 May: 15.

Yoshihara, Toshi. (2001) *Chinese Information Warfare*, Carlisle Barracks: Strategic Studies Institute.

Young, J. (1891) 'New life in China', *North American Review*, 153, October: 420–32.

Younger, K. (1954) 'A British view of the Far East', *Pacific Affairs*, 27.2, 1954, 99–111.

Yu, Bin. (1996) 'The China syndrome: rising nationalism and conflict with the West', *Asia Pacific Issues*, East–West Center, Hawaii, 27, May.

—— (1999) 'China and its Asian neighbors', in Deng Yong and Wang Fei-Ling (eds), *In the Eyes of the Dragon. China Views the World*, Lanham: Rowman & Littlefield, 183–210.

Yu, Qifen. (1995) 'The international military situation in the 1990s', in M. Pillsbury (ed.), *Chinese Views of Future Warfare*, Honolulu: University Press of the Pacific, 2002, 69–84.

Yu, Zhang. (2005) 'Chinese nationalism and the 2001 US spy plane incident', *International Studies*, 42.1: 77–85.

Yuan, Jing-dong. (2000) *Asia–Pacific Security: China's Conditional Multilateralism and Great Power Entente*, Carlisle Barracks: Strategic Studies Institute.

Yue, Jianyong. (2003) 'The United States and China in the age of globalization', *Chinese Political Science*, 27 July, <http://www.uscc.gov/researchpapers/2004/04_05_12editusandchinaglobalization.htm> (accessed 1 July 2006).

Zagoria, D. (1962) *The Sino–Soviet Conflict, 1956–61*, Princeton: Princeton University Press.

Zakaria, F. (1996) 'Speak softly, carry a veiled threat', *New York Times Magazine*, 18 February, 36–7.

—— (2005) 'Does the future belong to China?,' *Newsweek*, 9 May.

Zeng, Jize. (1887) 'China. The sleep and the awakening', *Asiatic Quarterly Review*, 3: 1–10.

Zeng, Peiyan (2001) 'The road map', in L. Brahm (ed.), *China's Century*, New York: John Wiley, 11–15.

Zha, Daojing. (2005) 'China's energy security and its international relations', *China and Eurasia Quarterly*, 3.3: 39–54.

Zhai, Kun (2002) 'What underlies the U.S.–Philippine joint military exercise?', *Beijing Review*, 14 March: 8–9.

Zhai, Qiang. (2000) *China and the Vietnam Wars, 1950–1975*, Chapel Hill: University of North Carolina Press.

Zhan, Yan. (2003a) 'An Annual Report on Military Power of the U.S. Defense Department I', *PLA Daily*, 9 September, <http://english.pladaily.com.cn/english/pladaily/2003/09/09/20030909001010_Commentary.html> (accessed 1 July 2006).

—— (2003b) 'On Annual Report on Military Power of the U.S. Defense Department II', *PLA Daily*, 10 September 2003; <http://english.pladaily.com.cn/english/pladaily/2003/09/10/20030910001007_Commentary.html> (accessed 1 July 2006).

Zhang Binsen (2003) 'China should abandon the foreign policy of "taoguang yanghui" "Bide our time, build our capacities"', *Chinese Political Science*, 17 May, <http://www.uscc.gov/researchpapers/2004/04_03_18taoguangyanghui.php> (accessed 1 July 2006).

Zhang, F. (1998) *China's Foreign Relations Strategies under Mao and Deng: A Systematic Comparative Analysis*, Hong Kong: Department of Public and Social Administration. City University of Hong Kong.

Zhang, Guihong. (2005) 'China's peaceful rise and Sino–Indian relations', *China Report*, 41.2: 159–71.

—— (2006) 'The rise of China: India's perceptions and responses', *South Asian Survey*, 13.1: 93–102.

Zhang, Jian. (2004) 'Chinese nationalism and its foreign policy implications', in D. Lovell (ed.), *Asia–Pacific Security*, Canberra: Asia Pacific Press, 108–125.

Zhang, Lijun (2006a) 'A passage to South Asia', *Beijing Review* 16 March: 14–15.

—— (2006b) 'Path to prosperity', *Beijing Review*, 20 July: 12–13.

Zhang, Ming. (1999a) 'What threat?', *Bulletin of the Atomic Scientists*, 55.5: 52–7.

—— (1999b) 'Public images of the United States', in Deng Yong and Wang Fei-ling (eds), In the Eyes of the Dragon. China Views the World, Lanham: Rowman & Littlefields, 1999, 141–57.

Zhang, Shu. (1994) 'Threat perception and Chinese communist foreign policy', in M. Leffler and D. Painter (eds), *Origins of the Cold War*, London: Routledge, 276–92.

—— (1995) *Mao's Military Romanticism: China and the Korean War, 1950–1953*, Lawrence: University Press of Kansas.

—— (1998) 'Sino–Soviet economic cooperation', in O. Westad (ed.), *Brothers in Arms. The Rise and Fall of the Sino–Soviet Alliance 1945–1963*, Washington: Stanford University Press, 189–225.

Zhang, Xiaobo and Song, Qiang. (1996) 'China can say no to America', *New Perspectives*, 13.4: 55–6.

Zhang, Xudong. (1998) 'Nationalism, mass culture, and intellectual strategies in post-Tiananmen China', *Social Text*, 16.2: 109–40.

Zhang, Yongjin. (1998) *China in International Society Since 1949*, Basingstoke: Macmillan.

—— (2001) 'System, empire and state in Chinese international relations', *Review of International Studies*, 27: 43–63.

Zhao, Huanxin. (2005) 'China, India forging strategic partnership', *China Daily*, 12 April.

Zhao, Qizheng. (1999) 'The US-concocted "Cox Report"', *Xinhua*, 31 May, also <http://www.fas.org/news/china/1999/990531-1.html>.

Zhao, Suisheng. (1997) 'China's intellectuals' quest for national greatness and nationalistic writings in the 1990s', *China Quarterly*, 152, December: 730–8.

—— (1998a) 'A state-led nationalism', *Communist and Post-Communist Studies*, 31.3: 287–302.

—— (1998b) *Power Competition in East Asia*, London: Macmillan,

—— (2000) 'Chinese nationalism and its international orientations', *Political Science Quarterly*, 115.1: 1–33.

—— (2004) 'Chinese nationalism and pragmatic foreign policy behavior', in Zhao Suisheng (ed.), *Chinese Foreign Policy*, New York: M.E. Sharpe, 66–88.

—— (2005) *A Nation-state by Construction. Dynamics of Chinese Nationalism*, Stanford: Stanford University Press.

—— (2005–06) 'China's pragmatic nationalism: is it manageable?', *Washington Quarterly*, 29.1: 131–44.

Zheng, Bijian. (2005) *China's Peaceful Rise*, Washington, DC: Brookings Institution Press.

Zheng, Yongnian. (1999) *Discovering Chinese Nationalism in China*, Cambridge: Cambridge University Press.

Zheng, Yongnian and Tok, Keat. (2005) 'China's "Peaceful Rise"', *Working Papers*, China Policy Institute, University of Nottingham, November.

Zhou, Enlai. (1955) 'China', in *Asia–Africa Speaks From Bandung*, Jakarta: Ministry of Foreign Affairs Republic of Indonesia, 57–66.

—— (1971) 'Why did our country accede to Nixon's request for a visit?', in K. Chen (ed.), *China and the Three Worlds. A Foreign Policy Reader*, London: Macmillan, 1979, 133–42.

—— (1972) 'Memorandum of conversation, Tuesday, February 22, 1972'; <http://www.gwu.edu/~nsarchiv/nsa/publications/DOC_readers/kissinger/nixzhou/12–18.htm> (accessed 1 July 2006).

—— (1973) 'Report to the Tenth National Congress of the Communist Party of China', *Peking Review*, 7 September: 17–25.

—— (1976) 'Oppose the two superpowers', in K. Chen (ed.), *China and the Three Worlds. A Foreign Policy Reader*, London: Macmillan, 1979, 183–93.

Zhou, Wenzhong. (2005) 'China's strategy of peaceful development and the future of China–U.S. Relations', 5 October, <http://www.china-mbassy.org/eng/xw/t215310.htm> (accessed 1 July 2006).

Zhu, Rongji. (1999a) 'Joint press conference of the President and Premier Zhu Rongji of the People's Republic of China', 8 April, <http://www.usconsulate.org.hk/uscn/wh/1999/0408b.htm> (accessed 1 July 2006).

—— (1999b) 'Luncheon remarks by Secretary of State Madeline K. Albright and Premier Zhu Rongji, People's Republic of China', 8 April, <http://www.usconsulate.org.hk/uscn/wh/1999/0408.htm> (accessed 1 July 2006).

Zinsmeister, K. (1998) 'Why China doesn't scare me', *American Enterprise*, July–August, <http://www.taemag.com/printVersion/print_article.asp?articleID=16959> (accessed 1 July 2006).

Zoellick, R. (2005) 'Whither China: from membership to responsibility', 21 September, Remarks to National Committee on U.S.-China Relations, <http://www.ncuscr.org/articlesandspeches/Zoellick.htm> (accessed 1 July 2006).

—— (2006) 'Interview, Deputy Secretary of State Robert B. Zoellick with Phoenix TV', 18 April, U.S. Department of State, <http://usinfo.state.gov/eap/Archive/2006/Apr/20-160622.html> (accessed 1 July 2006).

Zou, Rong. (1903) *The Revolutionary Army: A Chinese Nationalist Tract of 1903*, trans. J. Lust, The Hague: Mouton, 1968.

Zubok, V. (1998) 'Deng-Xiaoping and the Sino–Soviet split 1956–1963', *Cold War International History Project Bulletin*, 10, March: 152–62.

Zweig, D. and Bi, Jianhai. (2005) 'China's global hunt for energy', *Foreign Affairs*, 84.5: 25–38.

Index